After retiring from 47 successful years in business, Richard Alexander has taken the time to reflect on his past, origins and childhood. Truthfully recording memories of people, events or happenings, some funny, others scary, some very personal but all building the foundations for the person he is today.

My wife and I became 'grandparents' for the first time in April 2000. This led to often interesting discussions on what we knew of the life and times of our own grandparents. In about 2002, my PA at work suggested that it might be a good idea to 'write a letter' to our then grandchild and any more that we may be blessed with. So, many years after continued encouragement from these two special people, this book, not a letter, is dedicated to:

My wife Eileen for all the great years that we have shared together – a thank you for our wonderful children and all our grandchildren.

And a very special thanks to that PA, Glenda Lochner, who whenever opportunity arose, reminded me regularly that I had a story to tell. So many years later…here it is!

Richard Alexander

My Life On Request
Pieces of Me

PUBLISHERS LTD.

Copyright © Richard Alexander (2016)

The right of Richard Alexander to be identified as author of this work has been asserted by him in accordance with section 77 and 78 of the Copyright, Designs and Patents Act 1988.

All rights reserved. No part of this publication may be reproduced, stored in a retrieval system, or transmitted in any form or by any means, electronic, mechanical, photocopying, recording, or otherwise, without the prior permission of the publishers.

Any person who commits any unauthorized act in relation to this publication may be liable to criminal prosecution and civil claims for damages.

A CIP catalogue record for this title is available from the British Library.

ISBN 9781786290809 (Paperback)
ISBN 9781786290816 (Hardback)
ISBN 9781786290826 (E-Book)

www.austinmacauley.com

First Published (2016)
Austin Macauley Publishers Ltd.
25 Canada Square
Canary Wharf
London
E14 5LQ

MY LIFE ON REQUEST

(Pieces of me)

Here I sit seeking a way to answer all your probing questions. Who am I? What makes me behave, reply, act, react to all things in the way that I do? Could I possibly provide sufficient written understanding of my life's journey, even a small part of it, to properly offer you a tiny view, a microscopic insight as to who I really am, even perhaps why? In other words, what makes me be, well --- me? A difficult question to address with any real confidence, made more so because you see me at a time when I am moving towards the end of my life journey, yet you may be only at the start of your journey. However, never wanting to run away from a challenge, I shall try to reply to your question as best I can. But at this, the beginning of my written story, you must accept, comprehend even how utterly breathless I am with the fear of failure, and how full of exhilaration I am at the prospect, the possibilities, of success. Committed to the task I remain immobile, caught, terrified, like a rabbit in a bright light, transfixed, scared even to move, shuddering at the immense task before me.

So, where to start?

That I want to share with you, my Dear Reader, as much of me as may be humanly possible, is not at all in question. Should there be questions of any kind at the outset, they must rather be along the lines of my capability to complete the mission at hand due to a lack of any previously recognised talent as a writer! This lack of even mildly proven aptitude therefore leaves me in abject panic, considering how best to approach the subject of who I am, or may have become through life's impact, without boring you into apathetic oblivion. Having spent much time agonising over how to avoid the latter, I will start my story with some bazaar truths.

Essentially, these 'truths' with their accompanied strangeness, carry perhaps the first foundation blocks of or for my personal human character development. Potentially then these 'blocks' are the porous base pieces of me, structured to allow the life osmosis of experience to flow through; a set of 'truths' designed to shape, cultivating that which I have grown up to be. A filtration mechanism perhaps allowing or denying residence in my personality, organising who I am today. These 'quirks', these wacky realities, had given notice of their presence long before my physical arrival on this planet however, hence the use of the word 'strange' linked to 'truths'! These 'truths' may for the sake of descriptive simplicity best be placed hereafter under the collective heading of 'controversy'!

Like so many other matters recorded here in this initial period of my life's journey, these controversial strange 'truths', which alas I must state with certainty I cannot claim a single ounce of credit or responsibility for, were seemingly pre-ordained as the big plan for my unique journey through this life. They were already contained within an inherent 'error', a blotch in composition as I lay forming after the miracle of conception. This 'error' may simply have been the result of some genetic disorder passed on by others of my line who had gone before me. I therefore, initially at least, could not be in any way accountable for this flaw, this predestination error that subjected its host, me, to a pre-selected path in life, one of a living controversy! Not that I was aware of this at all at the beginning of my time; therefore any responsibility or indeed resultant accountability must have rested with those that came before me. Ancestors! Rest assured however that I would like to grab the limelight for some of this strangeness if there was even an inkling that I could get away with it – I would!

I have after all, become known not to be of a shy shrinking violet disposition throughout my life, never lacking a lusty need for exposing intrigue, not least my own! Sadly then I must concede openly to accepting the proper random nature of my conception. Claiming then that there was no control or influence during my womb development nor that I had utilised anything to alter, amend or change – or did I?

Controversy!

Oddly, as my life developed, this became a unique but nevertheless suitable badge of office as I'm sure you will soon learn. It seemed like a tag or invisible label that at the point of conception was attached like a leash to my innermost being long before birth. Whilst I may now often deny its presence, itself a controversial act, I do know that this design default, this chemical error, still exists in me even as I write today. Controversy then has shared the same life path with me then. It has accompanied me, following me around in everything like a lovesick disobedient puppy. I say, long before I was actually here, that this puppy was already within my shadow. Yes, this particular strange truth has to be the first of many bestowed on me, not entirely a unique status but my personal partner on arrival into the world of men. A shadowy conspirator justifying its own reason for being! I am confident that the context of this first truth-in-controversy had existed many times before the occasion of my arrival, whilst doubtless on many other occasions since. But this one time, this specific time, this actual point of universe reality was my time, albeit shared with this unwanted companion. It will for always be mine – just mine alone.

Well almost!

Birth!

An argument, an unquiet gathering storm of such insignificant sway or consequence erupted shortly after the moment of my birth. Of the potentially multitudinous matters, some serious, others not so, where amazing human emotions may give rise to cause for concern, or the collective very special feelings of wonder, joy, delight, excitement, to mention just a few at such an event as the birth of a new child, the puppy 'controversy' was born alongside me. Acting on its own but sharing my arrival, this invisible intruder created an instant doubt, a wedge of conflict previously not present but without warning spontaneously raising a question by forcing the now three attending 'adults' into verbal battle over the question of what time I was actually born!

Please accept Dear Reader that although being the star attraction, the subject matter of this momentous event, like all of us, I retain no accessible memories of this time thus I can only rely on those who were there to supply any real view of the happenings surrounding me. I must acknowledge then that the views influencing my written version of this particular controversy, based on the tales of just two of the adult attendees, will be biased in the extreme. Even if some magic allowed me to recall the event in full, that same magic would have needed to supply me with the ability to instantly read a clock alongside a good understanding of the spoken English language. Without these attributes, I would not have been able to assist in any way at all in preventing the storm arising. Anyway, how do you define actual birth? When the head of the individual is first seen protruding – it has to be now? Quick check the clock! Or, is it when the new born is physically, by cutting the umbilical cord, separated from its mother?

Perhaps it is with that first sudden intake of breath or loud wail or maybe sooner? When we plunge complete in full human form from the cosy comfort of darkness in one final push, a gush of final pain, with blood we pass through out into cold brightness? Are there any set guidelines on the time issue? Surely in this world where every infinitesimal detail of everything must be fully recorded in glorious political correctness gone crazy, there has to be a stupidly depicting statute signed by some erstwhile leader of men defining matters of such import, so as not leaving it to mothers or fathers who generally at the time have other considerations?

But back in the days of the late 1940s the time of my arrival, it seems the only resolution to such a dilemma was that of those embroiled in discussion on the topic, he, or as in this case she, who shouted the longest linked to the loudest pronouncement of her truth, was to emerge the triumphant winner of the squabble. Henceforth it was decreed that this shall be the registered day, date, time of this child's birth even if it is somewhat removed from and therefore not supported by any element of others' truth. Thus this argument of such blinding seriousness is settled! Or is it?

I get ahead of myself.

I have been told, clearly accepting with no reason to doubt the telling of, that there were originally just two people in attendance at the actual time of my arrival. My mother of course; her role of succulent incubation provider nearing its end-stage, was being attended by a strange personage employing skills of special, perhaps almost mystical knowledge of required practices, intricate, intimate instrumentation. A recognised stand-in, an entity of magnificent status who although neither one-thing-or-the-other, apparently conducted events with absolute authority, the local midwife!

Yes, not for me the joy of appearing for the first time on this planet in some lily-white antiseptic, pristine shrine to the medical science of birthing knowledge. Oh no! Not for me the spotless glowing inside of a hospital maternity department delivery room. Oh no! Not for me a gathering of watchers in white! Oh no! My arrival on this planet was a planned occurrence for special reasons of delight to my parents, that this glorious event should take place at home! This underpinning pre-arranged location, this 'fact' of preference, explicitly contains, in my opinion, the most likely reason for the simultaneous birth (alongside my own) of the first of the many controversies I have referred to. Had this potentially uncontroversial, most may say normally oft' happy event indeed taken place in the cold efficient delivery room of the local maternity production factory, the actual time of my entrance may possibly never have been a matter of dispute. It most certainly may not have been anywhere near accurate either but would have nonetheless been blindly accepted as being 'true, correct with no objection' by any interested parties to the event. In particular, those to whom the event was of the greatest impact – my parents! This was however not to be the case, at home was the demand. Thus was the stage set, the landing platform established for the very first of a long line of controversies to begin. Establishing its core position with an impenetrable earthly rampart on that wonderful night of my birth, controversy confirmed a presence which was already evident long before the event of my birth itself! Indeed, long before I was even present! That is to say 'present' in the official register-for-tax sense. Or in the (with finger tip pointing directly toward you, in-your-eye) your country "needs" you, sense. But something that destiny had ordained as it were when I was simply present as a growing, developing, embryonic globule, set by the very natural order of things to become the star player in yet another eagerly awaited future attraction.

The foreigner, that stand-in-wife, funny concept don't you think, was adamant that with her years of experience, her qualifications, her undoubted professional standing in the local community etc, only she was entitled, perhaps by some unknown God-given exclusivity even, to record my birth as yesterday even though both my parents, my father having entered his own bedroom to 'enjoy' the arrival of a new offspring, were both convinced that I was born today! This argument (I am told) abounded with growing passion as the normal process of cleaning then weighing the yet unnamed newborn infant (me), took place. Such, I am told, was the verbosity provided in this debate that the argument was never to be really settled. For all eternity though in all recorded documentation it had been, but the subject continued to be a discussion point for many years to come.

I recall as a child often being present when this subject, due perhaps to an impending birthday, would re-focus the minds of my parents which often attracted light banter, squelched giggles, all sometimes even shared with a little laughter. A silly excuse used to spark conversation about the awful state of this nation as a result of WW2, etc. In a leading world-war-winning country, questions, statements linked to socially common banter about not even being able to record the correct date of a child's birth, suggested that there was much that the civil society of the day had to achieve! So in this matter of birth date, day controversy, I have to confess I remain truly blessed. For here I must now officially, publicly concede to something that others throughout my life have only ever been able to snigger about at best. I am indeed one of those exceptionally, almost uniquely singular individual male members of our human race, who has always acknowledged with absolute certainty or fear of contradiction, that he has no idea if he was born yesterday or today!

Not only am I not sure, but neither are my parents nor deep down inside where she lives I suspect, is the midwife! So around the 19th or 20th of October each year a distinctly special privilege is available to enjoy; I can never use the simple statement often applied by others that "I wasn't born yesterday" – because I may have been! To place this minor issue in its proper perspective – if one arrives, after some time of being pushed down through the birth canal, then resting followed by more pushing, mother breathing hard, even yet more pushing, resting, then suddenly entering this world exactly upon the crest of the midnight hour, will the time of birth be recorded as yesterday or today?

In my case, even when outnumbered by a ratio of two-to-one, the totally uninvolved stranger, the stand-in wife who by the way, had never cooked a dinner for the family or made the beds or indeed undertaken any task in our house that could possibly indicate some form of wifely or even motherly behaviour, officially won the day. "Henceforth", she decreed across the damp, wet bloody birth sheets, my birthday, my arrival time, that day of days dominating all my human existence in the modern era was recorded by her for eternity – either as a reflection of a real truth or just plain guesswork – as one tiny second before midnight on the night of the 19th of October in the year of our Lord 1948, and not even one tiny second into the new day dawning, October 20th. In mitigation on behalf of the combatants in this fractious intercourse, I would like to suggest that my arriving safely with all the proper bits, coupled with an additional very sad confusion surrounding this particular delivery episode, my parents possibly simply relented, accepting the awesome might of the part-time interloper in their lives.

Due also to other obvious pressing matters of import, they abandoned the fight although they continued spreading the story for years to come that they, not the third party visiting attendee were correct! Despite these on-going protestations though, I always only ever had one day acknowledged as my special day, my birthday! No duo-parties for me at all, just the ordinary singular recognition. Yes, the 19th day of the month of October was, is known to be, the official date when the celebration of my birth takes place each year!

So, at the outset of my existence on this earth, the beginning of my own life's journey on our planet Dear Reader, something as simple as a record of birth date created a ruckus of a proportion way beyond its merit that I can see will only (finally) cease to be when I (finally) cease to be. I have no doubt whatsoever in my mind though that my demise will also provide for anyone interested or present at the time of the conclusion of this life journey, some similar controversy. If that is so ordained to be along the lines of 'is he dead' or 'isn't he' even, 'did he actually die or not' style of questions, then I will ensure that ghostly laughter will prevail for some time thereafter.

Therefore, innocent as I am led to believe I was at the time of my birth, the subsequent corruption of that innocence by life in general, led me to often wonder if I could have avoided at least this small number of the multiple controversies created, simply by arriving a clear second or two later or earlier? That way, my parents may not have been subject to the dictates of a complete stranger with a funny job title.

Nevertheless, sound the trumpets! I had arrived!

Well actually, in truth, alongside 'puppy controversy' two human babies arrived at the same time!

Thus this controversial moment in human history became somewhat more complex! One of the arrivals was simply a half developed empty shell whilst the other was – well me!

Or is that? Should that be...the other way around?

Controversy!

At this juncture my Dear Reader, you will need to know a little background knowledge, without which much that transpires here may prove to be cumbersome in its appreciation. My mother was the seventh child of a seventh child, a twin no less. Born, raised, nurtured on a tenanted farm in a farming community village in the county of Buckinghamshire England with the unlikely name of Juniper! (This is all true!) The significance of the seventh of the seventh in some sectors of the 'common' people is, in the first instant, that such occurrences are not very 'common' at all. Folklore for centuries when recording such an event, provided the basis of legend by reporting that the resultant being of the Seventh-of-the-Seventh, irrespective of gender, capacity, wholesome or deformed, is said to possess powers or 'gifts' that all other 'common' or so-called normal mortals do not. Such powers are widely known, have been recorded throughout the history of western civilisations, acknowledged with respect across varying social communities. Even to this day, such occurrences in the general European Gypsy (Traveller) community are treated with wonder, almost awe. Traditional storytelling of this wandering band of humanity includes many tales containing references to the exploits and the numerous wondrous abilities of such individuals. Indeed, any such individuals were highly prized by witch-hunters during the dark centuries of European suspicion. When an accused individual was subsequently shown to be a true seventh child of a seventh child, they were regarded as beyond the recognised capacity of a simple witch or demon, maybe even an emissary of or for the anti-Christ who, once caught, must be burned to death in full public view for the purifying process of protection for all innocence! Often these individuals were so hated by members of their own clan who, in fits of jealousy or spite gave up surrendered the individual to the vicious witch hunters in return for some trinket.

Where such a victim was one of a pair, the bewitched offspring of a seventh-of-the-seventh… TWINS, the rewards were larger trinkets, but still trinkets nevertheless! Yet even this exalted status was denied me as no matter how much I have on occasion wanted to emulate such powers, any gifts bestowed on my personage proved to be simply unattainable, well almost! Yes, I was one of twins. Conceived of, brought forth from, a real Seventh-of-the-Seventh who was also a twin but that is where any pretence of similarity ends due to some really significant differences. The first difference being that my twin, the other me if you like, did not survive the journey in the womb longer than a few months so whether or not I was born first or second, whether or not the action of birth itself was before or after midnight, the only fully developed human child that night to be born into this world by my mother was me. Yes, I was the result of the seventh pregnancy of a seventh-of-the-seventh twin child, but due to several prior miscarriages suffered by my mother before my arrival, I became only the fourth child carried to full term that was successfully delivered to my parents.

More controversy!

The Seventh-of-the-Seventh I was but in reality only the fourth child to survive the events from conception through to natural birth! Should I make claim to vast amounts of or indeed tiny portions of, or any form of extra-normal powers at all – should I?

Back to my mother!

Her family were typical of the tenant farming community of the age who had for generations been living on a hand-to-mouth basis merely existing close to the poverty line. Families, no more than traditional surfs really with no land to call their own, making up whole communities working the land for others generation after generation. Communities who were constantly subject to ill health and inter-breeding, often making early departures from this world through overwork, injury, illness or simply exhaustion. My mothers' family had survived, as many large families did in the early 1900s in rural England, living at a time when gratitude for years of loyal service was not generally perceived as a right! After all, each had their place in the society, their class, standing within their social pecking order role. To aspire to anything different from your God allotted place or expect clemency from those higher up the food chain from you, was just nonsense! Also, little or no adequate form of poverty protection via a state pension existed – just more work because the landlord could always find someone else! Her family consisted of mother, father, two sisters together with six brothers, therefore eleven individuals including her. Here were typical people regarded throughout the middle to upper echelons of English society of the day, as the 'salt-of-the-earth' or the 'real' people of England. You know; those that were always first in line to be sent away to war by the landowners, or told to "move on" at a whim. Then, having sent them to fight-the-good-fight for God and country, a better life for all, would cleanse their own guilt by proudly espousing their own stupendous suffering role played in the war.

However, these same gentry often had a differing view on the return to work of the men, some just boys still, who had survived untold horrors.

They were so often kicked off at will from that same land, from their 'tied' homes, if any poor sod returned from serving their landlord, their God or country – minus a limb or two! Those people that the wealthy 'Gentry' had for generations regarded as 'their' possessions – 'my manservant', 'my farmer', 'my woodsman', 'my milkmaid' including all their young!

When approaching ninety at the time of her death, my mother had been the only surviving member of her entire family entourage for many a year!

My father, on the other hand, had two brothers and a sister, was raised surrounded by abject wealth, living in several family homes dependant on the season of the year, across the breadth of the country. Sent away to one of the best 'public' schools for boys as a full time boarding pupil he was from a home where money was never in question. In fact, eventually as a young man, he was actually employed for a short while as a teacher at his school, just one of many very old, famous, well respected English 'public' schools. This then is where the male siblings were all educated as was their father before them. His one sister however was 'packed off' ("sold", he would often say) to the Roman Catholic Convent where after a lifetime of service, she was eventually to become the Holy Mother Superior, holding this high office for many years prior to her death. A long, loyal life dedicated to the teachings of the Roman Catholic Church by my aunt, transpired to carry her to such heights despite attempts by my father together with one of his brothers who, in the early years of her incarceration at the convent, joined my father in attempts to rescue their only sister from the grasp of or indoctrination of the convent. On one particular occasion, both 'kidnapped' their own sister, 'stealing' her away from the convent, desperately trying to show her that an alternative life existed. They wanted her to have the opportunity of choice!

They wanted her to be free from such a restrictive life. However, all such attempts were to be of no avail. As the boys grew older, this conflict within my fathers' family reached, I am told, quite devastating proportions. We will return to this struggle later on.

So, having armed you with this tiny overview of just some information on the background of my parent's Dear Reader, you may now be better prepared for the continuance of the story of my arrival.

Arrival!

That this disembarkation, this event that was the arrival of me took place at all, was something of a medical roulette 'wheel-of-chance' in the first place, but was also in the year that National Health was first introduced in the United Kingdom. A strange type of government 'reward' for the surviving population – 'free healthcare don't you think chaps?' For all the suffering the great British fortitude displayed throughout the war, we the nation need to show gratitude – free medical assistance will now be made available to all! Each of us will contribute to a national pool of money that will support this new exciting benefit which will from now on be called "The National Health Service." Just three years after the end of the most devastating, not to say the most expensive of all wars – World War Two. The people, the politicians of the day, were all desperately attempting to build a collective, national feeling of pride, of triumphant success whilst completely enslaved in a shattered society with an economy resting on its broken knees. All able-bodied citizens were being encouraged daily to help create a living environment for the creation in the future of a shared national sustainable peace, a lasting prosperity programme. At the same time, England had to meet its internationally agreed responsibility of financial contribution (Retribution?) by paying its part toward the re-building of a destroyed German infrastructure. You know – the land, homes, factories of those that were to be leaders of the 'pure' human race for the next ONE THOUSAND YEARS – but failed! All these foreign costs at a time when massive reconstruction needs at home were not being attended to with anywhere near the same level of political expediency or enthusiasm. My arrival year was also to be the year that a new country, a new 'homeland' was to be born.

The shocking 'discoveries' of over 6 million perished souls – the attempted murder of an entire nation (race/ethnic group) in just the few war years provided the energy, impetus, politically moral opportunity for the Great British RAJ/Bwana/Father to finally fight for the creation of the modern day state of Israel – 'with so much to recover from chaps, let's now wash our hands of that irksome issue'. 'Let us make it look as if we have carried out our responsibility at last in resolving the Jewish homeland question. Draw a line here – now here – yes, even there! Thus in the modern day, the state of Israel was born.

The ensuing war that continues to this day baffles all the so called smart brains in political circles across the globe!

Controversy!

Ha! The year of my arrival was also towards the final years of that utterly foolish, yet greatly politically expedient best-ever British foreign policy worldwide con-job. Perhaps even the best such expedience trick by any governing state in the history of man, the so-called UK 'baby-boom' – the 'Your country still needs you' debacle.

So, to be born at home when medical science at the time was at a level never before experienced by the common folk, but was not yet however full of 'scanners' or other sexy (forgive the pun please) exotic electronic advances. Much of all maternity activity continued at this time to be conducted to a large degree as it always had been – in a hushed almost secret-society way.

Mostly this activity was governed on the basis of 'what-mother-knows-is-best'. Put another way; 'old-wives' influences still held a powerful sway in the world of birthing!

Two of Us!

So, part two of the arrival controversy was that there were two of us arriving but I became the sole survivor of possibly identical twins! It was however, identical only in as much as both were developed as male but only one was fully developed at birth. My erstwhile companion of the dark, wet, warmth of my mothers' incubation chamber sadly did not make the final journey into this world. Perhaps he had an insight somehow of things to come, electing to miss this portion of his greater education. Maybe he somehow knew that FOUR boys would be enough, thus jumping ship for another family. Whatever the reason, having shared the initial stages of conception growing with me, he then failed to make a complete appearance on the grand day. That said though, with little money in the house and suddenly now with four boys to feed, perhaps it was for the better in the long term. This accident of nature was seen in certain circles as an issue to be explored for its seventh-of-the-seventh potential. This was because my mother – the real seventh-of-the-seventh – was also a twin! Quietly imagine if you are able, the dark oft bizarre expectations such an omen may provide. Yet another strange truth!

Nevertheless, the silly but somehow obvious question I have often tooled with during moments of stupid inner self-study of course is – am I him or am I me? Could we have switched places on the way? Was I born first or second? Would it have made any difference to the end result? Well whatever, there was to be only one new fully formed (hungry no doubt) child this day (sorry – night) on the 19th or the 20th October, who by gender was set to destroy or challenge the incumbent male sibling triad.

Now Four Boys! (I was a Daughter)

I was to create therefore from that moment, a grand family total of four boys when there could have been five. Eventually there were to be five of us, but no more boys!

The potential awful future of living with testosterone headaches of now four boys was surely a warning to my parents that their shared dream of a daughter was to remain just that, a dream. They of course took little or no notice of any possible warning!

They only ever wanted a girl.

Here comes our daughter?

So yes, perhaps Dear Reader you have guessed correctly – now comes part three of the controversy with some more strange truths – I was for almost nine months the girl that my parents had always wanted. Not yet physically in view but developing, nevertheless expected to arrive in the fullness of time. This expected girl – surely the signs were right this time – I even received a name to be savoured, tasted publicly and tested throughout the long pregnancy period. A name that was reflective of recent Royal history even?

That name was, Alexandra.

The Daughter That Never Was.

This naming of the unborn infant was to be the outwardly self-assured statement that, this time, indeed a daughter was on the way, perhaps even – if size or 'feelings' were anything to go by – maybe two daughters! The hanging of the house brick over the swollen belly test, swing left boy, swing right girl, had been undertaken so yes the innocent house brick indicated that the female spirit at least lay within! All was fully planned, prepared even to the extent that at the Christening, I was to be introduced to the family of Christ as Alexandra, the daughter now no longer in-waiting! The future had been planned in detail. Baby clothes of gender-correct hue had to be made to match the future dream for now this was indeed the final attempt at production of a female offspring. Amendments to the family cradle, the oft used crib, had to be made to ensure soft pink would prevail. Well, here I was at the end of the wait completely oblivious to these destroyed plans, these shattered dreams, that my naked, screaming body was displaying an obvious appendage that indicated that this child was most definitely not the anticipated girl!

After months of self-sure expectation – another boy! The deflation of such a long held expectation caused by my truth must have been catastrophic.

In a short period of heave, push, sweat, heave again, all the plans, the preparations for the desperately wanted daughter were obliterated! Despite this awful news, the let down once again, my parents soon banished these memories from the scene! I, this latest addition to an established male dominated pride, needed attention. "Oh, I don't want you," was my mother's cry on being handed her next son to feed!

Nevertheless, I was to be given a name in the true Christian way that reflected my obvious gender. Well I was actually given two Christian names as were two of the other boys who had arrived before me. My names therefore were proclaimed henceforth to be Richard, Alexander! Perhaps here was a possible compromise in the second name, a shaded recognition of the lost dreamed-of Alexandra, don't you think? Maybe so, but a quiet, silent compromise that thereafter was never to be brought into future conversations, either public or private.

I know the essence of truth in respect of this particular family strange truth as you will no doubt agree. Simply put, I have a brother, Greg, the first born child of my parents, who, as the 'exalted one', received not just two, but three Christian names – James, Gregory, Charles. He has however never, ever been referred to as James or Charles. In fact, when big brother Greg was married at age 21 (I was 14 going on 29 years old at the time of this wonderful occasion), I recall being astonished on hearing the vicar refer to someone with a deliberately slow enunciation as James, Gregory, Charles "who was to take this woman–" etc., suddenly wondering who the hell the old fart was talking about! This was to be the first time I had ever heard our big brother Greg called James! I remember clearly being startled by this, taking some moments before I realised that the guy in the long black dress with the silly white top was talking to big brother Greg! I had another brother, Andrew – the second born child of my parents who, as with the rest of us boys thereafter, was less 'exalted' than the first born, but setting the naming convention for the remaining boys by only receiving just two Christian names. Andrew was bestowed with the Christian names of William, Andrew. Here again though, Andrew has never, ever been referred to as William, or even 'Bill' or any other derivative of the name William!

Finally, I have a brother, Chris, the third born child to my parents (even less of an exalted-one than boy number two who was less exalted than the first etc.,) who was christened Robert Christopher! Maintaining the now truly established naming convention, Chris has never ever been referred to as Robert, Bob or Rob or any other similar names reflective of the name Robert. So, all three elder brothers of mine then were never encouraged to use their given first name. Then along comes boy-child number four, really no exaltation, not even a glimmer – you know that final attempt! The one who must be the girl – arrived – well as you now know two of us arrived, I just happened to be the fully formed breathing one – christened with first name Richard followed by a mild reference to the now defunct Alexandra – I was given Alexander as my middle name. Thereafter for all time never ever, not even once ever, to be referred to as Alexander! Do you see the pattern now – three boys with unused given FIRST names whilst me (the daughter that never was) with an unused given SECOND name always to be called Richard. The disappointment of Alexandra buried, opaquely shied away from, perhaps a painful memory of what nearly was or might have been.

Before I continue further with the great event that was my arrival on this planet, caution leads me to examine the text thus far to fill in as many of the obvious gaps as possible. This task Dear Reader has been rather like painting by numbers except in the telling hereof some numbers are missing. Possibly due to lack of clarity of memory on my part or perhaps I have forgotten where all the colours go or indeed what they represent. Your generosity Dear Reader is therefore required. I thank you for your fortitude.

Some Missing Bits.

The first missing piece is that of the vastly different backgrounds of my parents. I have indicated that on my fathers' side wealth was evident throughout his childhood until those early adult years.

There is an old very well-known heavy engineering company based in Bath, England having operations around the world including Edinburgh, Scotland. This was our paternal family business into which our father was born, also potentially into which we may also have been born. However, by the time of our collective arrival, our specific branch of this family had lost any connection to the family wealth due to the behaviour of our paternal grandfather. Nevertheless, in most ports across the globe, the giant gantry cranes used for loading or off-loading ships carry the makers' name…that of our family surname. The large metal roller hanger doors seen at most airports in the world are made by the same company. In the 19th century this company was selected to build the original railway bridge across the Firth of Forth in Edinburgh. Such business success over many generations ensured that during his childhood, my father together with his immediate family had the ability to enjoy the best of everything. Having completed his formal education then following a short teaching spell at his school, (it was by now the mid/late 1930s), our father had planned to attend university. Although never actually confirmed, I recall in conversation with my mother that she understood that my father had been accepted to start medical school with the view to becoming a doctor. This however was not to be for two unrelated, but nevertheless compelling reasons. One, the family money ran out and two, World War Two was imminent. In England as elsewhere at this time in the late 1930s, after a long period of economic recession, unless you had money to pay, a university education was out of the question.

Some scholarships were awarded to very bright individuals less well off, but very, very few. War was seen as inevitable, nervous tensions in capital markets as well as donor communities reduced the availability of access to funding, all adding to our fathers' withdrawal from university education before he started. The reason for the loss of the family money I will address some time later; at this point I am simply trying to provide you with a picture of how extreme the void was between the two people who created me. Further, my fathers' family had been for many generations, dedicated, practicing Roman Catholics – a family following a religious lifestyle that would subsequently be rejected by my father due to the treatment of his only sister. Also in his stated view, in his opinion, the single principle defining influential power that this doctrine had in contributing to his own father's demise.

My mother on the other hand was a simple farm girl! Reared as one of a very large, very boisterous family of old English farming stock, living a typical country life of the poor. Growing up through the 1920s, suffering through the great economic collapse of that decade into the early 1930s. Like many of the time, poverty was daily reality. Although little money was in evidence, her parents seem to have been land-wise or street-wise enough to keep their heads above water during these trying times. My maternal grandparents had followed English Christian teachings through membership of the Church of England, accepting with full participation in the established traditions of this august body. Schooling was provided by the local village 'Church School' which, with all its very good intentions, was lacking in sophistication at anything other than a basic level. The sudden ending of formal learning however arrived for our mother at just 14 years of age, a circumstance imposed due to the sudden death of her own mother.

As was expected therefore within the accepted 'tradition', in such circumstances the youngest female of the farming family, if there was one, shall take over the role of 'mother', allowing the rest of the family to try to continue with their daily lives as best they can. In discussion, my mother referred to this part of her life many years later as the time when, without much of an idea or practical experience, she held court over a household of many, learning to cook, feed the family including the domestic animals, darn woollen clothing, sew, wash, clean, make beds, search for eggs, muck out the barn – all in an instance. Her childhood cut short, no teenage time – an instant adult in a sink or swim situation. I think I was about twelve years old, maybe thirteen when she first spoke to me about this period of her life. I have no idea if she ever repeated the story to my siblings but she evidently thought I was old enough to understand. She informed me that due to the loss of her mother at such an early age in her life, she had very little understanding or even knowledge of relationships between humans. Perhaps as our father was not the sort to tell or instruct his sons on such matters, she had taken that task upon herself. Yes of course she had seen how farm animals reproduced, had actively assisted in the delivery of lambs etc., but she nevertheless had only some imagined whispers of similar grotesque activities between humans. She had no mother to turn to for information on such matters. By way of explanation of this conversation with me at the time, she said that when she was about age twelve or thirteen when her monthly periods started, the only thing her mother had said was that from then, on she must not under any circumstances play with boys! A real disquieting quandary for a young teenage girl who has six brothers! Thus it was she confessed to me just as my own sexuality was being awoken, that she had no idea what virginity was or what a prostitute was or indeed anything to do with carnal matters until her marriage to our father at the tender age of twenty.

Giving a shy laugh about this sad state of affairs when seemingly I was old enough to understand, I recall her saying that she had to purposefully seek information from those around her at the time of her wedding --- "What do I have to do?"

So the human history mix that was to create me was Public School Education, old-money Wealth-vs-Village Church School, poverty surrounded in worldly ignorance! That is not to suggest for a moment that my father's knowledge of things sexual was any greater than my mothers' total ignorance. I suspect that he too was on a journey of discovery of his own when they were married.

It is also essential at this stage of my story for you to know Dear Reader that I do have a sister! Yes, my parents continued to try for their dream, resulting in, finally, the always longed for daughter. My sister was born following two more miscarriages some five years after my arrival. Thus the final composition of my family was seven people – my parents, four boys together with, after oh so many, many attempts – a daughter! Equally as exalted as the first born of their brew, this new addition to our clan was provided with three Christian names, Penelope, Anne Susan!

TEA vs COFFEE!

I digress. There was yet to be another controversy surrounding my birth.

A controversy that to this day, as I enjoy the evening period of my time on this planet, has maintained such a significant influence on, about, and during my daily life. This controversy has its roots soundly anchored in that wonderful activity, that great, national British pursuit…the making, but more importantly, the drinking of a hot cup of tea! Yes, that all English beverage! Never mind the Empire where that stiff upper lip prevails, oh no, here on the hour by the hour, the English imbibe their tea; from the mean, meek, quiet to the magnificent echelons of society their drinking activities are nothing if not well regarded across the world. Stolen of course from Asia at a fraction of its worth, by the mighty merchants who roamed, raped rightfully pillaging the globe for centuries. This application of skulduggery by the Brits now masterfully performed in so many ways even today.

Back to that warm liquid, that nectar...tea. From India, Ceylon across many other exotic, subjugated nations of the world bludgeoned into submission by the British for the good of the Empire! Tea; that today comes in many guises, full bodied original to multitudes of mild flavours aplenty! Oh how the people of Japan celebrate it, espousing its mythical, perhaps even aphrodisiac qualities, apparently evident in this wondrous fluid. Such was its influence that although there was an obvious lack of money in the family, my mother was, even as a child, addicted to this remarkable slurp. Tea, the phenomenon that provides real answers to a never-ending, inexhaustible multitude of human ailments, real or imagined.

From early childhood, my mother drank tea on the hour, every hour, all day, every day, continuing to do so until the day she died at almost 89 years of age. Although one has to concede that during the last few years of her life, she shared this devotion to tea with some new, more potent liquid friends.

Only once in her life was she to abandon her faithful worship to the 'cuppa'. That, Dear Reader was when she became pregnant with? You guessed it – me!

Hence the next, very serious controversy!

Suddenly without any warning at all shortly after conception, the quickest way to get my mother to vomit was for her to attempt to drink a cup of good English or Irish or any other nations' tea! This appalling sudden state of change to an established life defining activity, took hold without apology, reigning supreme with full control throughout her pregnancy when carrying me together with the unknown other, my twin. This must be therefore success! Absolute certainty, here now at last will be the desired daughter!

The whispers in the passages! Silent, mythical exchanges of fearful yet knowing understanding between women up, down and across our street, oh something was amiss! Here then, at last, after all the years of trying, here was the sign! Surely this change, this altered human capacity in itself was proof-positive, solid confirmation of the foetus gender at the start of this, the now to be the last (Absolute Bloody) 'final' pregnancy. Get ready for the pink! It has to be a girl, it's in the God's…our daughter is on the way! After trying all these years – number one DAUGHTER!

Not one of the previous pregnancies successfully carried or not, had spawned such a life adjusting catastrophe as an abhorrence to the drinking of tea during pregnancy!

A strange craving sometimes yes, but not an outright rejection of the life defining social status activity of my mother… the drinking of tea!

By itself, the rejection of such an established beverage consuming habit by the expectant mother-to-be is, I am told, not unusual. It is often to be seen in sudden often sometimes perverse cravings. Very frequently in rapid changes in disposition that can even make the poor women cry for no apparent reason whatsoever. So, for any woman to not want to eat or drink their favourite food or beverage during pregnancy is nothing untoward.

Nothing that is unless this happens to inflict itself on the dear lady just after the devastation of six years of world conflict! Throughout Europe as a direct result of rationing together with mayhem, and six years of carnage on the high seas, there was at the time of this pregnancy little or nothing other than tea! If anything was available it was bound to be massively expensive thus way beyond current financial capability, but whatever was, would it ever be able to meet the quenching attributes of the loss, albeit temporary, of the one, the only beloved hot drink. After seemingly a lifetime of ensuring that the kettle was constantly on with tea brewing in the pot, my poor mother suddenly found that she had about as much interest in drinking or even making tea as I currently have in the mating instincts of the greater-spotted ants that are only found in the northern mountain reaches of Mexico!

Stop the world! Mrs S isn't drinking tea! Imagine the sheer panic of the local grocer getting to hear the awful news. His volume of sales of the adopted weed now under threat, with the related economic impact which had to be assessed! Maybe finances would have to be adjusted accordingly, it was certain that sales targets would not be met! Friends, relatives – with mysterious others – could be seen huddling in corners or in small groups in the street with bowed heads. Locals were caught in public whispering to each other about this strange, hitherto unheard of affliction. Something dark was afoot! Call in the gypsies, the soothsayers et-al, seek out advice from the voyeurs! Answers to this phenomenon must be found! During each prior incubation, with the end game being yet another subsequent delivery of a boy child, such a preposterous situation had not arisen! This must be a sign of the will of God to answer the parents' simple wish – a daughter was in her at last!

That this situation was as a direct result of her pregnancy was never questioned! That this adversity was a foreboding sign far beyond comprehension was fully accepted with the gathering of scandalmongers, however, no real answers were to be found.

There were yet many months to come of experiencing this strange burden, requiring continuous support by friends from near or far, cousins with family history and knowledge of repute, all called to question. Was there anyone able to offer suggestions to repair the damage, or to provide for an alternative, warm, liquid sustenance! Early March was a long way to go with no tea until October or even into November! It was set to be a very, very long nine months indeed! The real problem facing all with any interest in the matter was what to use as an alternative or substitute. I have been given to understand that many were consulted.

Across our end of the council estate, multiple meetings were held. Voices in regular but hushed discussion, separated only across rickety garden fences, mumbled in confusion with not just a little bewilderment. "The woman must be parched, she'll just have to drink water, or milk if she can afford it."

I am told that it was to be some time before a solution was found. But found it was, then offered in excited anticipation of acceptance by the poor inflicted woman who by now, was perhaps a very dehydrated mother-to-be. Ground Chicory! Yes, that stuff 'pretending' to be coffee, produced for sale in a solid glass sauce bottle similar to that of one dark brown sauce, which to this day remains a very famous supplier to the most royal house in England. This dark sauce, this burnt black, ground down Chicory was almost something from "The Dark Side" that could address the disorder. But this was no sauce though. Rather it was a thick black 'gumph' with perhaps a long very faint reference to any whiff of coffee. As a temporary hot drink of sustenance however, it did provide the solution. Although via its generations of pillaging to build an empire across the world, the entire known coffee bean production still lay in the hands of just a few English descendants throughout all the far flung corners of the globe, the ability to ship real coffee during the previous 10 years to England had been badly interrupted. The result, chicory based 'CAMP' coffee or thickly compressed brown 'stuff' in an upright bottle, would have to suffice. So for many months, the only warm to hot fluid offering nourishment to meet the needs of this pregnant lady, a situation requiring resolution due to enforced abstinence of tea drinking – not to mention to also have the kettle to be on – was substitute coffee!

So what? I hear you shout.

Yes, in the great universal scheme of things, this is hardly to be of any earth shattering consequence. Except that once I had arrived, mother was able to return to her lifelong hot beverage friend tea, breast fed the little bugger of another "unwanted" boy for several months, then attempted to remove the little sod from her breast by giving him (me) tepid tea! All hell broke loose.

You may have now guessed that this was not to be a pleasant experience for either party involved; such inconsiderate activity giving this child tea. Not only at her first try to supplant her milk but also at very many subsequent attempts, apparently! Finally however, the vile hidden truth emerged, RICHARD (the daughter that was not to be) – did not like tea. When replaced with tepid (pretend) coffee, the little bundle of joy gulped, then gulped some more with subsequent contented departure from his mother's nipple!

Was I born today or yesterday? According to the two people claiming responsibility for my wellbeing at the time, it was really today – I will never be sure who was right.

Which of the two boys am I? An interesting thought but one that to this day remains best left alone.

Not a girl, despite the omens, just another boy – boy number four!

Finally, how is it possible that my parents produced a child who rejected their shared favourite hot beverage when first conceived at a time when he was only a 'dot' in his mothers' womb? The effect of the tea issue thus far in my, predicted to be a very long, comfortable life, has meant that I have had no more than a dozen cups of tea ever and then, mostly only out of politeness or by mistake.

Also!

What, if any, 'gifts' had this partial seventh-of-the-seventh-twin received beyond those of the common people? Look to the future young man!

Having now successfully survived conception, the sharing of a womb where one of us fully completed the rigours of birth then, finally separated from my mothers' bosom, it was soon time for me to crawl through the process of exploring my environment whilst at the same time looking to establish my place in the pecking order of the family clan. Controversy would however be my unwanted companion as this boy-child sought to understand, to immerse himself in the adventures of his own life journey!

Different Pieces!

Having arrived, it was not to be too long before the realisation that even though my birth had been an earth shattering event, my first discovery was to be that the world was not just for or of me! Others had been this way before me! My parents were not simply in existence to ensure my comfort, no matter how much I was to protest the extreme level of my personal importance to them! (Well, I'm sure I thought so at the time). Even my attempts to convince all those other, earlier, invaders of my new world that the very continued wellbeing of this place must be dependent on my existence alone, fell on seemingly uninterested ears with no beneficial effects to me whatsoever! It was that nothing I could do at the time would allow for such a false state of self-righteousness or imagined grandeur to continue for too long. How quickly was that enclosed cosy, warm, very personal sleep-food-clean-sleep horizon to expand, encompassing others needs for parental attention? Despite my urgent very best efforts to stay in that new-baby phase where periods of constant warmth together with regular 'own' attention to every whimper surrounded my waking life, they were to evaporate, leaving me to my own devices for defensive survival. The secret ability of the new-born to articulate its singular particular distress to claim by demand ATTENTION! NOW!

You know, that start-up priority service at the cost of almost everything else, that auto-responsiveness awarded to us all for entering this life – all too soon was over, gone, never to be reinstated. I, like most of us I suspect, do not recall when I started to understand that this was how it works, that the world was not just a place of wonder designed specifically for me. This was the natural way of progression from constant care to some alternative that seemed to offer the same sort of protection but with much less individual attention, less notice even of or to my chosen priorities!

I can only assume that the 'cuddle', show-off new baby, put dry baby to bed, wash baby, cut tiny fingernails together with indeed all the multitude of new-born parenting activities, took place around me. That once able, I would crawl to investigate my surrounding world of comfort. Seeking out to explore opportunities for fun, for food, for learning where threat could harm. Perhaps the biggest initial shock to me as one of a multitude, a people filled family home, was that I was actually nothing 'new' at all! Nothing special, nothing exciting, just another noise, another clan member who really was nothing that had not been experienced before by my instant siblings or parents – just another boy-mouth to heed on occasion, make room for to feed on occasion!

Originally, unwanted as a result of my gender, surrounded by controversy, having denuded my human maker of her all time favourite beverage for some eight months or more, it was the time now for me to escape, a time to become a fully fledged active participant in the lives of this enforced family fraternity. From then on, my task was endeavouring to stake my rightful claim, my place in the clan on all the things that I thought mattered. Even some that didn't! Thus I set about the enormous although nevertheless justified mission of learning to hide from further wrath within this family community. A community swathed in a volatile dissonance of never ending action wrapped in sound. I now, looking back, seemed to have raced through all the usual years of crawling, learning to walk, fighting, indeed shouting or crying sometimes, all driven by need of succour or love or food.

As the youngster of the pack, that one at the back, suck-the-hind-tit-end-of-the-litter individual in all things, it was my duty to recognise, soon, however reluctantly awarded which was matched no doubt with like reluctance, my pre-consigned place in the group.

Having succumbed to this unexalted status, pretending to be the happy little runt of the litter, I survived reasonably unscathed. Some may well question the impact that this initial section of my life's journey may have had on my mental wellbeing as an adult, but hey – no one is perfect, right?

Remember also, this is the late 1940s, early '50s in England, where the nation is desperately seeking to prove to itself that the sacrifices, the carnage, not least THE COSTS of the recently completed world conflict, will indeed produce a long lasting peace for a better life for all! The taxman was kind to the parents of multiple offspring; councils were building housing estates with a view to catering for the growing populace. A battered, shattered, almost broken populace was attempting to find normality after almost a decade of abnormality! Above all, rationing was still in place, money was always something that those 'other' people had whilst the daily fight for the scraps was simply a necessity for the vast majority!

Today as I write this history of my journey, nothing of a very spectacular nature lives within my memory of those very early years. Perhaps I have just chosen to forget most of the first twenty-four months or so of life, just submitting that from birth to over two and a half years of age or more, I am reliant on others to fill in the many blanks. As I was of very little interest to those close to me, just another boy-mouth, my family have not been able to fill in very much. I am told that there are few of us however who have any real recall of the first two or so years of life. I am no exception to this failing or ordained infant development rule.

There is however a very opaque picture in my memory of me standing outside the garden gate of our house looking beyond the gate into the passage leading to the back garden – a very unhappy little person because something is wrong.

What that something is continues to remain hidden from memory-view though. Not too opaque a picture however not to be able to recall that nose excretion had somehow combined with salty tears to plaster with resultant 'gumph' portions, my screwed-up, albeit angelic, features. Distress is very evident but without any reason unidentified. Perhaps this distress was caused by the immense size or the structure of this (small garden gate) giant obstruction preventing me from moving forward. In this somewhat oblique picture, there is no memory of any sound at all, no dog barking, no shouting human – young or old, stranger still – no baby crying! I am holding something at the time, a toy, stick or cherished possession that perhaps others were intent on taking from me. Why this shadowy image is retained in my early memory of life remains today a complete mystery. Doubtless however I was rescued, managed to survive this particular episode without too much physical or emotional impairment. Although it may have been normal in such a largish family but the other thing about this recollection, was that no one really took much notice of the needs of my padded tail-end, so perhaps this may have provided additional impetus to ignoring the obvious baby-boy-frustration-rage. After all, they had all seen it, heard it before – hence the flowing snot mixed with tears by the garden gate!

My 1st real memory!

One event that was to become my first captured, my first 'fully retained memory', occurred one winter morning when I was about three plus a few months I think. It may have been slightly earlier but not too much.

I could have been around three years four months at the most, which would make it somewhere between late October to late February. It was clearly during winter as the narrative here will portray. I know for sure that it was, in child-time anyway, long before I started school. Logic today suggests that with my third birthday in October (the 19th not the 20th), together with the fact that the external weather, the temperatures particularly at the time of this event conspiring to play a role, then three years, three months feels about right. Irrespective of the foregoing though, this event has always been my first independent, real stored, more importantly, retrievable memory of my life.

So here then it begins. My independent memory, my own picture story, the official 'own' beginning of 'my' life story. That one unique recall of definition, separating me from any other that gives credence to this solitary first individual, totally mine, my memory! Not something shared! The beginning then, Dear Reader, of my own remembered life, a first of my individual truth memories. Whilst I cannot be certain, because at the time of this event, days or weeks or any other contrived human time measurement tool was unknown to me, I am convinced that the event took place on a Sunday morning in winter. The reason for such a statement of strong belief regarding this incident, one that left its physical as well as mental mark on me, is that it has the sudden angry intervention of my father at its resolution.

I can see him now quite clearly; red-faced, full of blustery vocal anger, not at me, but at the older boys. More detail on this later. During the first few years of my life, Sunday was the only day that my father did not go to work having returned to his wife, who already had a young family comprising two boys in 1946.

Here he was resplendently dressed in his badly fitting yucky 'De-mob' suit, having played his own role in the glorious defeat of the German Nazi War Machine. Father regained his pre-war job as a cinema projectionist. Not quite the occupation he or his family had been planning during his schooling career.

His new – non-military working week in those days comprised some 'flexible' hours because most cinemas' were only open from late afternoon, midday on some occasions, through to late evening each day, Monday to Saturday but also including Saturday mornings to cater for children's 'Saturday Club' at the 'pictures' or, as we knew it, "Saturday Morning Flicks"! It was not to be until many years later that cinemas were to open for longer hours then followed very quickly with Sunday opening as a matter of course. By that time however my father had created a career for himself in the electronics components industry with a company undertaking government arms development work. I remain convinced therefore that this impressive first life memory event of mine, the first of multitudes yet to come, must have been on a Sunday morning because he was usually late to rise after arriving home late the night before. That this episode took place in the morning after breakfast I have absolute certainty. As the physical washing of the breakfast dishes in the kitchen was the catalyst for this special family occasion, then with all things being equal, my first real memory reasonably intact including the arrival of my father on the scene, must have been after breakfast one very cold, winter Sunday morning. Maybe it was in January, definitely a very cold, very dull, dark grey day!

Family Rules!

Before progressing further, it is important that an appreciation is held by you Dear Reader regarding some aspects of our family culture at the time, a culture that remained throughout the raising of this particular family where responsibility for some household matters rested in particular with the male siblings. A broader comprehension of this 1st fully recorded memory in my head may be easier to appreciate when you grasp a small quirk of our directed even designed home behaviour!

A somewhat strange family rule amongst many such life rules governing social order across almost all activities in our household. Naturally, due to the dominant gender of the occupants of our three bedroomed house, life without structure or rules would have potentially resulted in complete anarchy with the accompanying constant hellfire dominating all. Strict rules therefore demanded adherence, taught control, but more importantly – they engendered blind obedience through fear of punishment. Such was the nature of that immediate human group into which I was attempting to ingratiate myself that I seem to think at the time, that I had not had very much success in winning any friends or influencing anything at all. One rule of membership on acceptance into the family clan was an imposition from on high, a qualifying edict imposed on its (then) collective male sibling membership! All non-adults or by default, those of us dependent on adult protection, irrespective of age or capacity but not of gender as we brothers were to discover many long years later, were subject to a decreed duty at the conclusion of any meal in the house. Irrespective of where in the house such a meal was enjoyed or by whom, or even to the exclusion of whom, we had to clear the table or tray, wash-up, dry the dishes, put everything back in its proper place after each such repast.

This, we were informed later when we were able to understand, was to ensure that our mother was always acknowledged for her work in the kitchen by never having to clean up the utensils, plates, pots or pans. This was to allow her to thus enjoy a quiet time of her own at the end of the meal.

Looking back on this today however, I could very contemptuously suggest that as my father's own childhood and early life was surrounded by maids or staff that 'did', he now wanted his own children to act as a subservient species to him in order to reflect to his wife that he was now truly the 'man-of-the-house'.

Having this view is not a judgement statement by me at all. Rather it is more a recognition of a lifestyle long lost in my fathers' life. Anyway, I do much prefer to see things positively thus I recall many happy hours sharing collective discussion, thoughts, comments, fun, argument, debate, often with laughter alongside my brothers over the years of growing up at these enforced kitchen sink duties. In addition to the basic chore however, these dish-wash times also presented an opportunity to share time with each other that perhaps other children in other families never experienced. These times were also for squabble, application for dominance one over one or one over the others, maybe two over two! Perhaps two of us (me when much bigger) may have wanted a particular advantage over the others, well, this was the place to attempt to win that right. It was a time to test, to challenge whilst altogether we could subsequently confirm the inherent status, the pecking order rights dictated by chronology of birth. Sounds good in theory but where needed victory either morally or offering physical gain in status, was gained by weight of sheer body power ability with associated punching using the hardest fist!

So here at the kitchen sink existed for many years a garnering of understanding of shared life experiences, a combined sibling ebb flowing often with the pride of the lives of four brothers who danced a shared a tango.

A learning, growing developing strange camaraderie existed amidst participation of an enforced labour chore of soapsuds often together with an array of damp walls.

(All this because someone still had to invent that all-time best ever domestic machine – the dishwasher!)

The day of this first fully remembered memory of mine, whilst full of potential to be another kitchen sink visit affording potentially moments of joy, turned out to be the exact horrible opposite! A winter morning when the external cold, dull, dark grey day morning assisted in building a visual quality of steamy murkiness in our kitchen. The sort of 'not-quite-finished around the edges' daylight that would still require the use of those now abandoned but powerful search lights employed during the recent world conflict to really infiltrate the murk to provide any definition at all! Single glazed, poorly fitted windows with one half trying to keep the external bitter cold from invading our warmth whilst the other side of the same piece of glass, was being subjected to muggy warmth generated by steamy hot water attempting to escape to the outer cold. Both sides of the same pane of glass conflicting fiercely whilst the internal side was fully encouraged by a constant stream of running-dripping moisture displayed over the pane, somehow supported by cloudy steam particles running randomly over the walls in the kitchen. Sloshing, foamy dish washing water dripped from 'almost' dry plates as they were carried by one of the dryer-uppers of the day from the draining board to the kitchen table. These once grease infested water drips splattered across cheap smooth shiny linoleum flooring which was slowly building a non-stick film of slippery stuff underfoot! All the while the thick coating of steam refusing to allow what little natural light there was to enter our busy kitchen, ensuring a morning atmosphere generally dark, dank, discernibly steamy, which was really quite unpleasant. Because we were now in midwinter, the coal fire had been alight in that 'strange' rarely visited 'front room' or 'lounge' for many weeks now.

It was simply kept going by the essential talents of adults who knew how to re-ignite yesterday's embers to procure heat for today. The existence of this living fire endowed our family with constant hot running water throughout the winter as the 'boiler' was situated behind the fireplace!

The kitchen sink with its draining board were placed by the design of the house under one of those broad double kitchen window units allowing anyone standing at the sink, the opportunity to look out across the expanse of the back garden to the other homes in the distance. When the weather was kind that is! It was not kind on this special Sunday morning. The floor was wet, the stacking area for the plates where cups, bowls together with all associated breakfast paraphernalia requiring washing, was also wet with damp. Leftover greasy slops were everywhere. The drying as well as the putting-away area on the kitchen table was very wet with soapy-greasy. The draining board had running slops urgently attempting to reacquaint themselves with erstwhile colleagues splashing about in the sink, which in turn was being stirred by the washer-person of the day who was busy creating more suds! A single 40-watt clear light bulb hanging from its central overhead position in the ceiling, itself covered in steam, gallantly struggled against all the odds to shed anything more than a faint smoulder on the scene below.

To offer successful management of the many tasks associated with the combination of chores in the execution of this kitchen responsibility, including collecting, stacking and washing the dishes, there had been a process created amongst my siblings, a loose sort of 'rotation' of responsibilities that was in situ long before I was.

Who would wash? Who would dry? Who would put away etc?

There was only a single sink unit therefore for all practical purposes only one person would be allocated the 'washing' responsibility. Before my arrival, each of the others would undertake a single task usually one washing, one would wipe-up, another would carry out the task of putting everything away to complete the established process.

This arrangement subtly changed on my arrival once I was at an age to participate. Yes, still one 'washer-upper' as before but now two 'dryers' then just one child to do the putting away. So here is a picture of domestic order supervised by seniority either expressed through age, weight or cunning! On this particular day, the task of 'putting-away' fell to me. The actual allocation of responsibility for the tasks that day continues to remain a mystery to me which is perhaps for the good of all of us. I am sure however that no malice was ever intended in the process of allocation of duties on that, or any other day.

I accept that it was, as always, a simple matter of "that's your job today Richard" so therefore without power to question, it would be! As you may realise, me being a toddler of just approximately three few months into my fourth year, I was little in stature in both the physical or indeed pecking order definitions. Neither was I yet vocally adept at this tender age to present any really effective qualifying resistance to the established proven collective willpower of my siblings. Many bruises from stupid previous defiance not withstanding! Even with personal events yet to come, I had not developed my wit enough to provide a challenge that could give any impetus.

Thus all was set for an event that has the dubious honour of being my first real full 'own' memory, one that represents the first piece of the story that is me.

Our kitchen was quite large, mostly the centre of activity for all things in the house. It was the place for food preparation of course that together with four growing boys, presented the need for constant stocking of the larder which was always challenging! No fridge, just a large marble shelf at the bottom of the pantry cupboard where there was a permanent open vent to the outside world for keeping things fresh. This piece of marble was a very effective way of cooling things during the heart of winter but not so reliable during the balmy heat of summer. Other than the usual sink, draining board, work surfaces, cupboards, cooker (electric, solid plate monster that required no less than four huge men to move it), there was also an old wooden farmhouse style table with an unimpressive collection of unmatched chairs in support. This table was where we as children spent most of our 'indoors' time usually because its location pre-determined that it was to always be one of the warmest rooms in the entire house for most if not any time of year. Well the warmest room into which we monsters were allowed to be, without seeking permission, anyway! The kitchen was constantly steamy with a wonderful cosmopolitan collection of warm smells from a wet dog or cat or bird or many other manner of stray animals or lost pets seeking shelter with us at any given time. This, along with the sleeping, scratching, sneezing, animal menagerie, in particular on washing days, one could also include that cloying thick smell of steamy wet washing wafting from the open top boiler – another electric metallic ozone aroma simply adding something special to existing gloriously exotic cooking fragrances. Boiling cabbage, carrots, green beans all steaming on the oven hot plates! Thus the kitchen then was the heart of our home with its pulsating, rushing life-blood being an effervescent constant flow of noise, people, animal smells, all accompanied by clattering chatter.

The kitchen was also the real entry to our house, a place where friends, local traders, in fact anyone visiting came always using the back door with the exception of the parish vicar on his odd visits, or when the family doctor or local police visited. These dignitaries always entered in style via the front door, the opening of which to allow entry of such visitors was indeed very rare. So the kitchen, with its own door was the life portal to our home, acknowledged as a welcome reception area to all life – human, animal, domesticated or wild.

Possibly, like most homes, the location of the kitchen was also of specific strategic importance because just outside the back door, now established in your mind I hope as the genuine prime entrance to our home, was the outside loo. When urgent need demanded a quick exit of the back door, there waiting to supply solace immediately located directly on the left outside, was the thunder box. This lavatory, to give it its correct name, was constructed of bricks, had a weather-beaten slatted wooden door that latched closed despite is constant warped shape, with a corrugated asbestos roof. This 'external' room commanded such respect that without any fear of God's wrath, it was a room known to have its' own temperature control system! Without any reference to the proper world or indeed recognition of or to any known natural laws of physics, weather or season, this room guaranteed that during our period of winter or summer even without the wonder of air-conditioning, a temperature far below freezing which was its very own, personal constant! An ice-box in which a call of nature was attended to only at the very last possible second – just to get the visit over with as quickly as possible! I can assure you, Dear Reader, that the placing of ones' naked bum or taking out one's appendage from its warm protection into a frozen chamber irrespective of the natural season at the time of such need, was something we boys all learned to manage with reverend respect!

Even at the height of what is laughingly referred to in England as summer, this external place of human waste disposal remained in constant defiance of Mother Nature by not ever supporting the concept of HEAT! In fact the cistern, that flush reservoir of cast iron hue suspended high above one's head like some ugly brown rusted catch-all of cobwebs, often stubbornly remained frozen, irrespective of season! Well that's how I remember this particular, special 'room'! To this day I can still remember looking up seeing icicles extending from the bottom of this rusty water container with similar ones hanging around the edges of the lid like glass stalactites, pointing with suppressed accusation at the visiting incumbent below!

The reasons for this lack of warmth, I have since learnt, rests entirely with the very poor design of the materials used in its construction coupled with even shoddier workmanship of the attached outhouse. Even allowing for the lack of materials, the appalling use of sheets of corrugated asbestos as the roof material simply nailed to the rafters without anything internally to protect the occupants, let alone the requirement of water storage with a flowing ability, can only be described today as gross stupidity. This 'popular' outside lavvy however with its hand torn squares of newspaper – courtesy of last weeks' 'Bucks Herald' or 'Bucks Advertiser' hanging on a piece of furry string – which itself was dangling from a rusting bent nail buried in the soft, flaking plaster between the bricks, was for the exclusive use of 'the boys' only. Whilst upstairs, inside the house was a bright, light, well-built and WARM bathroom that had been created by a deity caring nothing for little boys at all but who had determined that this 'bog' – sorry, loo, was to be for the exclusive use of adults only although in years to come – also one little girl, our sister.

Enough now, back to the 'event'.

Of the odd, sometimes strange, assortment of chairs I have mentioned located around the kitchen table, there had been for some years as part of this collection, a rather old but nevertheless really trusted three-legged farm stool. To this day I have no idea if this piece of furniture in our kitchen was rescued from the farm on which my mother had been raised or by chance, had been acquired from some secondhand, or perhaps in the case of this item, some twentieth hand shop for a few 'pennies'. Nevertheless, there it was. And there it had been for a long time before me, thus it had stamped its right to existence with our family long before my attendance. It was happily lodged under the kitchen table with a seemingly undeniable right to occupy a place with the other chairs!

The question, if any, revolved around the use to which it was put! For whatever reason, this object of furniture had been selected by one or more of my siblings that Sunday morning as the necessary piece of equipment on which baby brother Richard, the current toddler of the household would be climbing upon when he needed to 'put-things-away', especially things that were located high up on cupboard shelves. Shelves, whose own height above the ground exceeded, at the time anyway, Richards' miniature, although growing stature. Some of the lower shelves were simple to reach so this stool was only to be used by the toddler when a washed, dry (ha!) object or a number of objects held simultaneously had to be placed where height, upstretched arms with out-stretched hands, were needed to complete the putting-away task.

Now, to any reader who has a little or perhaps even no knowledge of a 'three-legged-stool' – you must first accept that these stools were not made with, by or for anything representing a particularly genteel activity, pristine location or occupation. Hewn from solid hunks of local wood, bashed, scraped, and drill-wedged into shape with no art or reason or need for delicacy in handling or prettiness of the final product.

All possible rough edges had been smoothed out of the somewhat curved initially, very roughly carved seat area, which had then been polished through constant use by rounded human buttocks completing heavy demanding duties usually on uneven, rough farm surfaces. The production of these stools was traditionally only to provide a seat, perhaps in a field, or farm yard, or less than smoothed muddied floors of farm shed or barn, although such stools could sometimes be found in large kitchens that had either flagstone or gritted brick flooring. As a seat though, they were often used in the task of milking cows for example, or to see to other essential processes in the business of farm animal husbandry. A much trusted solid seat then, a portable farming tool proud to be reflecting many generations' use.

The operative, therefore principal word I have used here of course is SEAT. They were not by any stretch of any right-minded, or even left-minded human imagination, designed even by way of default, to act as an elevation platform for a male human toddler! Especially not when the stool was in foreign lands never contemplated by its rural manufacturers, where its legs were required to grip on very smooth, very cold, very damp, soapsud splattered 'lino' kitchen floor on a dark, dull, grey Sunday morning! Indeed, never in such an environment on any other weekday morning, afternoon or evening during any season of the year! Imagine then, if you will, this toddler possibly with bulging pants, no shoes on, with one slightly damp hand, clutching several pieces of, at best still damp or at worst, still soap-skimmed crockery, standing, reaching on tiptoe, clasping with the other wet hand the damp steamy metal door of the cupboard for support, whilst reaching above to place his now high held trophy onto the safety of an inside shelf whose elevation was greater than his (mine). In order to facilitate the completion of this feat of mini-human endeavour, he (me) moved, albeit very slightly, just at the outer most stretching point.

Slippery damp feet standing on generations of bum polished seat of said three-legged stool pointing on tip-toes!

Oh confusion reigns for the stool is now unable to grip with anything, no farm mud to sink into. Oh no! No rutted barn floor to grip on, no large spread of human buttock even to counter any shift, just a highly polished 'flat' lino floor, covered in damp soapy slime where the centre of gravity is now so unstable for this piece of farmyard furniture. It was in such alien circumstances that what happened next was nothing other than a response to a three-legged stools' unintended dilemma!

The stool, having been expecting no doubt the usually ample spread of an adult human backside to ensure its own stability, now had just two small damp, and more importantly moving, toddler feet instead! The ability of the poor stool to maintain any equilibrium with a single point of reference was impossible. A moving weight – my foot – wobbling with me on tiptoe – the concept of solid or steady ceased to exist for the stool. Stability would have been hard enough for a four-legged chair under the same pressure on a wet floor however it proved unattainable for a simple three-legged farm stool. As human hands stretched, as tip-toes of little foot straightened for that final upward push to reach that extra bit more – the sorry stool started to tip, to give up, falling sideways just at the point of furthest human reach!

When three stout wooden legs, themselves smooth-rounded at the ends after years of loyal service, tipped over, reaching beyond that small inclined angle of no return on the wet slippery floor, the cast was set, the tipping-point reached, the result, the inevitable happened!

Crash!

In slow motion, toddler Richard flew with both hands waving, legs kicking in a twisted spiral seeking to attach himself with wet but now empty hands to anything with the potential to offer support. The stool flew in a different direction, attempting to keep upright but failing with awesome effect. The now clean maybe almost dry plates once gripped in the little human hand, also attempted to prove that flying saucers had no monopoly at all in the world but failing with an abysmal effect of flying crockery, unable to maintain independent elevation with a shattering thundering effect! All the players in this airborne comedy suffered combined, simultaneous failure. Not one, not the boy or the stool or any of several plates all having achieved instant flight in a joint celebration of chaos, had the ability to remain whole, although they were all desperate to do so! For some time, they were grotesquely intertwined participants in an unwanted but shared macabre destiny, suddenly performing an ill-fated, unrehearsed ballet where all dancers stop in instant impact on the slippery but hard, sodden floor.

The sudden split second silence, a terrible diabolical moment conjured by circumstance this cold winter Sunday morning in our kitchen, was nothing short of appalling!

As with all such moments that do indeed in 'real-time' last for just a real split second, but for the integral partakers in or those watching the action however – split seconds cease because time itself ceases!

Super slow motion in this period would have been considered very fast at the collective sudden point of impact. Time did not exist as the ballet unfolded, defying gravity, turning, swinging majestically through space. Here was a perpetual silence of a split second! A sudden STOP of all life, all movement, instant death of sound, a frozen world now surrounded us all in our kitchen that morning.

Totally obliterating normalcy! This was however a silence so fully pregnant – just ready to explode. This non-state of utter immobility of all things, this absolute quiet peace (it was Sunday morning after all) was eventually shattered (please forgive the pun) by an enormous ear-destroying scream! Hey! This was no fun at all!

Isn't it amazing how many tiny pieces a single plate can shatter into during such trying times! Not special crockery now, just the mass produced urban, everyday common stuff. Now multiply the picture in your mind, Dear Reader, by at least three such semi-fragile objects.

Add to this, the after effects of an explosive end to the existence of a three-legged stool; chunks, lumps, all alongside splinters of wood mixed together with the slowly creeping, seeping spread of dark red blood…from my head! A strange attempt, an experiment to merge by liquid osmosis, a human toddler, crockery and wood through a non-proven test into some 'other' being! This impossible mix, this beating of a strange inexplicable concoction was being watched by a now two-legged stool that also wanted to mingle with this creation across the damp flowing surface of our kitchen floor! My fully matured prolonged shout was of abject fear! Picture, if you can, the stunned faces of my siblings as they cast their eyes across a scene of destruction, knowing that the uneasy peace of this particular Sunday morning had forever been destroyed!

Perhaps even life itself as they had come to know it was now to be obliterated forever by their infant brother who at this very moment, lay ranting, simply screaming in the bloody chaos that was this particular Sunday morning after breakfast! Throughout it all, the floor remained covered with sloppy soap suds! The prolonged silence had created a powerful threat, a realisation of true danger manifesting itself in the minds behind those frightened, but fully focused, fascinated, even knowing wide eyes! Surely that powerfully extended screech of agony coupled with the nerve shattering commotion had been heard…from above? Racing thoughts that father had indeed been disturbed, was at this very moment thundering down the stairs, having hoisted himself from his warm Sunday morning cosy bed on this, his one day off a week! Incited by the explosion of human linked perhaps to non-human uproar downstairs in his kitchen!

He had indeed been recalled violently from his sleepy revere! Was currently ploughing a thunderous passage to the kitchen! He was greeted as he burst open the passage door into the kitchen from the hallway, with a scene that must have mimicked a real version of a dark story written by some bedevilled Gothic novelist. Four boys ranging in chronological age from little me to Greg at about eleven, surrounded by the remains of shattered plates strewn at random across a blood covered floor, with wood splinters in all directions! Steam dripping down, running across every surface with an external backdrop of a grey, dark, wet and cold Sunday morning! Everything, as he entered the kitchen, given raw emotion by the up-front in-your-face 'Banshee' screeching of abject fright, but of greater import, bloody indignation! I seem to think today that together with the three-legged stool, we had formed some instant secretly shared desire to see which of us could prove to be the best contortionist.

With the power of hindsight I think the stool won that particular trophy. Whilst I had managed to remain almost whole throughout the fall, one of the legs of the erstwhile farm implement designed for human bum had, by even stranger influences, been sent to Coventry permanently by the other two; it had been cast asunder in a multitude of large, medium, small even tiny non-symmetrical fragments, never again to be whole or return to its preceding ample human backside supporting occupation.

It seems almost as if it wanted to share in the shattering experience of the unfortunate plates. It was the final demise of this now multi-splintered stool leg that carried full responsibility for the addition to this spectacle of human blood. It was a slither, a fragment of wood which was cast asunder during all the mayhem that was to blame. A single, possibly lonely even, shocked or lost splinter approximately one inch or so long that had pierced the outer rim of my left ear lobe. Did I say pierced? Well actually not, pierced is incorrect! No. It was really more along the lines of puncture; a penetrating stab or drive through skin, fat gristle and thus it lodged itself completely through this flabby portion of my shaken banged-about toddler body.

Those whose business it is to know these things will quickly advise that any head injury where there is trauma of a large or small nature, is known to produce copious amounts of blood. This truth often makes both the injured party as well as those who may be present at the time, think that the damage is far greater than it really is. This Sunday morning event was no different for those involved as the red stuff sloshed amongst all the other fluid goo with globules of soap! However we, the cast of this particular drama, had no such knowledge to console ourselves with.

At the time it seemed appropriate to me I suppose, without any rational or understood reason, that constant screaming was what I should be doing to somehow protect myself from this particular evil. Adding to this was the perfectly correct accessory by me of yet more fluid – tears of pain clearly running down my screwed up face, adding their unique variety of chemicals to the already very wet, multi-coloured floor. I suppose that had I, as an adult, at any time walked into such a scene involving my own children, I would have reacted in perhaps the same way as I recall my own fathers' reaction to be.

Bloody Foul Murder of his youngest son had been committed on his kitchen floor by his other three sons! Expensive (not really) crockery had been destroyed, a three-legged stool lay in pieces with bits sloshing about around the curled up almost foetal-positioned body of son Richard lying in a pool of running, soapy blood! All this only just after breakfast on the morning of his one day off from work a week! To this day I do not know what words he used, I was only three plus a little bit at the time, suffering noisily, probably (knowing me today) secretly, perversely enjoying the fact that I was the centre of attraction, having been suddenly promoted from the everyday ignored, ignorant runt-of-the-litter status, now hoisted to centre stage! My comprehension of vocabulary generally but adult vocabulary to be more exact at the time was suitably limited. As I lay sprawled amongst the broken crockery, shattered wooden furniture, looking up at my three young-faced siblings staring in consternation at the one old face above me, the crying stopped. Not faded away via a whimper, just ceased. Once again a fully pregnant, terrifying silence visited this new tableau. My father's face just inches from mine, no glasses on his nose, just blue blurry bulging eyes protruding either in anger or fright. Then words!

The picture of my father I carry with me even today at this event is as a huge thunderously red-faced, slightly bleary eyed, dishevelled man whose mouth was forming such harsh shapes. The words exploded from his twisted lips with a power of such massive intensity that spittle in foamy globules hung for a few seconds in expectant collection at the corners of his mouth before dripping from his lips. Each droplet, each filmy drip falling into the outward rushing expelled air used to form those unintelligent (to me anyway) words, becoming an instant fine spray splattering everything close to me including the faces of my frightened, cowering siblings. Eventually by the natural laws of gravity, this was to provide yet more fluid contribution to the flowing mixture already fully established across the floor!

For what seemed like several lifetimes to me, the verbal onslaught of my brothers continued. Roughly I was 'checked' over by fumbling hands seeking no doubt information of the true extent of my injuries. Eventually though the reality of the situation reduced the anguish, the initial blind fear, to a level where a more delicate, though nowhere near permanent, peace by understanding, a fragile truce was established. Gentle egg-shell dancing by the bigger boys proved to add credence to the value of the on-coming acceptance that foul murder had not been committed, just an accident caused simply by lack of forethought had brought about this current Sunday morning family disaster. Things became calmer, almost settled.

I was scraped off the floor and subjected to a full inspection, the slither of wood extracted from my ear, I was washed, rinsed, dried then almost put away. A different cleaning chore was now needed once the kitchen was returned to its normal state with the balance of the original Sunday morning washing-up completed.

Then as often happens with such magnificently memorable events, this one, even with its wonderful earth shattering scary immediacy on that Sunday morning, began to fade into yesterday, soon too many yesterdays vanished into the past only to be recalled at the next explosive occurrence until over time – forgotten.

Except that is, for me! Today I have a perfect circle, a dark skin mark where the wayward splinter of the shattered stool leg punctured my left ear! A permanent physical reminder of an event captured in my memory for ever. My first private recollection, a real life story that is the beginning of me!

This 'bloody Sunday' event possibly signalled for the first time in my young life, maybe perhaps creating an awareness for any to grasp, that my ears, as an integral part of my body, would prove to have a significant role to play in my future. For it was perhaps a little over a year or so after this ear-piercing event that such a life changing significant episode about my ears first emerged. Yes, my ears, one with a puncture, the other whole. Those bits attached to my head were ready to set out their own significance when….

…I was about halfway through my fifth year some four years four months old when first I met, was mesmerised by, fell completely under the magic spell of, became completely totally in love with…the wonderful Mrs Peebles!

Well, I had no concept of human love at the time of course, but oh did this wonderful lady alter my life because she really could make a piano sing colours!

Mrs Peebles.

At the time, I think it was around the end of my first term at infant school heading towards the end of what would have been my first school year, had I started before my fourth birthday. But no matter the actual age, it was the impact on my life that the first meeting with this lady was to have on me. A meeting that proved to be astonishing, that would affect all that I was from, that moment becoming a central foundation to so very much of who I am today!

Dear Reader you must understand that I was, even at such a young age, no stranger at all to this thing called a piano. We had one at home! Yes, it was located in that very special place in our house, that place of parental haven from children, unless of course one, two or more of us were required for some reason or other to attend its interior. That 'out-of-bounds' sanctity, our quiet front room! However, as I'm sure you will be aware, knowing of something even as in this case actually living with such a music making machine, had not attracted me to seek any real knowledge or understanding of what a piano actually was! My ignorance was complete in any comprehension of its' magnificent potential at such an age. An appalling lack of feeling for this instrument which would have seemed to anyone who was then, or is today, really interested, as an absolute sacrilege! Especially as my father was a piano player of moderately good level. Whilst growing up thus far in my tiny life, I had recently heard my elder brother, Chris, plonking away under our fathers' tuition! So there it was, this big very dark brown wooden noise making 'thing' in our home that I had taken little notice of whatsoever.

It seemed to me therefore quite 'normal' at the time for people to have a piano at home. After all, if we had one why shouldn't others.

My father displayed a reasonable competency in his musicianship, playing our piano at home when the opportunity presented itself. In fact, his cunning plan was that when each of his sons reached an age that he considered was the correct stage of child development, they were each to be subjected to his paternal style of individual tuition in this instrument. His own initial learning had been as a child when it was his turn within his family to sit with his father. Naturally there was no consultation with any of us. No asking if we had any interest in or for such tuition! Irrespective of the potential for any of us to harbour alternative thoughts like 'no thank you dad, I'm not interested', the concept of any of his sons being a reluctant pupil simply did not exist in his mind. Even if it did reside vaguely as a potential, that one or more of us may not be inclined, this was not allowed to be expressed in any way. Seeking agreeable acceptance of the participation in learning from or of the boy-child was not then a consideration. Naturally having been taught to play at home during his own childhood, this particular 'gift' had to be passed down to his children as had been the process in his family for generations. After his participating in cataclysmic activities of the Second World War, it was as if he had not realised or even thought that perhaps the world including his own circumstances, had moved far beyond his child-time. Or that his life circumstances had been changed for ever. As breathing out was the result of breathing in, so he established our young lives to be as much as he could a reflection of his own; attempting to teach all of us the basics of piano playing, music composition or appreciation was simply a manifestation of this. Difficult for us today to accept or grasp any hidden torments of our father but surely they were there. This 'piano' stance for instance in the 1950s by a man who was himself a product of the early 1900s during which time the world subjected itself to not one, but two world wars. Even after shocking failures with Greg followed by Andrew.

Their apparent inability not to reflect a single ounce of interest or talent in playing the piano at all was initially I understand considered a challenge to overcome. They, nevertheless, had to continue for many hours over many months of their young lives sat at the instrument with plonking fingers! Father, although bitterly disappointed, persisted with his master plan however! By the time brother Chris, born just over two years before my arrival, was to experience this home piano teaching, our father must have been very downcast, perhaps even recognising that the world may have indeed moved on from his day. However, persistence often will provide rewards as it is said and so it was to be our dear brother Chris who presented proof to our father that his labour had not been wasted at all!

For Chris, the piano became an extension of his fingers, short, altogether podgy though they may have been at the time. His natural musical ability, his easy grasp of music theory was both nothing less than astonishing! A real talent.

But Chris has always been the really very clever one of us. Not just in music but in maths as well. Here at last were the brains, the flair, Chris the child, recognised by all the family as having the ability to absorb knowledge at a rapid rate, to store it, use it when wanted. How devastatingly ironic then that this same child of our parents, this bright one of their brood, comprised a character trait that was ruled by a 'sod-you' personality! This flaw, this characteristic, this finger-in-the-air to authority, perceived or real, this was reflected in all that Chris was as a child, throughout his teenage years and across his adult life. Via his attitude, Chris provided the reality that our fathers' times were indeed of the past, lost forever.

Simply put, our brother Chris was, of all the siblings, the one constantly following the line of 'don't care', the child of rebellion to all things at all things especially anything representing any level of authority.

Even where any potential authority may have been suggested or just mentioned! So then came to our fathers' own reality, a new very hard lesson indeed! Of all his sons Chris, who was without doubt, the one blessed with so much talent, so much intellect, with such thirst for knowledge, with a capacity to learn having reportedly an intelligence quotient level heading towards some high numbers, it was Chris who was to rebuff him time after time. It was to be rebellion at school, raged anger at life generally, together with an attitude of stubborn refusal in accepting any form of imposed civil order that became the outward evidence of these very traits, resulting in the destruction of such a wonderful array of natural gifts in our brother Chris. Other than by his own selection, was Chris ever to use these abilities, these talents for the benefit of himself or for us to admire throughout his adult life.

There must however be no doubt at all that dear brother Chris (Robert Christopher) is blessed with a natural, wonderful abundance of intellect that if used to any extent, would have provided him with the ability to be or do whatever he wanted to be or do. His success at being the angry challenger to all established things around him though was total, complete in the extreme. Exceeded only by his lifelong success of only doing what he wanted to do!

Back to the young pretender – me – with no knowledge of the piano whatsoever. When my time was deemed to be right, my father would invite me without option of refusal, to participate in his imposed learning process. Many further painful hours of irritating 'plink–plonk-plink' to be endured again by the family.

Back to Mrs Peebles!

I cannot today recall in real detail how it was that this lady actually entered my life or indeed if it was just before or after I started 'infants' school. I must confess however that I truly think it was in my first year as a pupil at the local infant's school – the one located at the far end of our road, the one past the junior school, on past Mr B's corner shop where recovery of the tea sales was back to normal, then across a number of small roads. I recall very clearly however being taken in the September before my fourth birthday to this infants' school one morning by my mother. We were sitting outside the office of someone called Mrs Low who was apparently the 'headmistress'. Whilst I knew exactly what a 'head' was because I had one of those (with one punctured ear on the left with another one still whole on the other side), I had no notion of the meaning of the word 'mistress'! As to why these two words should be linked as one, I also had no comprehension. I think however that intuitively, whatever the reason, the very sound of these words merged together then uttered generally in a hushed way, even enunciated in such a way as to demand awe, somehow carried a ring of threatened but yet vague authority. Similar in many ways to a punctuation mark! I remember walking back home a short while later, not knowing why but secretly breathing a sigh of absolute relief because the 'Headmistress' had told my mother I could only start at the school after Christmas – in the new year. A real stay of execution! With my birthday in October when I would be just four years old, it had been officially agreed that I should only start at the school in January the following year.

Thus as decreed previously, I was to be four years plus almost three months of age when I started school. It was January 1953.

This was not an unusual age to start school during the early fifties in England as the role of parenting at that time, was also a role of so-called re-building the nations' stock of cannon fodder or labour force. These were the final years of the 'Baby-Boom' period, encouraged by government to replace all the recently lost souls. There was even a 'tax' incentive to assist this process for all parents, reducing their income tax liability each time a new offspring arrived. The health aspects of the pregnancy period together with the delivery of the child, was for the first time, 'free' due to the national health initiative.

Incidentally, I know now that this whole incentive/baby boom social instruction – "every man is expected to perform his duty" etc., – was a political cover-up ploy by the government of the time, who were embarrassed because of the really low number of casualties actually sustained by England throughout the six plus years of conflict. Low that is when measured in comparison to the contribution of so many other counties to the total global losses! Such a national policy would, (some really believed at the time it did), send the 'correct' political message to all the allies that England had suffered just as much as they had. In other words, yet another infamous piece of British political propaganda to protect the truth.

Now where had I got to?

Oh yes, the wonderful Mrs P.

Over the many years since my first meeting with Mrs P, I have no doubt, embellished in my mind by latent corruption, how we met. As time passes, possibly more recent embroidery may have emerged from my once fertile imagination.

Suffice it to say though, that full recall of the actual event that brought Mrs Peebles together with the four-year-old me is unclear. So in the interests of truth, I will not offer here any definitive view of the how. It is indicated 'the when' must have been sometime after my fourth birthday, possibly during the first half of the fifth year of my existence. It really matters little but on reflection, when attempting to rummage around in the abyss that today resembles what once was a power beyond doubt – my mind, I seem to have the feeling that a friend, a schoolmate of similar age, enticed me to attend a lesson for beginners in the piano one weekday afternoon. It would have been an afternoon because infants school consumed all of the morning, lunch time together with a little of the afternoon. Richard (me that is) was in his first year at the school whilst brother Chris, was in his last year at the same school. Richard was left to find his own way home shortly after his very first day, after embarrassing his elder brother! It may seem appalling in the world of today as I record here the sheer level of confidence my parents had in that I was allowed to 'entertain' myself after school at such a young age, seemingly with little concern for my safety. This also applies to the 'walkabouts' undertaken by me prior to even starting school. With this knowledge therefore it would have been nothing unusual for me to take a detour to use up an extra hour in getting home after school, especially during the spring or summer months when daylight seemed inexhaustible. Anyway, I knew what a piano was. After all, I had made a noise on such a thing at home on my very infrequent visits to that 'front' or 'special' room.

Little fingers had explored this strange machine at home out of curiosity having recognised that this was where father sat from time to time making noise. I also knew that my turn was to come sometime soon when, as in line with my brothers before me, my father would become my very own teacher of pianoforte.

So I guess it would have been without any fear that I would accept such an invitation from a newfound friend to join a piano lesson, if indeed such an invite had been made. Surely it can't be something to worry about or be afraid of!

Oh how very innocent I was!

Any student of this instrument will tell of the anguish, even hate, together with the shear madness from frustration that this music-making machine can create. They will also talk at great length of the wonders of the same instrument. How it can transform you as you gain mastery to unimaginable places.

However I got there, the first time is of little consequence as, in any event, I had entered the home of one Mrs Peebles.

Have you ever had in your mind Dear Reader the perfect picture of your quintessential grandmother? Every inch of her giant towering five-foot-one-inch rotund frame, topped with grey hair tied in a bun, funny little half spectacles resting on her nose and constant cheery-red face, was offering friendship. Well this was Mrs P. She lived in a small house on Chestnut Green, just a short walk along the road from the infants' school I was attending which was about half a mile or so from our house. Her house was, I have since ascertained, approximately 50 years old at that time, young generally for England, resting at the outer end of the council estate alongside an old single track railway line running behind it on that side of the green. I could walk you to it today without a second thought. Chestnut Green is a large roundabout acting as an interchange for the merging of no less than five roads at one of the main entrances to our suburb.

Its name is derived from the dozen or more Chestnut trees gracing the entire circumference of the green that at the time, were already prominent but today dominate this piece of ground. The constant shadows, the ever changing colours of light through the branches of those splendid trees, continue to play in my childhood memories even today. The 'front room' of her house was also a very 'special' room looking out onto the green. But it was a special room that was oh so very different from the one at our home. This front room seemed specifically designed for special children! It had been converted into a studio (not that I knew that at the time) where within its confines proudly stood a 'Baby-Grand' piano (nor did I know that at the time) as the focal point of the room.

Sitting as perfectly as it could in the middle of the available space, acting as the hub of all human focus providing, it seemed to me, the sole reason for the very existence of the room, stood this black magnificent music machine. It held an invisible command, an aura of presence, almost a demand for calm obedience, often with lid held high as if in welcome. An instrument of real distinction! Around the walls were continuous bench/box seats except for the bay window. This had a selection of drawers built into the front of it under the window seat. These drawers I was soon to learn contained the 'stuff' needed to create the music magic. Stuff, that was to become known eventually to me as sheet music. Stuff, or paper or books only initially containing what looked like messy splodges...

Squiggles, dots, lines, some splodges with tails, yet others just circles. More – signs, more symbols, page after endless page of this 'stuff' to explore. Mrs P was, at that time, possibly the oldest person I had seen in my short life or who I had been in close proximity to. To me she was possibly the oldest person ever in the entire world!

Not that I had any real concept of age. In itself all this should have been a warning for me to run, escape immediately from the potential terrors such an aged person must surely possess. The only reason such really old people existed surely was to scare all little boys into blind panic or instant submission to instruction. But, on the occasion of my first introduction to Mrs P, she smiled at me, her round happy face shone as the summer sun shone. Whilst standing there in her home but also in her 'special' room, a truly amazing thing happened to me, I just could not control myself...I smiled back! Friendship together with mutual trust was born.

I cannot of course remember in any detail today anything of those initial conversations but I will never forget when she sat me down on the stool next to her, as her tiny fingers reached across the keys she started to play, my own private magical musical journey began. Dear Reader, to me at that time, the piano represented hearing the plonk, plonk, plonk of my brothers, still riding the waves of the piano lesson process at home, with occasionally perhaps some sweeter sounds when my father sat to play for his own enjoyment. This was the extent of my piano music universe, my expectation if you will, of the known sound issued forth from such a machine I had come to accept. A sound associated with home, our special front room from which we were excluded except by invitation. I had discarded any notice of these sounds except to know it was just that, sound. I did not expect my ears, one still whole with the other not so complete, to hear rolling violent colours, soft trickling colours of moving blue water receding from a cliff, and then quietly gathering red strength to charge with white thunder again against a cliff. I had never heard the colour of the call of an animal or bird across a green meadow or vast cavernous echoes of strange tinkling sounds, colours surrounding the stars in the heavens: of sweet soft sound or loud hard sound, the flow of rivers or the exquisite quiet of a gentle soul expansive melody.

I was lost, this cannot be a piano! I was hooked! I was shocked! How can this be possible? Let me learn to do that! Let me get lost in an ocean of sound to ride the fantastic winds of this music magic –-! So, guided by this wonderful lady teacher, I did!

Thus this was the beginning of a part of me that, in so many different ways during the next few years, I was to experience many very special moments. Addicted as I was instantly, it would not be too long before I was a regular guest pupil. Very soon I was invited to enter that magnificently magic world of Mrs P. two, then three times a week, often more. For perhaps almost two years I was to learn the basics on that wave-crest of beautiful colourful noise. Never even attempting or being allowed to learn more than I wanted to or needed to, just simply enough to muster sufficient understanding of the splodges on the paper to convert to sound! It was the sound that was the carrier of wonder, of joy, of peace, of sound-colour, building passion to this boy-child's life. Nothing at all like 'plink-plonk' after plink-plonk! Mrs P had adopted a 'let's play' not a 'let's work' method for those children who like me, were enthralled even mesmerised by the colour of sound! Time stood still, I once thought that there was so much to learn that I could never play with any skill or interpretation as my life continued. Visits to that special room became a blur of time. But time slipped – I was comfortable there, welcome – time slipped further – people grew, people changed.

I remained away from those changes which were wrought by real passing time, only changing in my way, in my time. Outside this almost private world of sound, time of the chronological world continued to slip past unnoticed.

Bloody nosed from school or home, read, write, play, charge, fight, eat or sleep, always millions of unanswered questions, throughout all this – Mrs P was a constant, my measurement, her music my unremitting core.

Time outside continued to slip until – the inevitable caught up with this wayward child, this silly child so full of apparently stupid questions never answered except in the womb of a music journey designed, protected by Mrs P.

Then came the expected instruction to attend piano lessons with father in our front room at home! Wash hands after 'tea', sitting upright, back straight with flat balanced hands across the waiting black, plink-plonk, white, plink-plonk keys – start to practice! I do not recall any objections from me at the time of this change, it had been anticipated. Knowledge of the expected transfer from a real child learning site to that of the 'Plonk' site at home had been as a natural inevitable to my truth for years. But time had slipped, learnings from Mrs P, I was destined to be different, more aware, cognisant beyond expectation, which eventually proved not to be at all good for me.

I do know that I was not the best of students at home as you will discover later in this journey but at the time, the expected hours of 'Plonk' plonking followed by excessive finger exercises were of no interest.

Lost was the freedom of music magic provided by Mrs P. Here was order, here was expectation of ability to learn, here music was lost to a heart rendering slog for the sole purpose to examine, measure progress. Living, feeling sound or colour music was totally driven away to be replaced with dark frustration!

For the purpose of family good order though, there I sat providing the traditionally expected noises of multitudes of generations of pianoforte students! From time to time almost in sheer desperation, I would meet with Mrs P if only for a short while where we explored the freedom of multi-variances in piano sound. But at best life is cruel. Our time together had slipped beyond the reach of both of us. I was early morning singing now, plonking practice in the afternoons. As with such things, Mrs P was soon to become a pleasant powerfully wonderful memory from an earlier childhood era. A lover of a different kind, one that helped shape me, making a contribution not seen, not heard – just private music colours, just mine!

I did see Mrs Peebles many years later when I was in my late teens. In appearance she looked just the same! She looked across the road to me smiling. So perhaps even today, due to some magical time-slip, she can still be seen, if you look very closely, walking across the

Chestnut Green talking to the elements, stealing their shapes, their sounds by the colourful multitude – with special permission of course – doing so to encapsulate them in her music magic for children, still giving music piano lessons to shadowy children, awarding sweets to her favourites with a twinkle in her eyes. A charmed lady making charmed musical magic with her fingers. I do not think there was ever a Mr P in evidence in all the time we shared together. It was possible I suppose that he was lost in the recent world war, thus the need for Mrs P to provide some income for her own wellbeing. However, I have no idea if money ever left my parents hands or mine for her services. Romantic thought I know but I would go so far as to say that I do not believe my parents ever met Mrs P.

As with many other things, Dear Reader, whilst not seeking your tears, my parent's interest in anything I did was very limited.

They had the first born son and all that was needed to complete their world was a first born daughter. The first time my mother ever heard me sing was when she received a special invitation to partake in an extra-special service at our church in September 1960 – my induction to the Royal College of Church Music as a registered chorister at the age of 11 years. I started singing when six years old so by the time of becoming a qualified, registered Chorister, over five years of training, voice qualifying stages completed aplenty, visits to sing in schools, churches in many locations, including Oxford. Until that day my mother had not been to a single service. Even when receiving such an accolade, my father declined to attend. My single soprano voice echoing in the vast caverns of this almost cathedral that had been standing for over one thousand years in the heart of our town. This particular special event took place just before my twelfth birthday. It was the culmination of many years as a choir boy, hour after hour of voice training with an ability to sight read music that started whilst I was still with Mrs P.

Some Practical 'Stuff'.

Sorry, I am now getting a little ahead of myself here again Dear Reader so I need to provide you with a little more understanding of our home topography.

Thus far, in descriptions of our house, you have met the kitchen, here, when growing up is where family life in all its guises was as a constant flowing stream of energy. Probably like many other families, the kitchen was the heart, the axis, where stories of exploits, true or dreamed of, were shared. Where our friends were welcomed, tradesmen stopped in for a 'cuppa', girlfriends were first introduced, animals roamed or just waited in great expectancy of help, sustenance or just a little human love. A truly warm space, a place often wet, but always magically bursting with life. Entrance to this cauldron was primarily via the back door to our house. This was the real entrance of welcome to visitors from the outside world unless such visitors were officialdom of any sort. If so, it was that Front Door place! Examples of those entitled to this mode of entry are the local Church of England Cannon for selling his version of human peace laws, or our doctor who would call when one or more of us could not walk the few miles or so to his surgery. It was also where hopeful politicians stood expectant of support seeking nods of agreement, where charity collectors, door-to-door travelling salesmen of every type knocked for their first time, to stand waiting in pregnant anticipation.

All these visitors only if invited entered our house through that 'other' door, the one at the front of the house, the one that remained constantly locked as we were growing up. A door which suspiciously was unlocked on the very exceptional occasions when relatives arrived! So it was the back door that was our friends welcoming entrance to that most occupied room, the family kitchen.

The kitchen provided that all important back door. Oh yes, you must also have realised that there was an internal passage leading to the kitchen – the one used by our father that wet, dark, cold bloody Sunday morning. Our kitchen then actually had three doors but one of them was never closed. The dining room door! I shall talk about the dining room later. This door was positioned directly opposite the back door marking the end of the oblong kitchen space. Halfway along the right hand wall when facing the back door from inside, directly opposite the kitchen sink with its thin window, was the hallway passage door. This passage led to two integral but very different structural features of our home. First, directly at the end of the passage leading away from the kitchen was that 'other' door to our house – the one that as explained already, no one ever used except the postman to deliver mail, the doctor or the vicar. Not that we often had any post but on the odd occasion such stuff arrived, it was pushed through a thin elongated slot that had been cut, somewhat roughly, into the heavy central wooden portion of the front door. This permanent gap or hole had on the outside of the door a brass covering plate with a spring loaded metal flap that strangers would lift then drop when 'knocking'. This was also the choice of any school teachers visiting sometimes with good news, but more often with unwelcome news for someone. At such times, teachers would be accredited, if only just for a very short time, with a status far exceeding their lowly station in life. I recall one such teacher visit for example when brother Andrew whilst playing cricket at school one summer, was seen standing with legs taut and firm, both arms stretched to the heavens with hands raised, fingers stretched out to catch an incoming ball. Apparently at the very last second, Andrew lost sight of the ball as it moved into then through his hands. Dear Andrew had missed the catch! Well. Actually the batsman was still ruled out because Andrew in fact did catch the ball, sort of technically speaking anyway!

It hadn't hit the ground! Not at all! It was held by Andrew but out of sight! On its downward flight, the ball plunged directly between outstretched fingers, rocketed down the natural channel created by raised arms, finally smashing its way through white front teeth then lodging itself firmly inside a wide open young man's mouth! The teacher in charge of the game, realising that he could not dislodge the now double-red coloured solid orb from one panicked boys' mouth, took said brother by car to the local hospital where the bloody foreign object was removed by white coated people endowed with medical expertise! I was never privy to the conversation when said teacher arrived at our 'other' door, and knocked loudly, to tell his story. I only know that he was brave enough or guilty enough to do so. This special portal then was directly at the end of the passage beyond the kitchen door.

The second structural feature to be found in the passage was, by turning sharp left before that 'other' door, and sharp left again, in other words turning back on oneself, there now stood a single flight of stairs taking any climber to the upper rooms. You should by now be aware that upstairs was a light, bright oh-so warm bathroom; the one specifically available to just a few members of the family. From where the boys were banned entry unless at times of illness, they could crawl across the landing from their sick bed for necessary relief. This bathroom contained that most dreaded of all things for most of us though – a proper bath tub. That place where, as children, we were each forced to occasionally strip, climb into steamy water to be subjected to a body wash. As a very young child, one of my male siblings would be charged with making sure I was washed properly although sometimes my mother would undertake this task. Or complete the task after a full inspection of my potential cleanliness! In addition to the bathroom at the top of the stairs, there were two quite large bedrooms together with a small box bedroom. Access to each room was by way of a squared landing area at the top of the straight stairs.

Of the two large rooms, one was the place of my conception, our parents' room. The other large room was mostly shared by brothers' Greg and Andrew with, due to squabbles between any of us, occasionally Chris.

Being large, these two rooms both had heating radiators for winter. I was permanently assigned to the small box room that had no heating whatsoever! Generally Chris would share this with me but I do recall occasionally enjoying the company of Greg as my roommate.

Downstairs again, the balance of the ground floor comprised the dining room together with that very 'out-of-bounds' to all boys in the house, front (Special) room. As I mentioned earlier, the door from the kitchen into the dining room being constantly open was simply a means to ensuring that the carrying of food, hot or cold, plates plus all the normal utensils from kitchen to table, was a safe pastime. Imagine little hands carrying dirty plates whilst at the same time having to negotiate the opening of doors! All shared family meals happened here. This was also where the older children who attended 'big' school would pretend to do their homework. Although there was a heating radiator in this room, it too was little renowned for its warmth even when Sunday lunch had been steaming for hours through the open doorway to the kitchen. Over the years, this eating room witnessed so very many family episodes of havoc, laughter, sadness, indeed angst of all types. It was at times also used as a utility room or a games room, often having to surrender its established purpose for some strange oblique reason.

My father for instance, being an electrical wizard, once commandeered one third of the table to spend many hours over many weeks, even months, with any spare time he had, sitting building piece by piece our very first television set! He had somehow purchased, or otherwise acquired, each individual part needed for this complex electronic adventure.

As with a number of such projects over the years, he commenced the task of creating this new modern wonder via electronic assembly with a huge amount of excited enthusiasm.

In addition to the commandeered portions of the dining room table, about half of the top of the low flat sideboard containing best crockery, glass, eating utensils, amongst other things, also co-shared its established role for the duration of the task. These selected areas were to become his private home workbench. Valves, wires, resisters of all colours, size, design-purpose or type danced to fathers' construction demands. What at the time seemed like miles of multi-coloured wires, some thick yet others so tiny that they were difficult to see, completely occupied one end of the table, all items carefully placed on a spread of old newspaper according to when needed. Simply waiting like lovers in eagerness, these were also sited around a 'base-plate' upon which the creation was to grow. To this day I can still smell the hot metal liquid solder used to bond wire to resister to valve to gismo. The reek of brown flux as it ran with its own light fizzing sound along with the melted solder, to solidify then cool to eventually hold firm the tiny joins that were destined to be joined as lovers forever. All the time my father commanding 'don't touch that soldering iron boy' it will 'burn you!' As he progressed with this project, progress became slower with the initial enthusiasm vanishing as time moved on, taking months instead of weeks to complete. Finally however the moment we had all once been very excited about arrived. The long awaited stage of 'testing'.

I can see him now sat at what was then regarded as 'his' although purloined portion of the wooden dining table, on a wooden chair with his feet firmly placed on a pile of old books as he plugged the power cable into the wall socket. Flicking the wall mounted switch with half-hidden trepidation, his creation very slowly started to hum!

It glowed as faint new light could be seen inking its way within, around, over, across the massed electronics. Heat emanated from the married groups of multi-clusters of its newly merged gismo stuff.

Like some mad scientist crazed with anticipation of discovery, an overly excited voice never heard by me before sprang with obvious urgency from his gaping mouth. "Do not touch me boy," he bellowed, "I'm live!"

For some reason I did not perhaps understand at the time, he had expected me to think that he may be dead, as if all his personal power had been drained from his body! Then "If you touch me now we will both be shocked!" In a display of ignorance befitting my age (around eight years six months), I asked him why he was standing on a pile of old books. Anyway I knew he was alive, he had just shouted at me in a voice that was not his! Here again was the overpowering need for me to understand what he had just said? The answer he gave to me was one that I could give no meaning to. He had drifted into a language of electronics as if in fluid conversation with a peer, describing in detail the need to ensure that whilst 240 volts of electrical current coursed through his body he needed to put his feet, stand if you will, on so many books in order that he didn't 'earth' the thing, or himself! Still, in that strange over excited utterance, he gave me my first lesson in things regarding conductors together with non-conductors of electricity. How ohms, currents (not those we steal from the larder from time to time apparently), watts, all forming, moving, invisible miracles – bouncing off each other at speeds almost past understanding with positive as well as negative energy.

Electricity was in the air! The building heat, the hum of electrical power accompanied by a new stinging, burning smell.

All this in that place where our family often gathered to dine in general comfort, except when electrical engineering work was taking place, during which time all seven of us squeezed together onto the remaining three-quarters of the table to eat.

Yes, the television worked. It was encased in a very dark Bakelite box, had a tiny 12-inch screen showing vague black on white or white on black, no such thing as colour in those days, moving pictures with sound emanating from a single small speaker situated at the side of the box. Initially the flickering images were only at their best providing the 'Twisted Metal' aerial was held absolutely rock-steady whilst apparently pointing in the right direction! The sound was OK but tinny, almost metallic in quality. It was not too long however before a proper aerial was installed as a tall silvery looking metal attachment fixed to the chimney of our house high on the roof. This was as if a flag of office or improved family status had been raised for all to admire. Even so, this metal appendage also had to be pointing in the right direction!

So this pointed object on high enhanced public awareness of our family status but all that was representing deep inside the house was a tiny receiver of a home-built television set. So small was it in fact that due to the size of its tiny screen, we all had to huddle together simply to catch a view of whatever was on. Imagine if you can, seven people at the same time trying to catch a glance of some exciting viewing! Each of us jostling for the best possible position but nevertheless still having to squint to really see anything anyway. Naturally such proximity, the pushing, eager determination to get the best view resulted in many grumpy moments!

The answer to this potential conflict for the family arrived very soon after the television itself was completed. We acquired a very large free standing purpose built magnifying glass lens that covered the entire front of the set. It had long flat 'legs' attached that slid sufficiently far under the body of the television that it was acting as a sort of counterbalance. These 'Legs' supported a large convex magnifying glass that was designed to cover the tiny 12-inch screen converting it into perhaps an 18-inch screen thereby providing a 50% increase in the area of picture.

With this purchased item, the evolution of watching television in the mid 1950s in our house took a giant step forward. At the same time, several members of the family were all able to view the pictures together without too much rancour! Prior to the installation of this multi-viewer equipment, watching anything on this 'box' was something of a physical positioning challenge. Get to sit in front first then you would perhaps stand a good chance of seeing something. If not, sitting at anything less than straight-on to the screen could mean that most of the picture would be lost to you. Oh wonderful technology! Our father was a very proud man. The most exciting change though was not the homemade electronic creation; it was where it was located that started to drive away some established rules of the house. This modern magic created in the dining room of our home played its part in destroying a hitherto family inviolable, the right of access at will to the front room. This massive change to our interactions as a family was due to us all being offered for the first time, an accepted right to visit without invitation that special front room. Sat on a small low table to the left of the fireplace, attracting excitement was our television. No more would we have to visit friends to watch this modern wonder. Television had arrived in our front room, the start of world invasion at every street level in the 1950s. Mass propaganda had arrived! Thus for the first time, as with many families across England, we started to experience the demise of self-entertainment. The piano sound faded in our house. Over time the regular exchanges of insults, cries of joy, anger, shared laughter because of some petty exchange of dialogue between us, just faded away. Board games, puzzles, flat water-colour paint tins, brushes in jam jars were discarded as they were simply unable to compete.

The scary influence of telecommunication arrived into our midst by our own innocent invitation. Favourite toys, books, secret playing places became casualties to be slowly abandoned, left to the gathering dust both physical along with metaphysical. Walks across the fields on long summer evenings diminished, finally becoming just an occasional interruption to 'watching the box'. Conversation between us on multiple subjects degraded to speculative chatter about really inconsequential television programmes. The potential to learn to speak with some type of American accent was huge. Our dining room had witnessed the birth, or in this case, the mad electrician's creation, of a modern marvel that was by its very nature, destined to become an invasion of the outside world into the lives of us all. Just one creative event in this dining room which held a direct immense future impact on where we all were at the time, influencing the thinking, awareness, but more importantly, the direction our lives would subsequently take.

There were indeed many dining room events over the years, the one of which I am about to tell, is mostly for its angst, for it's a tragic comedy, for its befitting location, squashed (you'll get my wicked humour in using that word just now) leading to the front room.

It was on a Christmas day!

This story, the actual mastication of food, cooked or raw, providing rounded goodness imbibed through a recipients' digestive system with the benefit of resultant healthy body, does not however refer to any such enjoyed activity by a member of the human race! Well obliquely perhaps.

Oh no!

Throughout our childhood years, it would be something of a wonder if at any time on any given day during any season of the year, there were no animals, domestic or otherwise, birds, fish, frogs, snails, slugs or spiders, rats, mice or hamsters or any other such oft child companions, sharing our home either on a full or part-time basis with the status of either a family member or current guest. In respect of this story I will portray a life or, as it turns out, the death of one amongst the more permanent boarders in our house at the time. A budgerigar, a feathered pet with the wonderfully unusual name of 'Hopperty'! Not just any old hopping budgie either! A real walking, talking, shoulder-climbing, curtain-staining, flying, spraying poop machine! Blue, green yellow feathered, vile of mood, vile of smell, long of beak, long of claws, just one that truly hated his lot in this world with such a passion that it made even the worst of us humans out to be really lovable, sweet, innocent individuals. Never an act of gratitude did this bird show during his long sovereignty as our mother's favourite pet! It was though, to meet its end in the arch between rooms late one special morning. It is the method of his dispatch, his untimely demise that wrought simultaneous tears, laughter for which we should have been chastised, but also, a really fresh meal for a fellow family pet. It was Christmas morning just before lunch! 'Hopperty', yes, that was the poor things' name, chosen I think by mother although I'm not too sure who in the family had actually created such originality! Nevertheless our bird, our family pet of some years, the special pet friend of Mothers, unexpectedly, somewhat very violently, became Christmas lunch for the then resident cat!

A fitting end perhaps for this particular bird in playing its part in the provision of Christmas day lunch!

It was clearly our fathers' fault!

You see, Dear Reader, from the dining room was a double-door archway into that front (special) room. The doors themselves were or seemed large but on this particular Christmas day the doors, which normally would be closed to protect that special room from the resident rowdy, often dirty brew, were both held wide open. For reasons now forgotten, which is probably best, they were both to their fullest extent to allow our father to fix up into the centre of the door frame, across the now double space provide by the open doors, a single hook. Onto this single hook apparently deeply imbedded into the solid wood of the door frame, he hung the cage containing our 'Hopperty'! Up to this point, the cage was on a free-standing upright solid metal arm which was fixed at its base into a very heavy circular cast-iron plate. This upright arm was well over six foot with the top curved over then downward where located at its end, was a strong sharp hook onto which the cage was normally hung.

Not this Christmas, oh no! The doors were open between the two rooms as a special arrangement, a recognition perhaps that with the television located in the front room, times were changing. Therefore, in additional celebration of this festive period, father had hung the bird cage high in the space created by the now wide open double doors.

It was as a sort of high focal point, a salutation, to recognise perhaps that these normally closed portals had at last been thrown wide open for all to pass freely, without invitation even! Although it did seem somehow excessive! A little over the top at the time! But hey, it was Christmas, maybe the family thaw was upon us. However, to the best made plans of mice or men, the very action of having both doors permanently in an open position proved to be against all previously established family norms or practices.

Oh how often had we all been shouted at down the years in vocal reminder of a statutory house rule, "Close the b–y door behind you, you were not born in a barn." Instinct or unconscious blind acceptance of or to this rule was buried deep in the essence of each of us. No notice had been published that things had changed this Christmas day. No family gathering emergency or otherwise announcing that even though temporary in nature, this particular family law had been rescinded! No patriarchal proclamation had been issued such as, "Don't close the b–y door!" Someone, who for the purposes of protecting the guilty shall not be identified here, when walking between the rooms in a state of adherence to such oft' espoused family rules, attempted without thinking or even looking up or sideways, to close the doors behind them as had become an inbred, long established self-protection behaviour!

There was an instant crunch as heavy solid wooden door obeying its own anticipated purpose, met with semi-stiff metal frame comprising some lightweight foil covered thin hardboard flooring invading its own official space! The cage, suddenly bent out of shape, swung madly with nowhere to go except crunch (told you I was wicked!) as it swung back against the other door with an enormously loud crash!

The result – the original square shape of the cage irreparably changed by its first encounter with one leading-edge of a closing door, whacked the same leading-edge on its pendulum swing return, instantly buckling! This rapid change of shape spilt the mucky, seed covered cage floor which, together with a very startled, unhappy, grumpy, no different from any other day, attitude to life incumbent, out into the world, falling to the room floor. Pieces of half eaten seeds, a plastic ladder with a noisy bell, a broken mirror together with falling twisted bits of millet mixed with a burst water bowl hit the floor scattering everywhere!

Hopperty, who until a few moments ago was resplendent in his home, safely hanging from a solidly fixed hook in the top of the door frame which had of course stayed firmly fixed in place, had no time to recover at all. At about the same instant, the re-shaped now broken cage bounced, scattering its contents everywhere. The current cat recognised a golden opportunity! It pounced! Well it was Christmas day after all when 'bird' did seem to be on the menu for the human occupants of the house – so why not? In a flash the cat grabbed the now dazed feathered pet flapping uselessly in panic. I suspect it died of fright rather than due to anything that the cat was doing to it. In the meantime, mother, who was busy in the kitchen with final preparations for the traditional family bird lunch, dressed for the occasion of Christmas protected by a pinny around her waist – screamed. The cat, now licking salivating dripping lips in wonderful appreciation of its luck, scampered across the floor carrying remnants of poor Hopperty leaving the building in urgent haste and avoiding any eye contact with human masters. Away ran the cat carrying its very own Christmas lunch!

Memories of mother remain permanently vivid as there she was standing in the kitchen, tears running down her sorrowful face, spilling into a mixing bowl of something or other; perhaps it contained stuffing mix for the larger bird that was to be consumed by us later. Also remaining in my memory of this particular event, is how after the initial shock of the death of Hopperty, on this of all days, a realisation of the circumstances of his departure introduced those famous family giggles.

Held back at first but once started however, the giggles would suddenly explode from one or more of us at odd times during the afternoon across the house.

There was more; mother was caught quietly giggling with suppressed tears of laughter not sorrow, shining in her eyes.

It was not much later that day when discussion turned to Hopperty, that each in their turn could not simply hold back the laughter, one causing all others present at the time to chortle again! A sudden unexpected end to a family pet on Christmas day provided us all with a symbiotic collective sadness edged with a celebration of life lost by giggles!

Yes, our dining room was a real place of fun, of shared laughter whilst growing up. This family room was often used during various individual teenage 'rebellious' rushes of testosterone, surreptitiously on occasion, forcing one or more of my elder siblings to attack the status quo. A really wondrous example of this was when at about the age of twelve or thirteen, but already heading to full teenage "devil-may-care" up-yours attitude, Chris, my brother with more 'balls' than wisdom but possibly knowing the potential outcome of what he was about to do, suddenly asked our father during the course of Sunday lunch, just at one of those awful silent moments in any gathering of people, in a shockingly loud voice...

"Dad, what's the difference between a prostitute and a pregnant woman?"

Aghast silence! The world with all in it slowed, stopped breathing! Greg, now about seventeen or eighteen, sat suddenly red-faced, eyes everywhere, searching anywhere in the room but not at our table, attempting with manic desperation beyond his mid teenage life experience to disappear beneath said table as if he suddenly needed to inspect the floor below at very close quarters! Andrew, eyes wide, paused with mouth half open as if about to catch another cricket ball! A pause! A stifled giggle from mother, her eyes not able to conceal her mirth!

Chris with innocent expression painted on his face with eyes wide open, eyelashes flashing nervously whilst attempting to maintain an angelic face of naive questioning! It was one of those lunch times where for his sins Chris was sat at the right hand side of the table next to where our father was at the head of the table. Worse even, because Chris did not expect it…the sudden quick flash of hairy adult male arm, striking out with a heavy hand that smacked with a resounding 'thud' the back of his head!

"Stop asking silly stupid questions boy, now eat your food!"

I watched mother as she, in desperation of providing some protection, stated in squelched giggle constraint.

"He's only asking a simple question Jim."

For the first time I realised that there were things in this world that our father found difficult to acknowledge. Rules of the house were OK, reading stories when we were young was OK, building television sets was obviously OK, but anything that had to do with male female relationship or interaction, caused him extreme difficulty. The question was never answered. Chris, fuming that he was not yet big enough to hit back, reluctantly attempted to finish his lunch. Mother hid her giggles whilst, as the eldest, Greg escaped from the room as quickly as possible, hoping that life would return to normal.

Continuing the guide then, round our house. In addition to the dining room that looked out across the back garden, there was that other very 'special room'!

The room which, before the advent of the television in our house we were excluded from, the front room! Only guests or adults allowed. Children on occasions when spruced for presentation to visitors, dressed only in Sunday best to be seen but never heard, once displayed to the sometimes frightening personage of a 'relative', then to be discharged as quickly as possible. This latter action often much to the joy of both child/children, but more particularly the visiting relative!

This off-limits room contained all the 'posh stuff' that was either kept out of harms (our) way or, on display high above the inquisitive reach of the resident young, be it animal or human! That place where parents could seek comfort often only if the children were asleep. A place where children were invited also to receive punishment for some terrible misdemeanour, real, actual or imagined that mother felt only father could determine the level of pain to "Teach the boy a lesson!"

But for me this was a room that contained two very vital, to me even intrinsically so it turned out, valuable items that were to influence my own entire existence!

A thing, an item of furniture occupying one half of a wall that I was to learn was called an 'upright-overstrung' piano to which I have already referred. This piano then together with another large piece of furniture dominating the room, a mahogany free-standing square cabinet box in which was an old valve driven radio! It was also a player of single mounted hard Bakelite music recordings, as well as massive 16 speed film soundtrack discs. Of course there was the settee, a comfortable armchair with all the usual bits associated with rooms of this type in the fifties. A sort of quasi private place within our house not usually available to children except as I say, on very special occasions or sometimes although rarely, by a spooky direct invitation.

So now you have a very quick view of the house into which I was to spend the first years of my life, sharing my world with six others.

Our home was a council house, one of hundreds on an estate erected directly after World War Two. Well actually the estate had been started during the 1930s but due to the conflict in Europe much of it had not been completed. It seems that completion of or construction of further homes on the estate ceased in early 1940, construction only commencing again after the war. My brother Chris was the first sibling to be born in our new 'steel' house which was one of eight on our side of the road. These semi-detached homes were tagged onto the end of an existing long road of completely differently designed council houses. Eight identical homes stood across the road facing us. Thus these homes were somehow seen as a foreign appendage, a sore, not quite correct, even alien additions, implanted to fill the final empty slots of this end of our road.

'Steel' refers to the fact that our 'new' homes, some of which had been standing half-complete for several years, were originally the same design as some of the others along the road. With the de-mobbed men returning to civilian life after the war, there was the urgent demand to finish all those unfinished houses that war had caused to be abandoned. So instead of waiting for the mass production of bricks to restart to meet the huge demand for such homes, many such semi-built council homes across the country were frantically re-designed. New materials had to be employed. The use of corrugated steel as the outer shell resting on the lower brick built half of the house provided, in what was to become in our case, an answer to the urgency. These redesigned homes can still be seen all over England.

Thus we lived as many others still do, in a house built half of steel and the rest of brick!

So this was my home.

Three bedrooms with a bathroom upstairs, that private 'special' room, the dining room, a hallway passage, and that really wonderful centre of our world – the kitchen. Once I was able to crawl, this massive home became a place for adventure as independence of movement as well as thought took hold, starting to shape me.

Finding My Place!

Now as a fully fledged growing family member beginning to demand acknowledgment of my own existence with its unique, inalienable right to participate in all that was on offer, I started to explore the world around me. With little interruption, providing I remained as inconspicuous as possible, I was awarded as much freedom as I needed to live each day seeking out new exotic smells, experiencing new shapes, learning not to fall, all within the hubbub of constant cacophony comprising light, sound and movement!

Our garden had many absorbing things to contemplate. Having been denied the opportunity to purchase a home of their own at the time because of the lack of cash, our parents had, on taking up residence in this council built home, created in the garden a large selection of areas for root vegetables such as potatoes, carrots and parsnips; in fact growing everything originally from seed. This included a patch of cabbages, broad beans with even tall poles holding long green pea pods above ground, all of which provided interest to this toddlers' enquiring mind! Gooseberries, blackcurrants! Tiny Redcurrants allowed for the inclusion of natural sugars in our diet but best of all, their bushes also presented delightful places to hide things in or from during the summer months, whilst savouring the early appearance of these tasty offerings!

Although I must confess that unless it was really red-ripe and ready to drop, I could not, or would not eat a single unripe gooseberry. Exploring my immediate surroundings at the age of three heading towards four years old, I was also aware of being really expectant of going to that place of fabulous mystery that my elder brothers all attended during my garden explorations – school!

I could already do small chores in the house; the washing up team was never a chore, just something that was a collaborative life necessity like eating or breathing. I would for example often be sent along the road to the local shop on the corner clutching a folded piece of paper containing a note to Mr B, the shopkeeper (who it turns out later was living in sin with his SISTER! Well according to local gossip anyway…) for some small forgotten household need. These personally independent journeys taking me directly past the front gate of the primary school attended by my two really big brothers allowed me to get to know the local roads, the journey to these places of magic called schools! So when finally I was at infant school, it was nothing for me to walk to or back from school alone, starting to take tentative initial steps away from my family into life experiences that were to be uniquely mine. I had therefore, since about my fourth birthday, been allowed to wander at random around the roads in our council estate on my own, crossing minor intersections whilst all the while exploring an ever increasingly wider domain.

Once again though I am guilty of excluding large portions of me that must be included otherwise Dear Reader, you will find it difficult to follow this child's journey; so, learning the piano, the arrival of my first guitar, all of which must be explained. Perhaps also an explanation is needed of the location of this child's journey with my easy access to the English countryside.

A lush countryside offering fantastic opportunities for walks in woods, across open fields, where ancient pathways meandered not only over the Chiltern Hills but throughout the Vale of Aylesbury, indeed intertwined between multiple villages in the county of Buckinghamshire.

There was countryside teeming with exciting possibilities for extraordinary adventures for children, no matter what the season. All around our historic market town as it still was then, the wondrous gift of being able to share time with nature was available to all who were interested. All wild things of all types big or small, animal or mineral were represented. There were rabbits, doves, sparrows, snakes, spiders, rats, mice. robins, rooks, crows, each in their own season. sticklebacks, frogs, toads, pike, cows, pigs, dogs, cats, ladybirds, butterflies, earwigs aplenty. Bees, house-flies, yellow striped wasps that would sting when angry!

Throughout our childhood, in our home, it was common for any visitor to come across a variety of animal guests of every sort, sharing our warmth or recuperating from some ill or injury! But the real star of all those special visitors whilst we were growing up was one very, very special individual, the wild funny, fabulously stupid bird – the very magical Percy!

Percy the crow, who one day adopted our brother Chris as its mother!

Also during the period from about my sixth birthday until about I was about twelve, there are many other essential elements to this story of a childhood journey, the arrival of my only sister for instance. Sudden expanding gums with hospital isolation! The amazing shared togetherness in the wonderful story of the

'Snowball Wizards'. The black pride, the fear, the belated shame of the Bonfire Wars!

As the youngest Boy!

Chronologically thus far in my story, I have now covered some important events from my arrival to approximately age six years, six months. Have you noticed how often 'a-half' year or six months has appeared in the telling hereof?

I am assuming that if I were now to really analyse in detail my life journey so far, as I write this tome I may find that those factors, those special events that had a greater influence on me than others, had perhaps always occurred when I was 'half-a-year' older or six months into an age defining milestone, a period, year or even half a lifetime, as exampled here with the already stated 'at a time when I was three years six months old' or halfway through my fourth year'. The half seems to have been an accompanying constant. Nevertheless, I will, I think, avoid the temptation to delve into this potential time consuming research project for now. Suffice it to say; I think there may be some extraordinary coincidences waiting to be discovered. One of the most important events, although at the time it was something that I was not too excited about I must confess, took place in the August just before my fifth birthday. The arrival of the next sibling! Unknown at the time by me but having since been made aware, this particular (happy) event became a matter of heated, rolling emotionally-charged debate in the family home orchestrated by my brother Greg apparently. There had been other pregnancies since my arrival with the associated, excited expectations. Each of these prior to the successful delivery of our sister Penny, had failed to reach full term. Nevertheless, arrive Penny did, who, being exalted even beyond the status of Greg the first born, was to be the long awaited daughter! In recognition she was also awarded three Christian names, Penelope, Anne, Susan. However, even with not one but two second name choices, like me, she has always been referred to by her first name, well almost, simply as Penny.

The Alexandra name lost forever!

The Greg issue surrounding the potential of another failed attempt at human creation was at this time, based around his concern that with four boys in the house already, another child was not seen by him as in the best interests of anyone! Least of all the existing brew!

So, at about twelve years of age, Greg was starting to flex his early teenage muscle, starting to challenge our parents, as to why? Again? Such a very brave thing to do for one so young after being subjected to an early childhood of Edwardian style authoritarianism! Now I admit that the event, as I recall, was of little or perhaps even no interest to me or my brothers, other than Greg, or anyone of importance in my little world. Mrs P was currently my personal delight so no interest there or indeed from that short, scary lady Mrs Low, that mistress of the head? I do not know if the local grocer was carrying extra coffee or not at the time, but I am sure that he may have been in some possible stress about the condition of Mrs S --- again! It was without doubt however an event that both parents were engrossed in due to its potential to answer their long shared dream. The eventual arrival of the most wanted, the one I should have been, the one Chris was going to be, the one that Andrew must have been (Boy first then a Girl – the perfect union result) but as each of us in his turn had failed to be – a daughter! Well it is often said that 'If at first you don't succeed etc.,' Or 'if you can dream it – you can do it!' Oh boy did they do it! In total, allowing for the Boy first Greg, there followed eight additional attempts in which they had produced another three boys, and four miscarriages before FINALLY – a girl. Not to mention a stillborn twin boy! (The 'Other Me')

As an adult even now, I cannot comprehend the depth of need, the real aching desire to achieve the shared wish for a daughter! I guess the closest to my understanding would be that of an adult male humans' sudden passion, all-consuming debilitating love for a woman (a very rare mania experienced by only the really lucky, the few or possibly the deranged!), their depth of desire, their strength of purpose, of drive, of absolute need by these two people, must be similar to this kind of uncontrollable deep emotional fixation. Well, at last – success! Now they could rest, basking in the warmth of their dream having come true.

That such an event as the arrival of Penny in our lives proved to be no less than the much needed catalyst for momentous change – shall remain perhaps the single greatest understatement of this entire epistle.

That Penelope (Penny) Ann, Susan (Alexandra gone, forgotten – ah well!) arrived at all was in itself something of a then modern extravagance considering that my mother was rapidly approaching 34 years of age. Unlike today, such an event at that age then, although not unknown was however, not common. I cannot tell if age was a consideration or not but Penny, other than being a girl, was obviously, completely, distinctly different from all of us boys. My memory holds no firm recollection as to if she was born at home. I do remember our fathers' beaming face showing her off to us so I conceded that in all probability, she too arrived on this planet in the bed of her conception! Even so, it was not long before our mother disappeared with her new baby to the local hospital anyway! Nothing exists in my memory at all during the nine-month period of Penny's incubation except a vague awareness of expectation around the house. There is no memory of any dramatic loss by our mother of her tea drinking habits or any other such complications. Mr B (who, I was informed on several occasions as I grew up, was said to be continuing to live in wicked sin with his sister) was therefore able to enjoy the normal expected cash flow from our family in his little corner shop. Not that cash ever did flow very often or much anyway.

Penny!

Penny? I recall a directive was issued one day early into the school summer holiday period calling for a gathering of the family. This was during my first year at school having just started in the January of the same year. So I was now on holiday having completed half (that word again) an academic year. September, the start of my next school year was simply ages away. A gathering, an announcement, oh yes, of an event of great import was to be made. We boys gathered unquestioningly (other than Greg who had questioned the pregnancy in the first place anyway); as usual I remember being full of excited expectation, as only boys can be by such an order. What really wonderful thing was about to be bestowed on us? New summer toys? A never-ending supply of free sweets to each of us was waiting at the corner shop? Richard was to be made King? Then the really 'wonderful' news – as of a few hours ago, we boys now had a baby sister! Wasn't that exciting? Thankfully, my brothers were far more mature than I. With the exception of Chris of course, they were better equipped with the requisite levels of childhood diplomacy than I. I'm sure they were able at least to present some signs of genuine interest. Maybe even Greg was happy that there would be no further pregnancy announcements. As for me, disappointment was huge! I remember clearly thinking – so what? I don't even like girls but now I was to share my home, my life with one! Girls were those nasty crying, scratching, noisy, horrid things that lived next door! Especially those ones living next door who speak with funny accents, often sticking their collective tongues out at me or making horrid faces! My only question was – when is mum coming back?

Announcement over, 'excitement' depleted, not even any sweets, oh well! Now we had this thing called a sister but that meant nothing to me really.

She was with mum anyway who I recall not having seen for ages either so it was back to my spending each day doing whatever attracted me. We all returned to whatever had occupied our hearts prior to that family announcement. With ungrateful thanks to an expression of loyalty by a neighbour just a few days after mum had disappeared, I was dragged off to the hospital to meet this new challenger to my own exulted status in the established pecking order of the pack – the sucker of the hind tit! I was comfortable with my lot now, I was not about to surrender any hard-gotten status easily!

Grumpy, not interested at all, even thinking that if she was to poke her tongue out at me, my world would sink way beyond bad, below despair even. What if she was to steal any small joys I may have collected, keeping them forever! So there I was, hanging onto the hand of a 'kindly neighbour' who had agreed to take me by bus. All along the way in that bus, I recall sitting attempting to show some interest but becoming increasingly concerned about the future of us all with a sister, a girl in our midst! Having reached the hospital, the ward that mother was in was quickly located by our friendly neighbour who initially sat me on a bench OUTSIDE the room where apparently my mother was resting with my recently arrived sister.

With an excited promise that I would see my little sister very soon, my protector for the day deposited me on the bench telling me to wait just for a little while. She disappeared whilst I waited in trepidation! What would I do if my own sister spoke to me with the same funny accent as the girls next door? Or worse, would she be in a dress sticking her tongue out? Although I appreciated that newborn children were small, several days had passed since her birth so she wasn't going to be that small anymore, was she?

Finally, just as I was about to do my own disappearing act somewhere, anywhere, having convinced myself further that girls were generally not a good idea at all, I was being gently pushed into the now imagined to be desperately dangerous zone of my mother's room.

I was presented into the privy chamber in which my mother was ensconced. The moment of truth had arrived, what did I do? This mighty midget of all midgets, this runt of the brood, this youngest of four brothers who thought he knew his place in life?

Did I go 'Goooo' or even 'Ohooo'! No! Not me. I didn't even smile I simply shouted incoherently, well shrieked really, panicked as if my life was in great danger, then turned running full speed out of the room!

Yes, I ran in hopeless, hapless horror, screaming from the room out to the dubious safety of the corridor with tears in my eyes, body shaking with fright! Daylight! I must have Daylight!

There was no little person with smiling blue or brown eyes having uncontrolled appendages waving around. No little sweet thing lying in a cot or cradled in my mothers' arms! In fact I did not see a baby cot at all in the room. In the dim very subdued light of this mother-baby temporary home, I could not even at first see my mother let alone my new sister. Then desperately, urgently seeking confirmation that all that underlying feeling of opaque fuss over the past months had not been endured due to some bizarre punishment, that it was now really all over – my young eyes had quickly adjusted to the light in just a few seconds enabling me to look around.

Oh what a stupid, stupid, little boy I was! Why did I, even then having accepted that I was simply an idiot anyway, why was I always wanting to know more about 'it' (whatever 'it' was at any time) seemingly before anyone else had thought of the question? Why did I have to explore, to answer the unanswered!

How many smacks had I received by then or smirks or laughter at my silly incessant questioning of everything, yet nothing had yet taught me to shut up! Why did I always have people yelling at me to stop asking so many questions all the time? NO. I never listened to their protestations then...or now actually. Oh, if only I had!

Penny, our baby sister, or something obviously animal in nature was NAILED TO THE WALL! Yes, nailed!

Well that's what it seemed to this nearly five-year-old inquisitive boy facing his fear of girls. If this was my sister, the reason for the bus journey across town for me to meet her, then here she was nailed halfway (yet another half) up one of the walls in the room, overlooking all activity as if in some macabre demonstration replicating a junior crucifixion! There on the wall hung my new sibling! The shock of this horrific sight meeting my enquiring gaze was nothing other than catastrophic! She, although it was difficult to tell at the time, was held upright in some sling arrangement that splayed her arms wide at the top whilst her little legs dangled out of the bottom. Her body was covered by the bulk of a sling structure with her tiny head protruding out of the top of this thing. Her head seemed to flop about from side to side!

Now, I had known by some experience in my small time on this planet, that girls were somehow very different to boys. After all, there were girls at school, you know, with two arms, two legs, also a body even. Hair, two eyes, head, hands, feet...well really they were just like us boys, but this was so shocking! How sad that their arrival on this planet at home or perhaps via a hospital, if indeed any of the girls at school had employed either method of entry, that their 'difference' required them to undergo such persecution as having to be nailed to a wall shortly after birth! No wonder they had to go to hospital – imagine having that at home!

So there she was my sister! Little arms incoherently waving, lolling head stuck on some protected body beneath the contraption holding her to the wall, almost as an afterthought put there by the creator of this tableau, were two chubby, wobbly legs. Seeing this thing hanging there in those split seconds before I ran, Penny looked like the crucifixion of a tortoise! This picture was made oh so very much worse because this moving thing, this sister on the wall…had no hair! Hence the panic! All this together with the lack of air in that darkened room prompted me to believe that sudden noisy escape was not a choice but an imperative. Sudden this determined, very raucous departure from my mothers' hospital room was to me a life preserving essential.

Anyone reading this with some general knowledge of things medical may be aware of the 'official' name of the anatomical development disorder that I am about to try to describe here. Although Penny was not 'premature' in the most common of understanding of premature, the thing that shuts off to ensure that food or fluid enters the tummy so avoiding the lungs then opens when breathing generally, was at fault. In other words, although she was ready to be born, Penny had not completed the development of this vital anatomical flap or valve prior to birth. The result of this delayed anatomical development was that initially each time she was fed then laid to rest the consumed food would simply 'run' back out of her tummy.

Therefore, it was necessary in those days, between feeds at least, that she was hung upright in the makeshift sling fixed to the wall in order for the food/fluid to remain in the tummy to be properly digested. This initial lifestyle of my sister lasted many days or if I recall correctly, weeks after her birth. Even when she was finally brought home, the family baby cot, used by all of us in turn but now pink in colour, had to be placed on bricks at the 'head' end until the offending 'bit' of our sister completed its development, enabling her to retain in the normal way her daily sustenance.

So now the family was complete. Well Greg was definitely hoping so anyway. As the youngest of the boys, Penny was just a couple of months off five years younger than me, making her a huge twelve years younger than Greg. My memories of growing up seem mostly to exclude the existence of Penny for some reason. This may have been due to the age gap between us or simply that I was never really comfortable with these things called girls. So throughout most of my childhood adventures, although Penny was obviously in the background, she is excluded from so many of the memories I have of my childhood exploits. In conversation with Greg much later life, he grants that he only got to know his sister at all when as an adult visiting England from his adopted country, South Africa, meeting Penny as a late teenager or early adult. Sadly, the adult relationship the other two boys had with Penny was at best strained contempt but at worst, just commonly hostile! As for me, well I have such an admiration for my only sister. Yes, she may be rough –

she grew up in a house full of flowing testosterone after all. Yes, her manner can be hard, often lacking in acceptance of others' incongruities. However, inside where she lives, is a shy sensitive individual who is not fully able to express herself properly with confidence. This insecurity is often protected by an outward projection of hard bravado. She is though a truly real person with real human qualities nonetheless.

Once again Dear Reader, I digress.

I will now attempt to provide you with a collection of 'Pieces' covering shared 'family' events that reside in my memory today, extending across my childhood years from just over six years (possibly that half again) to my early teens.
I require your indulgence, even your forgiveness that only one of these episodes includes any reference to my sister. This is not a display by me today of a sexist, or incorrect political correctness approach – I just do not recall her 'being' present at the time!

The old market town of Aylesbury in Buckinghamshire where we were raised can trace its origins to the pre-Saxon days of England. For centuries, Aylesbury was the centre of trade for the large farming communities which today comprise all the counties sharing the collective title of 'The Home Counties' of England – Buckinghamshire being just one such county. In fact, even though there is an ancient town of Buckingham in the county of Buckinghamshire, it is not the 'County' town. That title has been held by Aylesbury for many centuries. My arrival on this planet took place in the then 'new' council built suburb of Southcourt. This is a very large, sprawling suburb generally located to the south-west of the original town which was at the time of my childhood, almost completely surrounded by farmland with open English 'Home Counties' countryside in every direction. As a family with four boys growing up in such an area, we were fortunate as our lives were constantly enhanced by the proximity of the open fields with established woodlands and natural watercourses of all kinds, all of which were accessible by a variety of 'Public' footpaths. I must confess there were times where through playing games or passionate exploration, we would find ourselves well away from the footpaths.

I do not think today that this activity caused any damage to the local countryside at all. Most of the area that captured our imagination as children is today completely covered by a collection of large housing estates which reflect the towns' expansion into becoming a suburb of London. Growing up, I for one spent many a happy hour or more exploring the seemingly endless, inexhaustible supply of magnificent countryside. Throughout all the seasons, we were lucky to be able to experience the wonders of our natural environment. The smell of damp, rotting foliage underfoot in the autumn, almost an intoxicating, pungent drug! The dry grass that, after the harvest felt that it would catch in then scratch ones' nostrils if we got too close.

The very extraordinarily, really pungent smell of a new countryside springtime could often sting the eyes of those who were subject to attacks of hay fever. Bouncing across bales piled high in a hayloft, collecting chicken eggs left in hiding places by free range birds that play hide the egg games with the humans by just depositing eggs anywhere around the farm. Walking, or rather attempting to walk in knee-deep powdery snow across a meadow in mid winter, with a crystal clear blue sky above. In summer, picking wild berries from the hedges of those same fields, fishing for sticklebacks in nearby rivers or bubbling streams. Summer daylight filtering through green leaves of every hue. The sun casting changing ripples of shadow in every direction throughout long, warm sunny days. Across the road, a neighbour in the early evening after a day of work could often be heard lazily mowing his lawn with a noisy push-pull mower as we children lay in bed trying to sleep! That lingering sweet smell, that almost vibrant taste of the newly mown grass invading our senses on those long summer nights, offering to keep us awake when sleep was calling. The abundance of wildlife existing within just a stroll down to the local brook often provided hours of opportunity for entertainment to any interested child.

Then, should we to get tired of all this, a short walk into town provided all those other things we thought we needed from the then modern world at the time.

There were many families in our end of the street. There were some with a gender mix of offspring, others with just one or two, still others with several of the same gender, then again some families that had been devastated by loss from recent war or ill health – a cosmopolitan mix many of whom were then the first of the London population over flow.

The occupants of our end of the street (notice here that I have avoided using our "half" of the street) represented a wide variety of backgrounds, all playing their role in creating a busy, growing-up community.

Although we all would have argued strongly that it did not exist at the time, there was a shared awareness by most of the families that 'this is as good as it gets' so let's all help to support each other. I recall clearly the collective sadness whenever a local inhabitant passed on. There existed a shared interest in 'the next' arrival, a real concern for a sick child or if anyone was hospitalised. Yet all this caring was constantly coupled with an insatiable need for that most precious of sought after knowledge, knowing of local intelligence, put another way...the latest local gossip! Although naturally, gossiping was an activity that we, the more sophisticated collection of residents at our end of the street took no part in whatsoever. We (the collective we) were more stylish, more classy than to participate in local gossip; we (the same collective we) had proper gardens with lawns, even some flowers planted if money allowed. However, THEY, those residents at the other end of the street, had patches of unruly, muddy grass where old pieces of broken household furniture had been dumped to rot. Also displayed to the world in many such an unkempt front garden, were bits of old bikes, of both the motor, plus parts of the 'pushbike' variety.

Later, as apparent wealth changed, these discarded bits of human flotsam displayed to the world were to include many old broken cars as well. Old tyres, chairs or just large bits of human household debris could be seen in the front gardens of many of the homes within the 'other' half of our road. But! At our end of the road we had lawns, flower beds, shrubs, trees even household pets that were kept under control, who only did their business in our gardens, other than cats of course who only ever use a neighbours' garden anyway! Not like those up the street who did it in the street! (The pets, not the people who lived there – I hope!).

We had washing lines in our back gardens to hang washing on, not just sagging, twisted chicken-wire fences between the properties acting as the location to show off almost clean clothes. In all this broad civilian mix of residents, this council estate of poor humanity, where expectations of a 'better' life following the sacrifices made for peace in Europe were dashed, lost forever over time. Where the 'spoils of war' always, when available, seemed to go to 'others', this council estate in the 1950s lived, loved in festering despair of their lowly place in the human life chain. The gathering of humanity resident at our end of the road was where external visual presentation of the incumbents reflected a vastly different style. This community of ours was to develop over time almost subconsciously, into a strangely cohesive group of locals of which I was to be a part.

A 'Band of Brothers'?

We boys, we rival siblings, we, these independent individuals who by accident of birth, simply tolerated each other were to become a steadfast unit, a solid defence, a powerful 'band of brothers from number 44' who, but only when needed, ran in harmony supreme!

Just at our end of the road of course!

Growing up in that forgotten decade of the 1950s in a small forgotten town on a council estate for which we had to thank the nation, located just forty miles north of London, created in the minds of many of our peers a collective time, an unspoken desire, a shadow cry, a knowing that things just had to, just must…change. Reluctant but nevertheless wanting to create the spark, but yet not old enough to drive the changes that would build anew to make a significant difference.

It was not until the second half of the '50s that the brewing demand for change started in earnest. Change in popular music, in the arts, in the theatres all started the challenge to authority with small steps that would grow to such magnitude, to become a driving force to attitude change in the newborn, rapidly growing population. May 6th 1956 a new play "Look Back in Anger" opened to shock the theatre world with its blunt 'kitchen-sink' reality reflecting the real world for millions of families who to a large extent, had been ignored for generation upon generation. The approaching decade seemingly just waiting to provide the vehicle for the groundswell that soon became an unstoppable focus for change, in particular for freedom of expression. Despite banning from the public airwaves by the government of the day, Rock-n'-Roll was starting to be broadcast via ships stationary in international waters off the coast of the UK soon to be listened to by millions of baby-boomer teenagers across the nation. The government's indiscriminate censorship of all published material including books, films, along with popular magazines, started to face a stark rebellion to the status quo of collective submissive acceptance. Here then was the start of the upheaval that resulted in the arrival of the swinging '60s. The days of collective, unconscious acceptance of total government authority began to collapse, reflecting the gathering of frustration as the Baby-Boomers grew up during the late 1950s into the new, new decade of change!

An almost spontaneously unified release, a common outcry for self-expression erupted. The youth, together with millions of now young adults, shared a collective energy with just one purpose in their demands – a cry for change, for freedom.

This tsunami eventually forcing lifestyle change, building areas of personal opportunity for expression, put an end to the forgotten people of the forgotten decade of the 1950s. From structured, planned repression to a crescendo of demand driven by a new self-awareness, an attitude of life defiance!

What a change it was to be.

I make the above observation simply as a warning to you, Dear Reader, not to misunderstand my intention here. The title used earlier, 'A Band of Brothers' is my own creation as I am writing this journal. However, estranged as we were throughout our growing up, when needed, we brothers were to 'Stand Together' in any adversity, real or imagined! Whilst this title is of my own creation, it is still nonetheless how I recall our collective reply when challenge required it. Even with constant scrapping with or between one or more of each of us, there were to be times that sibling rivalry was put aside in the face of the local public, when collective defence, or defiance or reply to a challenge against the family was demanded. However, to even hint at the possibility in your mind Dear Reader, that the reference to 'the band of brothers from number 44' indicated any form of bonding or lasting, loving friendship or partnership between the four of us or any such combination of us, would be a total corruption of the truth. No, this collective defence attitude was very rare indeed.

After all, Greg was seven years older than me, the apple of his mothers' eye, as the first born; the poor sod on whom our parents, from so vastly differing backgrounds, were destined to practice their own particular brand or 'version' of parenting.

Yes, it was Greg that continued to suffer the challenges of being the 'eldest' from both parents. Expectations of him by his parents with yes the constantly changing responsibilities of those offspring who were not the first born but were simply following in his tracks, must have caused him to labour in his own childhood for years under almost impossible pressure.

A yoke slung across his shoulders with which he strained as we were all growing up. Not likely then that he would regard any of us as 'friend'. Had the second offspring of our parents been a girl, maybe this particular burden would have been much less.

At the opposite end of the brats' pool was me – not the apple of any ones' eye, again not the much wanted 'daughter' yet here I was demanding constant attention, seeking ways to explore a safe passage though my early learning years, often angrily rejected for always asking stupid, apparently dumb, questions. Constantly seeking answers at every turn to the wonders of the world around me. The 'Blithering Idiot' was my label, my unwanted badge that was constantly vocally awarded to me by my father then often to be followed by, "who is best ignored with his insistent stupid questions". Then between Greg leading this loosely aligned pack whilst I occupied the rear, existed the other two personalities seeking to satisfy their own particular needs! Chris, challenging anything that resembled authority with a lightening wit but with simply awful timing!

Poor Andy, all he wanted was simply to be seen to be as good as big brother Greg in everything – but constantly failing abysmally! Never did he realise until much later in life, that he was a whole independent person not some adjunct to the senior sibling. Thus the home environment was not really one that encouraged large amounts of brotherly love. In fact, fights were regular, bitter squabbles that could last for months at a time, always reflecting those natural divisions that existed between the strong, the weak, or one or more of the rest! Each of us was primarily concerned, ever committed to expressing those concerns about our own earth shattering needs, desires, expectations; but also above all that, our individual obvious importance. This title then is my way of enjoying the moments when, as one, we stood together. Not that our dear father would have approved of such combined behaviour! His saving of potential catastrophe, his policy of divide to rule had no room for complicity! Regrettably. Although later in life he did start to open up a little, I was never really able to conduct a conversation with our father on things like philosophy, raising a family, his life or our family history generally. Not even his thoughts of or on the recent world war. I could not gain a proper feeling from him or to get a view of his inner feelings on any such matters. Very little was ever spoken by him in terms of his own life history. As we grew up he would offer tiny observational insights about his background almost in a 'throwaway' fashion. Unless the recipient was able to not just digest but remember these tantalising morsels, they were at the time forever lost. If any insight, some tiny crumb of information had had any real substance in its imparting to us on such occasions, each of us today lack any real detail or focus of or about who this man was. This secret individual, this boss of our childhood universe was then something of an enigma. He did, much later, share some things with me about his own parents, his childhood upbringing, but even this was to prove to be precious little in reality.

An adventure with our Father.

On one eventful time with my father when I was at home recovering from a six week stay in hospital, he 'invited' me to go to London with him on what for me, turned out to be a really shocking adventure.

Well 'invited' is not really true. "Why not take him (me) with you?" my mother asked one late spring day when I was about eight years old. As it was late spring, I was six months (that half year again) into my ninth year. It was just after breakfast time when there was only Penny at home as all the others were at school. Having been encased in a hospital isolation unit for a long time, my parents were advised that I should take the rest of the school term off. So it was that having been scrubbed, tidied, made to put on my Sunday 'best-set' of hand-me-downs, I found myself 'walking-out' alongside my father towards the local railway station.

Now this was new! We were going to London! Filled with wondrous excitement to the extent that unable to stop myself, I was just a constant blabbering noise of questions that were studiously ignored all the way to the station! I wanted to explode! What joy! I remember thinking with secret thought that from now on, I must conspire to be ill more often if such an opportunity to go to London, to "The Whole World" in fact, was to be the reward! A day that started with a walk full of suppressed excitement, even a little fear of the unknown after breakfast, was to end in the early evening, arriving home in a giant of a big black motor vehicle!

A sleek, powerful six cylinder car, a Vauxhall Velox! A car of our own! It was simply a very magical day indeed! Excitement of a train journey was enough on its own to cram my nerves with juddering tingles, allowing my legs to float. I was indeed walking on air. Then that huge city, London! The sound, the colour, the people all moving in multi-colliding directions except up! Yes, some even went down! But so did the two of us!

Down the longest moving stairs I had ever encountered, traveling into the unknown depths of this massive city I went, standing erect, holding on for dear life, eyes ablaze yet attempting to look as nonchalant as possible, detached but failing terribly. All the way down still flooding the world with questions, pointing in all directions, asking continuously for answers to how? What? When? I was overtaken often with fear as we continued into the deepest basement of this great city. Marylebone main line station was our entry to the city by rail then by making use of the Bakerloo Line, we continued our magnificent journey into the heart of London. Trains in tunnels, more trains! By now I was unsure of myself, simply clinging to my fathers' coat, hand or anything that was attached to him!

There were more people in the world than I had imagined any chance of ever counting! Perhaps they were all riding these underground trains. Eventually we emerged at whatever location my father had intended when the sky seemed so blue that the reprieve from the false underground night was sudden bright sun-driven soft wrap around me, a warm, reassuring comfort. It was also raining gently so even this colossus, this special place in the world produced conflict within my physical senses. Apparently we had arrived early for some appointment that, at the time, I was unaware of so I was taken on my first visit to a 'Lions Tea Room'. It must have been lunch time because all I can remember today is eating in this large, light, airy room at a table that had been set for four with my farther eating something with green peas! I had no idea that such places ever existed. The real surprise though was being allowed to 'select' a cake from a stand at the counter! How proud I was that it was me that had been so ill! Things could not possibly be more enthralling, or could they? After the lunch treat we walked along crowded streets, past shops of every design, whilst multitudes of smells, accosted us. Surrounded by volatile chatter, almost stagnant traffic, including giant red buses!

The world of the city was busy! Today I was there, a part of this visual rainbow of activity! Eventually we walked into what I thought was a rather dull open display area covered by what seemed to be a wooden awning. Scattered about this area was a collection of cars, a car showroom in fact. Now 'uncle' Laurie (lorry) who lived next door had a car as did Mr Chapman who lived alongside the brook. Often cars of all sizes would travel along our road. There were occasionally trucks, coal deliveries for example, with also every morning that small milk float thing too. So it was nothing unusual to see cars. But this was London City where there were oh so many vehicles all moving in a Stop Start fashion.

My father seemed to be looking at some of these cars within the showroom collection, opening doors, sitting inside, talking to another man who I had not seen appear from anywhere. By its absence from our house, I had come to understand that money was something that 'others' had. After all, the most we ever had as a result of running an errand to the local shop, was a 'half-penny' often just a 'farthing'. We never had any more money for clothes after the initial expenditure for 'new' secondhand stuff for Greg! This was then handed down the line having been mended, repaired where needed then altered to fit as best as possible, the next user. It was a constant struggle, so mother often said, "to make ends meet" so simply not having money was a way of life. Imagine my shock at what happened next! I, like my father, was gently touching these shiny cars on display, thinking how wonderful it would be if we had such a magnificent thing, knowing full well that this would not, could not be, for the likes of us. Then I was taken into a room at the end of this display area where the man who had been talking to my father now sat behind a large desk that was completely covered with paper documents. There were two battered wooden swivel chairs in front of the desk in which we each sat.

The adults talked, I swung around in the chair…their talking continued for some time more, then apparently this strange event was over. Or so I thought. Both men suddenly stood, I thought it was time to leave, but they reached across the desk to shake hands. My father was smiling, the man was smiling, some documents needed to be signed so father leaned on the desk from a standing position to sign them.

Then the impossible of all impossibilities unfolded before my eyes! I had on occasion seen a brown 'Ten Shilling' note but only very rarely, a green 'One Pound' note.

I had never seen more than one or two of either in the same place at the same time in my entire life – until that moment! I have already indicated before that my father was wearing a coat, I had held on to it in the tube, crossing busy streets. It was a long, pale rain coat with side pockets and a wide collar that could be raised against wind or rain when required, all tied around the middle by a belt. On standing up after signing those papers on the desk, my father put his hand in one of the pockets, the one closest to me, then without hesitation withdrew a bundle, a wad of notes all tied up in string! My gaping mouth was as massive as my disbelieving eyes. There was money beyond comprehension, a stack of the stuff! He, that person, now a complete stranger, who looked like, even sounded like my father, perhaps even actually had been my father until a few seconds ago, carefully placed this pile of money on the desk! He, this stranger, undid the string, slipping the bits of string back into his raincoat pocket, then he started counting this money! My face was frozen, I was giddy, astonished, what was this person doing? Where had all this money, the stuff we never, ever had at home, come from? Where had my real father gone? However, before I could get to ask my first question, it got much, much worse!

Having finished counting this remarkable fortune out on a cleared space on the other mans' desk he, this man who looked exactly like my father, who still seemed to be pretending to be my father, this known hard task master, this person who managed us by fear, reached into the other pocket of his raincoat on the other side from me, then again proceeded to extract another bundle of cash identical to the first one! Again the string was removed, more counting took place. Having found a way to breathe, perhaps even forcing my gaping jaw back to something resembling my normal expression, I stretched my body in the swivel chair to look across the untidy pile of paper to the now mountain of money, then at the man on the other side of the desk. There seemed to be a glint, a gentle soft smile as he watched the progress of the money counting.

He too looked a little dumbfounded but his demeanour carried with it an almost invisible glow, an expression of happy satisfaction.

Thus so it was that our family became one of the first in our street to be the proud owners of our own motorcar! A big, black, moving tonne of metal! A dark-brown walnut wooden dashboard, a real brown leather bench seat in the front with soft padding in the back. A gear stick on the steering column with a leather bound steering wheel. Electric controlled direction pointing indicator 'arms' on each side, the bright shiny 'Vauxhall' arrow on the massive bonnet pointing the way along the road! The 'Velox' had a straight six cylinder engine with over two thousand two hundred ccs' of power. Today this car, there are a few still running, is regarded as something of a classic with its own very active UK owners club.

Exhausted, excited, frightened, full of pride sitting in the front alongside my father, he drove that massive machine all the way from London to our home in Aylesbury.

I discovered many things that day about our father which raised so many questions. This man, who had always remained forceful in his resolve to assure obedience, seemed to have a second, hidden mostly, nature. Clearly there was a secretive, very private part that I had not seen until that London visit. Another shocking discovery of that eventful day, as if the money was not enough in itself, was that for the first time, I became aware of actually how small our father was, something that, until then there had been no reason to even think of or question with regard to our parents. All parents are the same aren't they? Well this was the day that I for one was to be exposed to another truth about parents; they were actually, well almost nearly but not quite really, like us!

It was as a direct result of this car purchase that I came to accept that our father was not a giant in the world of men. Not a bigger, stronger father than any other but was in fact, rather short in stature. The incident leading to this discovery, although small in reality, provided a giant awakening of reality for me. My father was small! A realisation of this truth, because that was what it was, quickly guided my thinking to accept that other adults must also be small or others tall, some thin whilst others were big! I'm sure all children of similar age to me at the time of my day in London, had never considered the fact that parents were really variable in size! What an awakening! This brought with it a sudden knowledge, a vista of realisation that like size, some parents must be even older than previously thought! It was some while later when I recognised the obvious; if some were old, others must be young. All this on a surprise day out in London with our father.

Age aside, our father was really small!

So short in fact that when he came to sit behind the steering wheel of his big, new to him second-hand car, he couldn't see over the dashboard, but more importantly, out through the windscreen! Here was this big, powerful person who influenced all our lives at home, being exposed for what he really was – seriously challenged in the 'height' department. In fact, he was not much taller than I was at the time, yet I had never noticed it. This lack of stature then caused something of a problem at the time of wanting to drive away in this newly acquired automobile from the car showroom. If one cannot see over the steering wheel of a car, how can one drive it? After what appeared to me to be a perplexed discussion, actually just background noise to me as I was by this time fully self-installed on that front bench seat of this amazing vehicle. I was living almost in denial, this cannot be true!

Nevertheless, eyes a-sparkle, chest heaving with unashamed pride – we had our own car! No more waiting on uncle 'Lorry'! Our very own car in which I, the runt of the litter, the sucker of that hind tit…was in the front passenger side, attempting to look as non-concerned as possible, holding my breath because there now seemed to be some possibility that due to my father's physical size, or lack of, we may not actually keep it. Perhaps we will have to go home by train! Oh please no! The problem though was solved by a gesture, a compassionate act of goodwill by the man who had sat behind the desk earlier, with that satisfied ghost of a smile on his face.

Due to the desk requirements of his job, this person also had a large wooden chair on which rested, for comfort purposes only I'm sure, a number of large, soft but worn cushions. Several of these were provided to my father for him to sit on, thus raising him up high enough to be able to see over the steering wheel!

I cannot imagine how he managed to drive across London sitting on a couple of worn, gifted second-hand cushions in his second-hand car where the cushions under him were resting on a shiny, highly polished leather seat! But drive he did. Or should that read 'Butt drive he did' perhaps! Although I have no real memory of the journey home, I'm sure that he must have slid around on that seat all the way back to Aylesbury. At the time of this great adventure, there was no law about having seatbelts so even the possibility of a strap to hold him steady on the journey home did not exist. But arrive home we did with me beaming with unconcealed pride as mother watched us extract ourselves from this four-wheeled big, black chariot on arrival. Some of my siblings emerged from our house similarly carrying expressions of excited wonder on their faces.

So thus it was that we joined the ever growing mobile populous of the mid-fifties, becoming members of the AA, that magnificent motoring support organisation, displaying our membership badge proudly on the front grill of the car. Always when travelling thereafter as members of the AA, we enjoyed the status and we constantly looked out on long journeys in great anticipation of meeting an 'AA Man' coming toward us on his distinctive motorbike, with the attached sidecar resplendent in his full uniform. We waited in the back with hands ready to see, that all was well with our vehicle. This knight of the road riding his trusty steed would in full view of all, snap a perfect military 'salute' letting us know there was nothing he could detect as a problem with our car then he sailed past. How many times did one or more of us offer a 'salute' in return? Always! That six cylinder, 2.2 litre solid motor surrounded by real metal, real wood, real leather was to become a classic that today, as it does with our family, maintains its place in motor history, generally in addition to a warm place in our individual memories specifically.

Ownership of this car provided much fun to us all. I recall being woken in the small hours of a summer day, standing vacant, bleary eyed in the kitchen as the family gathered for a five or six hour, sometimes more, journey to the seaside for the day.

If the day was chosen correctly, at the end of the early morning journey waited hours of sun (well perhaps) ice-cream, sand, even the seaside! From around lunch time until late afternoon or early evening, we would make the most of these one day visits. Later exhausted, we would all climb aboard the big black monster motor for the long journey home. Often the very act of climbing into the car would result in sharp exclamations of pain!

Being closed up on such days for several hours whilst parked in the open, our shiny black car had held as if a gift for us on our return to it, half of all the heat of the day. Often we could not sit on the boiling leather seats for some time after discovering, usually in a truly painful fashion, that our already naked sunburnt legs, backs, arms and thighs in particular, woollen swimming trunks or not, also suffered additional burns from the seats! Nevertheless, such days were always fun, tiring sometimes even stressful but always ended with complete exhaustion. We did arrive back at our house very late in the evening on these days so sleeping in the car after squabbling about space was not excluded as being all part of the shared experience of the day. Counting the heads of each child to ensure the number was correct took place at various stages of the return trip.

At the beginning of the journey home of course, then if we stopped anywhere for bladder or other necessary body relief, even for the spreading of more soothing cream to a particularly painful area of someone's anatomy, the counting heads was a statutory need prior to continuing the homeward journey. Experience had set such a protocol…yes, someone had been left behind on previous outings!

Then off to bed frequently around midnight! There were indeed last minute checks that all souls were safely in bed before the house was closed up for the rest of the night. Sometimes these counting sessions did result in an unexpected panic either due to miscounting resulting in thinking that someone was missing, or indeed when someone actually was missing! We who were in the correct place on such occasions, were shaken in desperation, partially raised from deep slumber by shouted demands as to where the missing sibling was when last seen.

Our garage was not attached to our house nor indeed was it anywhere in our street! Its location was actually just a short walk from the house around the corner past the new church.

Often then after such days, we children, having fallen asleep on the way home, had to be awoken, perhaps even in the early hours of the next morning, finding ourselves in the car which as if by some magic, was by now parked safely in the garage. Struggling to carry picnic bags in a semi-slumbering state the short distance of about five hundred yards from the block of garages located at the church behind our house round to the end of our road, then on toward home was very strange indeed! It was dark! All the locals were sleeping; the world was a quietly eerie night time place. On more than one occasion, having got those of us they could awake enough to carry the array of away-day necessities to then meander, stumble in sleepy stupor not really awake at all, our parents would carry those that simply were far too gone to walk or help carry 'stuff'. The car was locked, the garage door locked whilst this rag-tag tired group weaved a weary line home. Things, people were dumped in the house, some in beds, whilst others sat in full sleepy mode on a toilet then via a completely dazed zombie method, somehow got into a bed. Often not their own, only to discover this the next day!

House lights extinguished, doors locked, the empty milk bottles placed quietly on the front door step for the attention of our milkman who would be delivering in just an hour or three! Silence! Then suddenly...

"Where's Chris? Has anyone seen Chris?"

My mother, on making the final check to make sure her brood were all accounted for, suddenly realised that Chris was nowhere to be seen!

Panic, open everything, doors unlocked, check the outside loo, check the shed, he may have missed the backdoor turning and simply falling into the shed! But no, Chris was still in the car, lying curled up on the floor behind the front seat fast asleep! Back they had to go, along the street, around the corner, past the church in the middle of the night to the row upon row of lock-up garages to retrieve their third-born son! The same thing happened to our sister Penny once as well, so although a worry at the time, giggles about such episodes in the car soon settled into our collective memories of shared times in this marvellous vehicle.

Eventually of course, as time rolled past, time itself separated the siblings chronologically so that one by one, the 'boys' participation on these days-by-the-seaside trips as well as the annual camping holidays, became less in number. Our big black transportation, that monster of the road whose acquisition I had been privy to, its regular weight demand of human occupants began to reduce, Greg, a late teenager no longer wanting to go on holiday with his parents.

Then Andrew declined these trips, quickly following Greg because he always seemed to force himself to follow in the footsteps of his elder brother, sadly never with the same successes. Then Chris was next, leaving school as early as possible full of testosterone, fully aware of the potential of the female form that suffocated his waking day. There were just too many of them for him to manage, together with knowing that his refusal to continue to attend these family events carried yet another defiant message to our father, so Chris also stopped participating. To some extent I think that our shining black knight of the road recognised that its family community of passengers was diminishing, so slowly accepted that soon it or we would 'move-on'.

The parting of us from this car was to happen rather suddenly during a camping holiday one summer during my early teens. Although I was a part of the arrival of this magnificent vehicle to our family, regretfully I was not to be anywhere near at the time of its demise – its departure from our lives. I was excluded from the event when this wonderful family friend without any warning, ceased to play any further part in the lives of our family. I felt sorry that I was not to be a part of its departure but inevitably the time came for us to separate. The final parting took place unexpectedly. It was the last such holiday that Chris was to share with us before other 'teenage' pressures were to encompass him. We, that is me, Mum, Dad, Chris and Penny were all on a weeks' camping holiday. Having arrived on the Saturday at our chosen campsite for a week of relaxation by the sea, we knew that next Tuesday however Chris had to return to Aylesbury whilst the rest of us were to stay for the remainder of the week.

Arrangements had been made to take Chris early on Tuesday morning to the nearest main line station to our camp site so that he could catch a train home. Initially I was to be our fathers' companion on the round trip to the station, drop Chris off, then back to camp for lunch.

At the very last minute on that fateful Tuesday morning just before climbing aboard I decided that I did not want to accompany them, but instead wanted to stay in the camp to do my own thing. This resulted in my being the only person to remain at the camp site. There I stood waving off the family on their journey to the station. I was left to enjoy the solitude of self-entertainment for what was intended to be just a few hours. What I did not expect at all was that it would be early evening before I set eyes on any of them again! I can only report what little I recall of that fateful day, as my memory is peppered with what I was eventually told.

However, I shall try to reflect the events of the day as correctly as possible. It seems that the initial objective of getting Chris to a station then on to a train home was completed reasonably quickly in line with expectations. Having discharged their duty to Chris on this fine August day, the rest of the family decided to explore the local countryside. This entailed them taking a casual drive along country lanes back to the campsite to re-join the reading, walking, thinking and generally lazy Richard in time for them to arrive for lunch. I do not recall knowing the actual time but after an hour or two of driving and enjoying the local views, it was then decided to make their way back to the campsite. No sooner this decision, when disaster intervened! Having located an 'A' road that would help them to find the road to the village where we were holidaying, they joined quite a lot of traffic heading in the same direction. Unknown to them but some distance ahead of them, slowly climbing up a steep hill, a lorry had been involved in an accident. Traffic was only just starting to move past the accident site after some of the debris had been cleared from the road. As the slow, almost static, line of waiting traffic were guided past the scene by a policeman who waved them through, each vehicle started to pick up speed when climbing up the hill continuing on their journey.

My family members at the tail end of the queue of cars started to climb the hill. However, about halfway up, although I have no way of knowing if it was halfway or not, our sturdy giant black friend encountered a thick patch of oil.

Forward traction was lost instantly! Despite the best efforts of the driver, the car started to slide backwards gathering speed very quickly, so I was told. Whilst there was no other vehicle close behind at that moment, there were other cars at the bottom of the hill about to start their climb up. Our heavy car, gathering backward downward speed with tyres unable to grip, steering being quite useless apparently, brakes not working at all, the car began to slew sideways at speed. Dad pulling hard on the handbrake managed to lock the back wheels causing the car suddenly to swing towards the side of the road. The car hit the curb-stone at the edge of the road at an angle at a downward momentum, lifted itself into the air then hitting the ground, rolled over!

Apparently just seconds before hitting the curb-stone, the back wheels, now in free-slide, encountered a section of dry tarmac. Rubber burnt, the heavy slewing momentum from the massive weight of the engine at the front of the car, added serious impact pressure as one back wheel crashed into the immovable curb-stone. The entire vehicle started an end-to-end tumbling over on to its roof, sliding to a crunching stop half on the grass on the roadside with the other half still in the road. There it lay like some giant black beetle lying on its back with legs akimbo catching a sun tan. There stood our wonderful Vauxhall Velox! No seatbelts for passengers in those days! Fortunately however, there was a lot of traffic with a lot of people to come to help the rescue of my family. Within a few moments the police were at the scene, but by then passers-by plus other drivers had rescued the occupants. Injuries were initially attended to then a little later the family were taken off to a local hospital for check-ups. Mother had a deep cut to the top of her head, Penny just a few abrasions from the upside down roll-over experience whilst father had a grazed hand! They had all received minor bumps. Lack of serious injury was put down to the strong car coupled with a relative low speed on impact. All this happened around late morning apparently, at about the time when lazy Richard, back at the campsite, would be looking for some lunch! I have no idea of the sequence of things so shall not attempt to even draw a specific picture. During the balance of the day, our now somewhat bent but loyal transport was righted, recovered, then delivered to a local garage where estimates of repair costs, time to complete were given to our father.

The damage was apparently quite extensive! Knowing that he needed to do something urgently to replace his transport, father offered what remained of our wonderful vehicle to the garage owner in part-exchange for a second hand Ford Consul, that was just one of many vehicles the garage owner had for sale on his forecourt. The deal was done that afternoon, insurance cover was granted allowing the lucky escapees from what could have been something quite awful, to drive away in their 'new' car back to the campsite where I was now becoming just a little concerned. Food had not been a problem for me during the day or indeed water, but wondering where they were all the time, instinctively knowing that this non-return by them indicated that something must be wrong, had taken its toll on me. Imagine my utter astonishment then when this strange but really more modern car arrived with my family members in it who immediately started to relay their story!

Thus, during what was possibly the last camping holiday we would share together, the long happy relationship we had enjoyed as a family for many years with this Vauxhall Velox registration number HTR 937 was lost. Gone was the warm internal glow of mine that I was the only child, not any of the others, invited to be in attendance at the very beginning of this relationship on an exciting, money revealing visit to London!

Personal Family Foundations.

My mothers' view on life generally had been built or nurtured on the simple things of a farming family in the Buckinghamshire countryside. This she immersed her own family in, sharing, love, the conquering of hardships, the pure survival struggle of the age. The necessity of actually making clothes, shirts, boy's short trousers from almost nothing when no money was available to buy them. Darning socks, replacing buttons, attending to cuts, together with things such as bruises sustained from the everyday goings-on around a fully active 1950s young family. Feeding her ever-hungry, ever growing brood, she had this inner acceptance of her 'lot' without too much or too often attempting to challenge such a status. She was I think to a very great extent, largely content to perform her role considering it to be her duty as mother, her role as wife, but also as had been ordained by a higher authority. Alongside her real specific fear of things that go 'bump' in the night, there remained unexplained, her continuous sometimes morbid fascination with her own family history, of the reportedly real association with the European Gypsy community. She always maintained a timid interest in matters of future fortune, soothsaying even, together with the potential (or actually real) obligations imposed upon those who are born as twins to the 'seventh-of-the-seventh' twin. Here was myth. Here was fabled superstition! Here was the unexplainable stuff of strange powers! Here within was the font, that unique well, a fearsome fountain of rare endowment not bestowed on just normal mortal souls, but only on those born of the 7th of the 7th who alone have been provided with remarkable abilities. Of the gifted to the gifted offspring of the gifted offspring! These along with the wild natural wonders of Mother Nature, were her anchor.

Animals of all types, insect life in its teeming multitudes across the planet sheltered within natural flora, acted as her guide to all things in life. Those providing or needing suckling or protection, were all welcome. Comfort given to God's natural young were at her centre of being, giving constant joy through her life, personal reflection in her quiet times. Intuitively she offered sustenance to all without question. It was not to be until much later in my story that I was to see a change in this general demeanour of our mother.

I think that due to our fathers' strict Edwardian upbringing, the "do as you are told without ever a question or answer back", the "stand to attention to acknowledge authority of country or the Catholic Church", he never truly recovered from or allowed himself to recover from the public shame, indeed the humiliation of lost wealth. More particularly however, was something far more damming to his family, the suicide of his own father. Our father therefore, to a large extent, remained closed to all those around him, well, at least to his immediate family. Playing with a ball, riding a bike, sharing a child's cricket game or otherwise with his children in the garden was not within his capacity of or for life. Having been in the RAF involved in aircraft electronics repair during the war then once things had settled in the early to mid 1950s, he changed jobs spending the rest of his adult working life in the employ of a company supplying military electronics equipment to the British Military including the Aerospace industries. The work he undertook was government project based therefore for obvious security reasons, he was unable to talk to us about what it was he did all day. I recall thinking at his funeral that other than his immediate family, there were two obvious government goons in typical dark suits buried beneath raincoats on that cold grey day.

There were no personal friends in attendance, no one he had maintained contact with during his adult life either via work or hobby or outside interest and clearly no one from his childhood years. His sister was with us on that day of course but his one remaining brother was not. Just us! There, standing respectfully in the background on that cold, damp March day, just those two unknown men representing his erstwhile employers. Forty plus years as an adult with no one called 'friend' to say farewell at the end of his life's journey. So the management technique he employed for his four male offspring was expressed simply. Governance designed with determination along the principle of divide, rule...then conquer! An administration of the (his) applicable rules by fear and fear we did. Not really then a conducive home environment for us boys to 'bond' as brothers. Here again then sat the opposing personal life experiences of these two people; the life influences of both our parents resulting often in conflict, regular confusion creating a juxtaposition requiring each of us to stand clear, alone, or be embroiled in turmoil.

BUT!

On the odd occasion when one of us at any time was threatened by any outsider, the four boys would stand together in public defence as one! There are so many examples of this that it would not be possible to convey them all here so I offer the following brotherly protection story in the hope that it may contain sufficient content to afford a view of this incomplete sibling support. Incomplete only in its application where outsiders needed to be castigated! A boy who lived across the road, whose dad owned the push-pull lawnmower, real name Roger but was better known by everyone as 'BUB' (we never worked out why he had this name), who was seven years old at the time of this event, was widely known to be the local child bully.

Well BUB, who had for some time been frightening infant school children on Monday mornings, charged up to me, at a time when I was just five years old, one day on my way to school. With very threatening behaviour he really frightened me into surrendering my school dinner money with the menacing promise of violence had I not complied! The entire street knew that he had been doing this successfully to the 'younger-than-him' boys, even to some of the local girls for some time but he had never actually been caught at it by anyone. On this morning for his own ego, he had a go at little me! Although I had no idea at the time – this experience was my first opportunity to record that I was on the one hand basically a coward, yet on the other, I was even then remaining the same to this day – a pacifist! I abhor violence of any sort! With hot tears, shaking, whining fear I surrendered my one shilling that was to provide my lunch meal each day of that week at my infant school. Later that day covered in shame, still trembling and somewhat astonished at my own weakness, I told Chris what had happened.

The very next morning as we were leaving for school together, in itself something very unusual, Chris was by my side! Usually we never walked to school together but on this particular day big brother Chris was at hand! As expected, so was my tormentor of yesterday! Without a word of warning or shouted explanation, almost casually even, Chris strolled directly up to BUB, who was convinced that he was 'King of the hill', master over all things, who suddenly found that he had a very urgent, very unexpected, very fast visit to the centre of his face by the hardened solid fist of my brother Chris! What had been up to this violent encounter, by all things a normal morning with children being walked or sent off to school was so suddenly broken, even blown asunder never to return to its former normality.

A sudden explosion of real, actual, truly painful brotherly retaliation was inflicted on the BUB boy! I cannot be certain of course but I remain sure that the split second before reality set in, Bub must have at least thought ---'I'll get this other boy now!' Then the pain started which must have been accompanied by sheer shock that anyone would have the nerve to do such a thing to…HIM! This was just too much to take. Pain, blood, humiliation all accompanied by a very loud shouted warning by Chris to leave his little brother

Richard alone or he, Chris, would ensure that he (Bub) would never stop bleeding from his broken face! This confrontation, this violence took place as children were going to school on what was, up to then, a perfectly normal Tuesday. Children being accompanied by their mums but there were several other children walking together, who all acted as observers to this incident. This unexpected violence, this shouting followed by the sound of crying with plenty of blood, all collaborated to attract attention. It was not too long before the street was in an uproar! Blood was gushing forth from the broken twisted nostrils of the big (former) bully BUB. There he stood transfixed, rooted to the spot, screaming for his mummy who just seconds later emerged to investigate and who was now pounding across the street. Taking in the situation, she held her injured offspring who started babbling through tears, blood, dribbling nose, and pointing with shaking blood covered finger towards Chris. Here she came purposefully striding across the road to wage war with our mother, who like other women had emerged onto the street due to the commotion! The sound had attracted a large number of other mothers out of their homes. A communal expectation garnered in anticipation of a potentially sizable conflict between mothers of the two local broods who were about to protect one or more of their litter! The shouting boomed! Mother stood her ground.

Carefully, in controlled voice but loud enough for all to hear, she informed her now irate neighbour from across the street who clutched her now pathetic, whimpering, bleeding son to her side, of that individuals' known bullying reputation. What had the exciting possibility of a really fantastic verbal boxing match between the two mothers soon developed into a combined passing-on, a sharing of knowledge by many of the other mothers confirming the 'Bully' status awarded to her son, the currently cowering Bub! Such was the conviction of the gathered community of motherhood that Bubs' own mother, realising the situation, eventually turned on her now tear stained, bloody-faced second son. She grabbed him by an ear in full public view, smacked him hard across the head whilst turning to walk back across the road shouting all the way that he must – 'just wait till his bloody father gets home, he'll give you a beating you'll never forget!'

There were many such instances throughout this period of my life from people cheating while we (one or more of us) were playing games with 'friends' in the road during non-school time. To name calling etc., etc. But always, as we were the only family in the road comprising four boys, the 'band of brothers from number 44' were regarded as a single unit that others should not, finally did not, attempt to challenge or suppress. Such was the reputation of this group of brothers that there were often times that all of us were the subject of, even sometimes the collective drivers of, all sorts of happenings; some to become famous, although I cannot grasp why such things should be, but also, some to become infamous! Some were of sufficient renown that the interest of the local printed media was aroused whilst others attracted the interest of those feared men in blue – the protectors of public peace – the police.

Were we sometimes guilty of a collective planning of these events, oh yes we were! But such collective protection of each other was an instinct of the pack, an impulse driven by pack protection not at all because we were friends. These moments of standing together, this public expression of all-for-one etc., seemed simply to show the world around us why we should not be threatened or challenged by anyone – other than by each other of course.

The Snow Ball Wizards!

One such event that attracted newspaper interest took place in the winter following my ninth birthday. I seem to think it was to become known as the Patterson Road, 'Snow Barricade War'. I am sure that via a search of the annals of the local weekly rag, the "Bucks Herald", it will not be too difficult to find an old picture of the 'Band of Brothers from Number 44' standing behind a large snow barricade facing across the road to a similar structure behind which stood a motley collection of all the 'others' in the road. It was mid-winter, possibly during a long school recess or a weekend in January or maybe early February. Snow had paid a visit to our land in what must have been a very excessive volume at a time following bonfire night activities – us against the rest of the child inhabitants of our end of the street. Life, as usual, was not at a calm or peaceful level. The result – an explosive daylong snowball fight took place across the street. Them-vs-Us! As with most extraordinary events throughout the known history of human time on this planet, this day could not have been planned by man alone! From small beginnings, the event grew by spontaneous participation, somewhat like a forest fire started perhaps by bright sunlight on a tiny piece of glass lying in the undergrowth.

That there was deep snow is without question but just how or what was the ignition, the flash, that spark, the accelerant leading to this particular incident resulting in this frantic activity, I have no recollection whatsoever. But come it did! Initially I suspect that one or two of us maybe had been mucking about throwing snowballs at each other or anyone else in or across the street. Perhaps we had attempted to build a snowman at some earlier stage in the day. Maybe it was throwing the odd snowball at some brave or foolhardy souls from across the street that commenced the eventual returned barrage of similar missiles in the form of snowballs. We already had something of a barrier to hide behind. Not to be out done by us (again!), the Higgins boy opposite accompanied by the Miles boys and perhaps sometime later the two Manley brothers, enlisted the help of two of the three Hales brothers to build their own protective barricade! Within a very short space of time, in fact by early afternoon, there stood two massive snow barricades like castle walls on either side of the road that separated us – it rained snowballs! Over the top, round the side, 'cover me I will throw these from the other side at them', fluffy snow held in glowing pink warm hands hardened, compressed into cannon-ball shape, several carried by one individual for letting fly a sudden barrage of stinging projectiles. Whilst some gathered to create the little piles of 'ammo' strategically stacked behind the barricades and protected on all sides, others with stronger arms or recognised throwing accuracy, moved along to pick up the waiting piles then returning to their firing positions, letting fly at the enemy! Although this activity was decidedly antagonistic at its outset, as the day progressed, as attack then counter attack continued, it became something of a great game of gigantic proportions attracting interest from anyone who happened to pass by or visit our end of the road that day! In fact it became a shared occasion, an experience that members of both groups started to recognise was actually becoming something truly special.

An episode contributed to by us all that simply turned what could have just been another cold very snowy almost dark day, into a celebration of or by the youngsters of the street. Even those really horrid (soon to be looked upon with much greater interest as they grew up) girls next door stood shoulder to shoulder with us until one by one they tired, running to seek shelter in their home. Secretly we (us) knew that we were so outnumbered that it must only be a matter of time before we were washed away by the shear physical weight of now roughly round shattering globules of snow, crashing constantly around us from the opposing party. But under stress, after several hours of snow war, almost possibly ready to do the unthinkable – run like hell conceding defeat – the local press arrived to save our souls! Some clever people of our town had contacted the newspaper telling them of this great event! Armed to the teeth with camera equipment, they had sent some poor sod to investigate yet another Patterson road event! Not known however for being particularly prompt at any occasion, very regularly requiring a liquid hydraulic sandwich lunch to garner the courage to investigate this happening, the intrepid reporter arrived at about four pm or just as the brilliantly dreary light of the day was turning to brilliantly dreary gloom of a late midwinter afternoon. Also just when we knew that the game was up, the defenders of the keep on our side of the road, us, about to crawl away, beaten, exhausted! Flash! Flash! Again flash. How our energy suddenly returned. With renewed heartiness we once again girded our loins, gathered whatever energy we had in reserve, and managed to produce a massive display of flying snow for all to see!

What a pose, what a picture – what an impostor! Children at Play in the snow! Stand straight! Look like you are throwing it! Now all of you get together around one of the barricades for the grand finale!

So the band of brothers who were about to concede defeat, survived to throw snowballs another day! In our minds though we had won! Yes us, supported by the four girls from next door who spoke with a funny accent! Together we had held off a far superior army of snowball throwers comprised of the combined youngsters from many of the families opposite. This epic snow battle lasted from around early lunch time well into late afternoon. Oh yes, we had won. No doubt about that! The published picture in the rag of the following week shows quite clearly who the 'Snowball Wizards were'. Although in following years some planned, some almost semi-planned attempts were made to recreate that amazing day, I seem to think that the snowfall was never again enough to meet the challenge, to match the sheer breadth, height or stature of the barricades we had built. After a night of very tired but somehow painful sleep, that grey cold dawn of nine o'clock in the morning arrived as always the next day. The barricades were still there providing magnificent silent witness to the majesty of yesterday's snow war. A symbol to which those who had fought could pay reverence whilst those who had not taken part could only stare at with regret, awe, perhaps even jealousy! Both barricades remained for some time producing in the hearts of those who had participated, a warm energy, a proud glow of knowing, of shared understanding of the magic of that splendid day. However, those snowy ramparts of defence slowly diminished, faded, melting away with time as the season moved on. Memories also faded of that wonderful event receding in the hearts of the majority of the participants. Nevertheless, this particular event had forged a depth of knowledge not previously seen in public display, that within our end of the street even with an underlying antagonistic, regularly hostile world, collectively we could build a slender shared pride. We could, even had, when appropriate to any situation, enjoyed a community spirit, a common interest in collective fun.

I well remember the resultant frostbite, the tired aching worn out arms, the bright pink hands. But greater than all these memories are the chilblains! Little toes bright red, sore, swollen! However, there was nothing ever more swollen as the collective pride of that intrepid foursome, that 'Band of Brothers from Number 44'!

As stated, there are many such instances of the 'Band of Brother from Number 44' protecting stance, pulling together where it was needed. It would be impossible to capture here more than just a peek into those times so I will move on blindly trusting, Dear Reader, that such a small view will convey a much greater picture! Suffice it to say that sometimes in times of conflict, enemies do default to camaraderie over shared experience.

Having mentioned the interest of the printed media in the 'Snow War' there are other stories in which our family attracted the local media. It would therefore now be badly amiss of me if I did not set aside time to introduce you to the enchanting Percy.

Percy was not a friend or classmate from school or choir. Percy was not even human! Yet delightful friend he became. Yes, he could sing but he was just an uncommon member of a common creature of nature that, for just a while, almost, really almost...became human.

This 'wild-thing' entered the life of our family by guile, seeking sympathy, but was soon attracting the attention of the police and the printed media whilst causing complete strangers to duck aside or strike out in fright!

Percy the Crow!

A crow of extraordinary bravery, compassion, enchanting, full of abject fun! I will not suggest that we add our surname to this feathered creature, but I'm sure that if, as well as all the other non-birdlike things he did, he could also have talked, Percy would indeed have adopted our surname as his own.

However, I must say, as reflected in this story as you will see Dear Reader, the full story belongs to my brother Chris.

My memories of this very extraordinary special relationship that Chris was able to develop with this wild bird will I'm sure, differ from his own or indeed any memories held by my siblings or parents.

Any differences then will be entirely my fault as it is incumbent on me throughout this epistle to recount only my own memories, not those of others. Chris the one who retained a unique capacity to link with all things wild, the collector of injured animals of all sorts. Chris the animal boy, clearly led the way in providing support, love, warmth to all wild creatures great or small! Not surprising then that this wonderful event should have him at its centre.

Here then is my very own memory of things that today remain in my head. Memories of a period of about eighteen months, two summers in any event, where magic really did befall us all. I accept that passing years may have incurred memory erosion, enhancement or alteration, but imagined or real these are mine only!

This though is Chris' story; however, each of us in the family enjoyed some small part in the extraordinary bond that was to exist between these two very different species, a wild, crazy but enchanted Crow and a light-haired, blue eyed human boy-child.

'Percy finds Chris.'

Having presented so far I hope, some view in your mind Dear Reader, of how easy it was for us to access the wonderful countryside surrounding the southern parts of the old town of Aylesbury, it will not require a major leap of faith to accept that such access also provided us with the opportunity to meet an extensive variety of English wildlife. Included over the years of this portion of my life, we, the boys that is, were to act as rescuers, nursemaids, even surrogate mothers to all sorts of creatures. In fact, we as a family were a veritable supplier of bandages, splints, cotton wool shelters, and matchbox homes to large numbers of injured, lost or orphaned field mice, birds, rabbits, hedgehogs, fish, even on the odd occasion, a snake or two. Our services were often called upon to help with many domestic animals as well including stray or abandoned cats, lost dogs etc. However most common visitors were frogs, tadpoles by the dozen, pigeons, sometimes coloured rabbits, often escaped hamsters. Our home was a constant busy flow of both human together with lots of wildlife traffic! In fact, I believe that the goblins living in the woods across the other side of the fields on the way to the grounds around Hartwell, had conferred with the fairies living by the stream along the road, together with the local elf population who were resident at the bottom of our garden, well according to mother anyway. So thus it was that the entire wildlife population in the area was aware that THIS particular human family provided care to lost or injured members of the non-human community.

Although during our teenage period, that care or protection or comfort would occasionally extend to some stray humans as well!

Often, particularly in early summer, it was not difficult to hear one or two of us pleading with mother to assist with the mending of yet another broken wing, or asking how do you protect yet another rejected bird properly or even to provide tiny bits of rubber for us to cover with warm milk to feed seventeen abandoned baby field mice! Along with the joys experienced in the 'fixing' of this varied collection of local wildlife then, when recovered, returning them to their own environment, I remember many a time when we could only watch as the poor creature surrendered to its injuries, departing this life, hopefully moving on swiftly to its next. Sometimes we would carry an injured cat or dog or rabbit or tortoise to the other side of town close to the cinema where dad had worked for a few years after the war to wait for the local vet, to have an opportunity to look at yet another natural friend in need of care beyond our paltry abilities! Some we saved, many we were told that the best we could do was to keep them warm providing comfort until they died. Some of these unfortunate wild or domestic friends would be taken away by a nurse at the vets' with saddened eyes, who spoke softly to us indicating that there was no hope. We never questioned what became of the injured animal. Not having any means of transport or money for buses, we knew that having carried the poor creature first from its natural environment in the woods or fields nearby to home, then having to run, stumble, walk a couple of miles across town, death arrived long before we reached the vet. It was only childhood wistful optimism of the possibility that miracles could happen that kept us going on such occasions.

I look back on the number of really young birds that had been kicked out of their nests that we were as a family able to save. I feel very proud of the role we all played but often wonder if others are continuing this support.

Again the local media were to print warm rescue stories by our family on a regular basis. "Bird Raised in Matchbox" is one good-news story I recall along with many similar such published activities. Whilst I think it is perhaps fair minded to say that at any time we, each of us, had a hand to play in the life of many a wild friend, it must be recorded that for each unfortunate animal I, or Greg or Andrew were responsible for befriending to provide help – it was Chris who most often happened to be in the right place at just the life-saving right time. As a child, Chris had an automatic perhaps some may say magical, affinity with all of natures' creatures. I think today that he was really far more tolerant of nature than any of us had known or ever suspected during those years of childhood. Maybe it was Mother Nature offering a way for him to be calm, at peace, a non-threatening place with no display of authority for him to challenge. That the two of them, Mother Nature with our brother Chris, were in so many regards symbiotic, was plain for all to see. This powerful mutual acceptance by Chris of the natural order of our planet, this very wonderful ability was never to be nurtured or encouraged at home, it was a 'just so' meaning perhaps sadly to be simply accepted then to be ignored. Finally forgotten! "Get on with your homework boy!" For each injured wild friend that Greg, Andrew or I would bring home seeking help, Chris would find twice as many again. Therefore, the wounded, lost creatures of the Vale of Aylesbury from the Chilton Hills across farmland, in brooks, rivers, woods or fields ploughed or planted. In long or short grass, or lying in the gutter, if in need of help at all such a victim would, as if by divine destiny, attach themselves at a time of need when brother Christopher, the truly angry one of our human dynasty, was available to offer succour.

Then came Percy, who was to prove to be absolutely no exception to this natural unwritten Christopher life rule, securing for ever in my mind the knowing that our brother Chris was a true child of nature.

As you may know Dear Reader, a crow is a scavenger! It will steal anything from anywhere at any time. It would of course be most offended when accused of such behaviour because, please, look into these deep dark eyes when its head is turned in a sideways manner holding a twinkling glance of the question; "would I steal?" Butter would not melt in the mouth of this cunning bird. Oh no! They are grey-black, big and smelly, they duck, dive, weave in flight committing, amongst many, many other things, the ultimate sin – stealing the nests or possessions of other birds. So they are regarded even by their own kind as 'lazy-good-for-nothing' troublesome misfits! (A regular title bestowed on dear brother Chris by our father – strange that?)

Firstly, I must confess that I have no idea how this particular story of a wild bird in our family actually started. I know it was summer. I know that I helped Chris on his arrival at our house with this bird. Chris though, everyone will agree, was the major player when one day he simply walked into the backyard of our home with what appeared to be a dazed crow (introduced as Percy later) nestled under his jumper. Chris had been keeping the bird steady using his left arm across his tummy to ensure that the bird would not fall out, almost as if the bird was sitting on his arm. The effort of carrying this bird with use of his jumper covered left arm as protection for some time from where he had found it, was etched on Chris' face. He seemed quite shocked, exhausted, even perhaps not just a little scared. Memory also eludes me as to why this young feathered thing had become so entwined initially with this young human boy.

I seem to think however it was suggested that the bird (Percy) must have flown into an overhead power cable somewhere across the fields, then stunned, fell to the ground. Chris just happened to pass by at the correct time (for perhaps the three hundredth or more time in his young life, being instantly available for yet another animal rescue!). He would have gently picked up the dazed creature thinking it to be dead perhaps, realised that it was injured or in shock so somehow attempted to revive it. Assessing the extent of any wounds and seeking the possibility of survival, our brother would then have reached a conclusion on the best course of action. Accepting that this bird, by simply allowing Chris to tend to its immediate comforts was an indication of its potential disorientation or trauma – it needed help! Maybe for just a while Chris sat with it where it had fallen, attempting to sooth the poor wretched feathered thing. Keeping the injured bird warm for some time, even covering it with or tucking it into or under his jumper or coat as further encouragement to survive. Once responding to this attention by showing with some movement perhaps, the bird would have been set down to see if it could recover from its accident so be able to travel independently. As each of us in his turn grew up, we were all taught to be aware of how dangerous it can be for very young birds as well as even some young animals to carry a human smell back to burrow or nest. I know therefore that Chris would have been very careful in how he handled the crow even knowing that this particular specimen was obviously an independent creature having flown the nest some time previously. As children we also at this time understood that Crows were acknowledged to not be the most pleasant of creatures in nature! They are even today indeed the most annoyingly cunning pests of the winged variety! Perhaps Chris lost his heart by being taken in by this injured party. So bring him home he did. Across field, brook, fences, across roads, via ally-ways, through parks then eventually down the length of our road until finally, entering through the back gate then heading towards the back door.

The resultant impact on our family of such a decision by Chris remains at the heart of a wonderful childhood incident that we were all to become a very privileged part of.

Apparently damaged, most definitely dazed, then being offered warmth together with gentle encouragement to fly – I can imagine the birds' thoughts – "now what have I FOUND HERE?" Could this strange gentle (angry) human potentially be an answer to a crows' prayer. By his true love of nature I suspect very much that Chris had unwittingly been caught; succumbed by concern for the apparently injured, at this stage even pretend injury. By his act of kindness to this flighty (ha!) bird together with his obvious compassion, the foundation was already set, the dye cast. So it was that an amazing journey of such an unlikely companionship between a wild, crafty, smelly Crow with a very special human boy unfolded.

This strange journey was to become a family legend. No urban myth, no creation of fiction but a real legend! A journey viewed, told a thousand times across the decades with memories imagined or true, a chapter in our collective lives so unique, so real, yes so very enchanted.

The first clearly remembered issue was that Chris was not too happy with having this large, although still young, bird tucked under his jumper almost perched on his arm that was held stiffly at an unusual angle across his abdomen. The arm itself was also not sure in its own right how much longer it could retain this fixed position. It had been quite a long and cumbersome journey to get home for Chris with his new companion. Having walked some two miles or so across country, through fields, along paths, clambering over styles, then crossing roads with some traffic, all the way from where they, Chris, the Crow, Chris' arm had met then merged, albeit of a transient nature. Although Chris was quite a strong, solid child (able to throw a good punch as you know), he would have been about eleven or twelve years old at the time, perhaps an early teenager when experiencing this strange creature mix. However strong he was generally though, the shakes of muscle strain were clearly evident by the time of his reaching home, having to support his left arm with his right hand to ensure that the whole unnatural unison remained fairly stable, Chris knew that something had to change quickly! Adding at the time no doubt to his concern, was the fact that we as a family had at least one cat as a permanent resident at home, often more cats visiting or recuperating at any time, therefore in all probability on that day perhaps, there could have been several cats watching with interest the bizarre mix of human child antics with a new-found feathered friend! Aware of the rarity therefore of such a situation being shared by wild bird with not so wild, just anxious junior man, it was essential to ensure that the human portion of this strange fusion received immediate support. At the same time it was vital that the obviously concussed, confused bird did not panic, creating the possibility that it could potentially injure itself further by attempting to fly. Such behaviour could have, perhaps, caused the bird to fall, ending its existence by suddenly becoming an unexpected meal of one or more of the then resident balls of fur or any other visiting masticating creature that just happened to be lurking in the shadows. As in similar previous rescues of those larger natural friends, the inside of our house was always 'out-of-bounds' so boy, with bird, with painful stiff arm, staggered into our garden shed where Chris was at least able to sit down, an action which offered instant relief! Now was the time to explore his next move.

'Garden shed' is perhaps a description that requires some definition.

This shed for example, was not actually in our garden! Its title therefore was already misleading in terms of its function. Do you remember the 'unpopular' lavvy located outside the 'real' door to our home – the back door? Well passing through the back door on your way outside, you would find that you were in a covered porch leading to a garden path. To your left, within the porch, is the 'lavvy', to your right, a floor to roof wooden wall. This wall was the end wall of our 'Garden Shed'. Incidentally, the ceiling or roof of the back porch, like the entire roof across the 'lavvy' indeed the shed as well, was made from corrugated asbestos! Still in the porch, at the base of this wall on the right hand side, was a sliding hatch used to collect the coal for the house fire (located in that special place – the front room) during winter time. This end portion of the 'shed' then internally held that very important status as the house coal bunker. That place where dirty-faced, often foul mouthed, grumpy adult men would, by entering the 'shed', dump sack after sack of rough coal that had been gouged from the earth, transported by rail to the local depot before reaching our tiny shed corner for storage. When stepping off that porch by the back door then turning right towards the entrance gate to the yard – some twenty paces away – this 'shed' accompanied you on your right side all along that end section of the house to the gate itself. If however, on leaving the porch, you turned left instead, you would find yourself entering the garden area of our home. So, 'garden shed' was something of a misnomer – it was not in, nor adjacent to nor even attributed to the existence of – our garden! Rather it was located almost as a partially forgotten adjunct to its purpose, along one entire end of our house that, having entered by the garden gate, all visitors human or otherwise, must pass to reach the porch containing the lavvy, the coal hatch and also the all-important back door.

Halfway along this walk to the back door so well before reaching the porch, was the 'shed' door through which Chris eased himself with his new feathered companion. The inside of the 'shed' was actually quite large. It did, with the exception of the back porch with its lavvy, run the entire end, depth, of the house. Whilst inside one end, space was taken up with the coal bunker but was perhaps only about a quarter of the available area enclosed under its own (since declared illegal) roof. This then was our garden 'shed'. A space acting as a general storage area for things like half-full paint tins, old garden implements including a steel wheelbarrow with bent spindle so the wheel never actually went the way you wanted it to when pushing it! There was a long handled hoe, a selection of garden rakes some with long handles others short, mainly because they were broken. There were also some cranky old shelves fixed to the far end wall on which rested dusty boxes of nails and pins alongside a selection of old jam jars with half-eaten, as if nibbled by insects, flaking paint brushes now stuck for eternity in mucky-brown mysterious stuff. A solid congealed gumph. All this was covered in cobwebs but had once been covered in workable damp, although now dry, stiff cloths. These shelves must have seen much better days as I can only ever remember how they were constantly resting at nothing less than a forty-five degree angle most of the time. This incline, this tilt, reduced the capacity of the shelves thus much was stacked on the dirty floor below, sharing dark spaces there with pram wheels, pram wheel axels, hammers, screws, a small broken cupboard, an old chair, including parts of a broken three-legged stool! Generally, the sort of home 'stuff' not often needed or simply that which would not be welcome in the house or had been rejected forever. The forgotten cast-off's, the flotsam of our collective everyday family existence.

High up on the wall, on the same side as the door, was a very small, dirty window so covered in spiders weavings that very little light ever penetrated the continuous gloom inside. Our 'garden' shed then, in reality, was no more than a large glory hole, our private graveyard for any discarded or broken furniture, toys, bits of wood, old cardboard books, and broken tomato box bits. A place where rats, mice (often guests – sometimes not) could be found attempting to avoid the awareness of others, a place for the now neglected, where broken was ordinary, was accepted. This was our garden shed!

Once Chris with his newly found friend were inside this household depository, it was soon of urgent need to find something that would act as an inviting attraction to the bird for it to disengage itself from its human perch. All of us at some stage had had to remove injured birds, to find locations of comfort for them over the years. To the best of my knowledge at the time, we had not previously had to find a suitable comfort receptacle for quite such a large a bird as this. In the past with small wild friends, it only took a moment of time to locate a small box/bowl of sufficient size to provide suitable accommodation. It must have taken a while before locating plenty of old torn newspaper, cushion stuffing, dry bits of grass, some fluff, which was comprised of bits from mothers' darning wool including someone's old socks that simply could not be darned again. All this effort was needed in order to build a comfortable place for our latest visitor, an injured black Crow needing somewhere to rest. Having provided what was thought to be a nice friendly, welcoming soft place for the bird, it was then time to separate the bird from the boy! Eventually, after what seemed ages, Chris coaxed a very dazed (quite possibly an Oscar winning performance!) bird into its temporary shelter.

From then on Chris was able to start his own recovery process by initially attempting to regain proper use of his left arm! With the human comfort underway, it was now time to take up the urgent matter of properly inspecting what damage, if any, had actually been inflicted on our new house guest. Here I believe he was christened with the name 'Percy'! In reality it transpired all this was to be for as crafty a bird as possible that had found himself starting his own recovery resplendent in this contrived five-star luxury environment!

WORMS! Yes, worms, you know, those little underground slip sliding, often silky-wet delicacies, alive, full of juices! The staple diet of our new guest, also ants or any other small bug with, oh yes, water mixed with a little milk. Percy, the cunning little horror, was in his own version of feathered heaven! So as the family became involved in this rescue story, out we would go digging for live food in the hope that we can complete the rescue sufficiently quickly to restore this wild bird to a level of recovery from its injuries – which were never actually seen at all. Nothing physical anyway! Only when fully recovered, would it be safe to return him to his own environment. There was no obvious broken wing or leg so our original expectation was that with food, warmth together with a goodly portion of 'T.L.C.', the recuperation process would last a day, perhaps two or three at the very most before we were able to return the subject of our tender administrations back into the wild. Sometimes, subject to the animal, insect etc., this return to the wild would happen simply within a few hours or most commonly after just one night of our special brand of care. Not the case with this Crow though, oh no! When we were set to release the bird the next day, it discovered that it was much more interesting to fly in a little circle, flap pathetically, wobble a lot then literally drop onto the shoulder of its erstwhile human perch – Chris.

From that day on, until Percy flew away with his chosen natural partner nearly two summers later – these representatives of two so different species, a human boy and a wild bird, were as one.

Although during his time with us Percy did disappear for days at a time, he would always re-appear to stay around for month after month. Percy did not live in our shed for too long. Oh no! He managed to find somewhere local to perch so as to always be outside the window of Chris' bedroom each morning. It was such a regular sight, Chris walking to school, big bird on his shoulder or flying nearby. Chris, in school playground, Percy could be seen keeping a watchful eye from a nearby tree or building roof (the proximity of too many humans was hard for our feathered friend to bear). If you saw Chris in the open without Percy during this time all you had to ask Chris to do was to call out loud "Percy" then from somewhere nearby, a dark flying object would appear. To suggest that Percy was brave, as I have done earlier, can only have meaning to you my Dear Reader by me attempting to depict the 'dancing game' he would play with any one or more of our cats, or as many as may be around when he was. Imagine if you can the sight of Percy 'hovering' some four to six feet off the ground above the head or heads of reaching angry paws of our ground fixed cat or cats! 'Hover' is not really the correct expression. Percy was not a bee or humming bird but a simple Crow. Hence the range of four to six feet, he seemed to be almost swimming through the atmosphere, sort of applying the breaststroke with his wings whilst maintaining a perpendicular poise looking down with contempt at the furiously frustrated action below. This was a popular game for him on summer days watched by any of us around at the time. As the months passed, his trust in Chris, including those of us he 'recognised' as a part of Chris, was absolute.

If, as we often did on lazy warm summer evenings when perhaps we were 'with' Percy in our garden for example, he would show no hesitation in landing on the grass near us to peck bits of food from our open hands. Even taking proffered bits out of our mouths! Alongside 'food' games he would often lie on his back with his two stick legs in the air whilst we tickled his feathery underbelly with our fingers! It was so funny to watch because when we did this, his eye covering would oscillate whilst his tiny black beak would swing from side to side.

Naturally the adoption of such a human by a bird as its 'pet' created, yet again, media interest with once more a member of the family pictured for the local press. Undoubtedly a further search in the records of the local rag may reveal references to this unusual but very happy relationship between A Crow, a Boy sharing time with each other as if an everyday thing in the lives and times of either. There are lots of single episodes to recount. For example, when Percy would for no known reason think that it had found Chris walking along the road and swoop down at a speed equal to its excitement, landing feet outstretched to perch itself on the shoulder of a total stranger! The stranger, often female for some unexplained reason, not appreciating the very special relationship this bird had with a fellow human, received such a fright that the erratic waving of arms with the shouting of expletives some socially acceptable whilst others not, was quite a commotion to encounter. Percy also enjoyed football! Not play-play, the real thing, not running on the ground with so many humans to score a goal playing! No. I mentioned earlier that he was shy when there were too many humans around but as a small group of children playing in the street with a football, Percy could always be used as an offensive weapon!

Not everyone liked the idea of having this big, heavy feathered bird becoming so excited, swooping down at you squawking, flapping, smelling, as you are running to intercept a fast pass of the ball from a team mate across the road. But if Chris was playing, so too was Percy!

A Boy Chris, a Crow Percy, a daily living partnership so natural that even when Chris was seen walking into town, Percy could be seen on the roof of the nearest building or, on shouted request, diving to land on an outstretched arm. Local's sometimes asking for a photograph to be taken of them standing next to

Chris with his non-shy, cunning, feathered friend perched on his arm, shoulder or head! Some brave souls even having Percy perched on their own shoulder or arm.

The following 'Percy' memory remains in my head although it may be more imagined than completely real so I request a small measure of indulgence for some poetic licence. I am sure that the following conjures the essence of the relationship, the pure magic of this amazing natural friend.

This particular personal Percy memory lives within my heart forever, happening on a day late during the second summer of his astonishing infatuation with Chris. This was just before Percy left us for good. The essence of the description below, Dear Reader, is absolutely true. I returned home as the final part of the battle below was raging. I stood at the pathway entrance to our back garden watching it in complete, stunned awe!

Three men arrived at our gate that morning on a mission to paint the outside of our 'steel' house. This service was supplied on a regular basis by the local council as part of the then on-going general maintenance of council property.

Now painting of the house would not normally be an issue at all but unfortunately no one had warned these poor unfortunate painter people that they were about to enter a world that was somewhat different from the average! A world where small humans co-habited with a variety of wild friends, with this summer being further removed from normality due to an especially deranged bird who, at the time, shared space with the human occupants. Perhaps they simply had not read about a crazy bird located in this house in any of the locally published rag stories. To compound their lack of simple expectation of the days' activities, no one had warned them about Percy! Oh well. Not a major headache surely?

It cannot be stressed enough here that creatures of the wild such as Percy, find security, even comfort in knowing their surroundings, especially after building confidence in having constant familiar sights, sounds, smells, around its' environment. In this birds' case…including around specific people! Well actually one person. All these stable, environmental elements had proven conducive to providing calm, succour, ensuring peace reigns with tranquillity. Acceptance of all things to a timid, although cunning, being of nature. To Percy this was a world of protection, warmth, with magical fun. No one had told these painters that to enjoy peace at their task ahead, absolutely NOTHING must change. The very core of such bird tranquillity, with assurance of its continued wellbeing, is that the status quo must remain! Should just any single one of those established secure constants in a poor wild birds' life be subjected to unexpected change – passive, accepting nature will, without need for explanation some may say, become viciously violent to downright hostile.

However, in the event that not just one but all of those known, recognised comfortable elements change in short rapid succession, the outcome will be screeching pandemonium! Such an outcome was set for that day as the council painters arrived. Inevitable chaos would be arriving unannounced!

How on earth, I hear you ask, can such a simple thing as painting a house cause any change let alone a change so shattering, as to send an already crazy bird into wretched squealing insanity?

Well to begin with, not one of the family members were at home when these painting contractors actually arrived at our house. The painters simply knew that this was the address. After all the job card had been signed, the equipment loaded as normal, along with all the paints. This was already on the truck when they had reached the depot first thing. As this was an outside job anyway, there was no need to contact the tenants to let them know that they were on the way. Also being summer, a quick survey on arrival had shown that most windows were on the latch thus not creating a challenge when painting such fixtures. Along with the painters came a whole collection of ladders, scaffolding boards, cans, paint brushes, presenting together a very large collection of new, exotic smells – sheets of canvas with linking pegs, buckles, buckets all taken off the truck to be piled at multiple angles on our back lawn. A wheelbarrow, a collection of scraping, scratching bladed implements, together with a hand held gas blowtorch. Thus an ever-growing foreign menagerie appeared on the lawn. We cannot tell if Percy was at 'home' either at the time of the arrival of this small work force, simply because we were not.

General assumptions have been made however that the painters only started to crow (excuse my word, fun here!) once they had covered the entire rear of our house with scaffolding, having also set the ladders at the necessary angles. They had settled to commence the initial preparation work at the top of the house attempting to burn, then scrape off the existing blotchy blue colour to start applying an undercoat. It takes quite a while to secure two storeys of scaffolding, lay the walking boards then collect the required working implements ready to start the task.

Presuming all the preparation took place prior to lunchtime, I assume that the actual work only started on this, day one, of the two day plan by middle to late afternoon. At that time of the day some, if not all, the household inhabitants had returned to the um' nest (smile please!) including our wonderful feathered friend.

Without the advantage of foreknowledge of the 'special-ness' of the resident family, our happy painters reacted as most offended humans will do when suddenly, viciously ATTACKED or DIVE BOMBED by a screeching, flapping, black monster arriving out of the sun at four-o-clock in the afternoon! Alfred Hitchcock had yet to make the frightening movie "The Birds" but I am convinced that had he been able to spend time studying the faces of these three innocent house painters that fateful afternoon, he would without doubt have employed our Percy in the leading 'Bird' role.

It's simple really.

The bedroom occupied by Chris was located upstairs at the back of the house. There were two windows upstairs here overlooking the garden.

A single frosted glass window of that posh bathroom, you remember, the one for adults excluding all male offspring but including any female children of the house. Yes, that's the one. Always warm from which boys were banned! The second window was a double one for the large bedroom that, at the time, was occupied by Chris, who was sharing with Andrew. This window had an outside ledge that Percy had claimed as his private perch – because inside this room was where his adopted mother, our brother Chris, was most often to be found when known by Percy to be at home. In addition, this window was especially recognised as 'belonging' to Percy each morning at the time of the dawn chorus. It was this ledge from where a very rare contribution to the morning daily song of nature was provided by Percy to the sleepy world at large.

Suddenly, from a birds-eye-point-of-view, this location representing the foundation of security being where Chris resided, was disrupted beyond imagination! Poor Percy's comfort, mother even, was under attack!

Everything had changed! It was now time to protect – MOTHER! The consequential commotion was cataclysmic!

The crazed attack on the community of once jolly painters was not very short. Indeed, flapping wings mixed with waving paintbrushes, bits of working cloths spraying in every which way, buckets of slosh ejaculating their contents over painters, scaffolding boards, incidental equipment as each human suddenly was attempting to protect his own flesh whilst trying to climb down to the possible safety of mother earth, almost two floors below!

Paint tins, some with lids attached, fell then rolled from what once was their relatively stable platform, to burst on impact with the lawn, adding a hotchpotch of colour to the spectacle. As was common in those days, two of the painters were smokers thus adding a final dark potential to all this turmoil. Cigarettes that a short while ago sat between human lips glowing gently, spilt from their tenuous holders to flick then bounce dangerously amongst this unprotected gathering of very inflammable material.

For his part, Percy was blinded by his fear of possible loss of Chris. He just kept coming, attack followed by attack.

He was relentless in his determination to return all things to 'normal', well his very own version of 'normal' that is. He was hit several times by hands or soggy paintbrushes during this fracas but still he would not give up! Once the men had reached the relative safety of the ground, they started to survey the rearranged garden landscape. Only then did things begin to get a little quieter. Chris was able to recover the now exhausted very tired but strangely colourful Percy. Resting on Chris' arm, slowly a calm settled on Percy. My mother was able to provide that cure-all, a warm cup of tea, supporting the recovery to calm where fortunately the only injury was to the pride of the painters. A job that was to last just over two days for these workmen eventually took over three! No matter how much we tried to clean all the paint from Percy, he retained a broad splash of matt white undercoat paint across his folded wings for the rest of his days. This story also made the local news hounds so laughter was heard for some time to come, especially from painting contractors, throughout the remainder of that summer. A painting story to really crow about!

Again time slipped.

We continued to grow, moving on, Percy moved on. We were all very sad when it became obvious that our wonderful feathered friend had returned to his natural environment. It was a slow realisation that those regular few days of absence at a time, that had become longer, were due to the awesome power of nature. After a magic bond lasting some eighteen months or so, our brother Chris had to accept, along with the rest of the family that for him, together with his special feathered friend Percy, the time had come for each to explore their own unique futures in their so very different worlds. Such was the natural demise of a magnificent friendship, a friendship that we had all come to hold dear in our own way.

I for one remain so very thankful to have been able to be a small part in a shared portion of two very different life journeys, wild Magic Bird, with little human boy who just happened to be my brother. For some time when a crow was spotted in the distance or overhead or on a fence or perched on a chimney high above, each of us would secretly search, point, look, seeking, silently praying, even wishing in fact, longing to know the answer to a single question – was that a patch of white paint on that crow over there?

The Bonfire Wars!

Weeks in isolation in hospital!

Eric the Deaf & Dumb bricklayer.

Guitar playing then Acting Lessons!

Girls!

Leaving Home.

Also still to come, the joy of singing driving this young child along a path so removed to that of any of my other siblings – a direction of no interest at all to my parents. Thus life was constantly moving me all the time further away from my family. To me though, it was sounds, colour, allied to the absolute need for seeing around the next corner! To know the answers to millions of things seen or read.

A natural independence of thought either due to my own essence or some unseen external guide.

The Bonfire Wars!

These were not 'wars' in which tribe fought tribe, nation against nation, mainly because one such conflict had recently been conducted across the world. The former glorious triumphant allies, having played the victor then sharing the spoils, were now divided in mistrust. Open hatred had created a warped bonding of power blocks dividing the world into pacts of East-vs-West-vs-East, then the all rest. The previous pretence of warm, complimentary friendship now much cooler, replaced with seething distrust accompanied by global political posturing stances. Whole nations now were split apart. What once were streets or roads in a country shared by people of the same national heritage now were divided by walls, separating former family from family, neighbour from neighbours.

Ideology now held sway so that between former allies a cold war now darkened any hopes of enlightened friendship, peace, and co-operation for the common good of all. This was the 1950s.

No, these bonfire wars contained no tanks, no foot soldiers trained, standing ready for the slaughter, no gas to choke on, required no 'H' bomb to bring to an abrupt end. But each year as the last of summer faded through autumn into winter, the usual antagonists formed their own alliances, gathered their forces planning triumphant coups, forcing others to salute their particular dogma.

This though was an annual 'war' never really publicly acknowledged as actually being such, but there it was nonetheless. I have actually no idea when, why or even how this perverse one-upmanship, this gigantic urge to usurp others to gain an invisible prize of fantasy, for this is what it really was, had started.

Who could claim to have had the best, the biggest, the brightest, the most colourful bonfire firework evening? In fact, such an approach to a generally popular annual activity must have been well entrenched in the lives of the participants in our street long before my arrival as a member of what turned out to be the continuously winning side! As true as good old England, with a touch of help from the colonies, having crushed the Nazi war machine, so too on that annual occasion of celebrating the explosive festival of Guy Fawkes, the gunpowder plot, our family flattened all challengers resident at our end of the street by building the biggest bonfire and supplying the most spectacular fireworks display.

By the time I was that climbing, waddling toddler helping in the kitchen, putting away slightly damp crockery the stage had already been set, the dye cast, the war of the fires, the flashes, those instant colours cascading from the heavens was already a grotesque annual contest that was to last for many years yet but was even then truly established. Perhaps, if we had been living less close to the open fields of the Buckinghamshire countryside, even perhaps if our sister had indeed arrived ahead of the rest of us, yours truly may not have been here in any event, but if Penny had been earlier to arrive then things may have been substantially different. But living as we were, adjacent to Mother Nature, having not just one healthy growing sturdy boy, but four healthy sturdy lads who could collect material for burning, no doubt contributed to our far-reaching solid participation in this horrific activity. An event that, when looking back today as an adult, I find it hard to comprehend, such stupid activity, although still to this day, all across England around November 5th the celebrations continue! No excuses though, everyone was doing it, there was no law against it, in fact as a national historical event November 5th was, we were told, a day to remember.

Pride! Simply pride. This is all I can offer Dear Reader as being the fundamental basis for the following annual event in which our family partook. Not though that wonderful swollen pride of exhausted achievement of the erstwhile Snowball Wizards. Oh no! That pride was one that was encircled with bittersweet warmth of pleasurable elated recognition, of shared passionate determination.

No, the Bonfire Wars 'pride' was encircled with a different passion. An obsession, a fierce determination never to be second best to anyone in this war! Our family had to win! Not just once, not just by chance, not just by any margin, but by miles!

Every year! Such a laid down dictate required that 'Band of Brothers from Number 44' always to know their role leading up to this event. As summer waned, as the nights started drawing in, as the first fall leaves were for the collecting, it started. August, still on school holidays there we were noting the location of fallen boughs that will be for the gathering soon, keeping their location secret. Early September, the collecting of twigs, leaves, the stacking of old newspaper in the garden shed began. October, we could all be seen dragging logs towards home, finally culminating on the final day with yet another, even better than the last bonfire-night breathtaking extravaganza. On reflection perhaps, the requirements of this event had been created in our family to provide for a possible male bonding opportunity for the boys; perhaps such a need had secretly been encouraged by the creator of this particular band of brothers – their father. Maybe as a result of his own inability to accept that he had four sons to account for when he only ever wanted a daughter. His own daughter who, by his assurance, would never see the inside of a convent! Catholic or otherwise! A way of providing atonement, an apology perhaps for his being forced to abandon his only sister after several attempts to 'rescue' her?

Here he was with the responsibility now for a rowdy growing male brew so control was to be imposed with that masterful of all management tools, divide and conquer! He may then have used this annual tragedy to allow for the boys to work together through a bonding of male siblings, hidden in the activities of preparation for an annual public, national, family ritual! I am far more inclined however today to regard this whole concert, this manic annual performance as just our fathers' unspoken way of telling the world around him, 'fuck you' for all the hard times it had given him. I can only speculate today why such a thing transpired then but I cannot deny his obtuse role in this annual activity.

Before continuing I must say that even though at times we children were subjected to what would be regarded today as potentially great danger of injury as a result of these annual home events, we all survived those antics with no permanent physical damage. I cannot say the same however for any psychological damage that may have been sustained, if any, by any one of us.

Yes, bonfire night in our house was the culmination of much hard work by the boys. Often having carried or dragged wood for miles across open countryside. In addition, we had also gathered sacks full of dry leaves stacked at the back of the 'garden' shed. There was also a huge amount of paper, much of it collected from behind shops where much was discarded by shop keepers. The night approached with mixed emotions of trepidation, but also anxious, excited anticipation. This was the one night when irrespective of whether it was ordained to be, it always was a splendid occasion filled with wondrous, glorious sights and sounds with magnificent smoke smells. A night when our back garden became, after dark, after dinner, a noisy conflagration full of sporadic massive conflict side by side with shadowed awe! Painful aching ears were shocked by the powerful silences between each explosive chapter!

Perhaps it was so fierce that in some way it helped to appease the demons of his past that my father made this particular celebration, the second biggest family night of the year. An occasion high in importance in our young lives second only to that of Christmas. One that demanded our attendance in that each of us must play his part. My early memory of these annual events, perhaps the first being the November just after my fourth birthday, is one of being under the kitchen table screaming for it to stop! Hot tears running in unison with snot down my face in combined terror! Hiding in the kitchen where the house lights had been turned off – for the greater external effect of course – I crouched terrified under the kitchen table, with one table leg to hold on to, leaning against the cold metal cupboard door which was at my back. I was way beyond frightened, way beyond scared, holding on to, as best I could, our cat – a white Manx called Brumas, named after the famous polar bear. Our cat was but one of the animals who happened to be sharing our space at the time. Each of us seeking desperately some quiet alternative place of peace but failing to do so. Distraught, clutching a wide-eyed shaking cat, I tried covering my ears as if thinking at such a young age that somehow I could stop the incessant din. My ears were being subjected to the constant bang, thump, whoosh, whiz bang again, flash, whiz, another bang as firework after firework spun, jumped, screamed into the night sky exploding one after the other. On it went seemingly never to stop. In the painful silent gaps of this bombardment, I sometimes could hear the family in the garden as if in a great distant place where calm in the storm of noise existed. They seemed to be conversing in very loud voices as if they too were finding it hard to hear, having to shout to hide their own excited fear perhaps. There I remained in the kitchen cowering because the whole world outside was being blown apart. I was left to fend for myself! Yes, this little wet wimp was just over four years old at the time.

However, as this little wimp grew older, the need to display considerable bravado on such 'special' nights was of paramount importance if he was seeking to achieve a more respected clan status. Thus as each year slipped by, when each such loud occasion took place, I in my turn became just as involved in this gross stupidity as others in my family had before me. To say that we celebrated some old insane idiots attempt to blow up the Houses of Parliament in London, would not really be a correct reflection of these occasions.

It was as if on that one day each year we wanted, no needed to, burn everything in sight, including our souls possibly, to make such an explosive contribution in colourful noise as to confront the natural order of the universe! November 5th in England, the early winter was well advanced, nights' dark seeping cold generally so that the conflict between the natural evening temperature with that heat of the erected raging inferno located in our garden, presented a challenge to human comfort, requiring stepping in then out of the inner to outer circles of conflict in an attempt to keep from being consumed by fire or freezing. Several hours of such behaviour often provided one or more of us within a few days with the first of many runny noses, coughs and colds, which if managed well, may result in an opportunity to miss school for a day or three.

Why should this recognised family activity be the cause of such consternation? Why have I referred to the exercise as a 'war'? Well, like the Christmas tree each year in our house, our bonfire had to be the biggest. I do not just mean when measured against next door or any other family garden up, down or across the road – I mean the biggest in the entire street. On the entire estate! Big in height! Huge in base circumference! What was the purpose for a fire of this magnitude? So that it would still be blazing long after all the others had tickled their last flying spark to safety.

If at all possible, long after sunrise the next day – our fire must still be burning! Visitors, friends or enemies alike must speak of the marvel of our fire for days if not weeks to come after the event! Year after year, out across the fields, we boys would seek to collect, bundle, hide, pull, push or slide, whole branches of trees struck by summer storms, some often thrice the weight of the individual boy, whose task was to encourage these former signposts of nature to cross stream, hedge, field, road or pathway. Sacks full of autumn leaves stacked floor to roof in our garden shed to act as ignition.

Where possible cardboard of any type or thickness kept safe, to assist when required as an accelerant. With newspapers by the tonne! All this was gathered to be stored in the garden shed in preparation for the big night. Often the amount of wood stacked in a corner of the garden had to be protected by waterproof covering in the event that rain may dampen it! From the month of August through to the magical day, the pile of wasted wood grew so it had to be protected not only from the elements but from 'others' who during the real depths of the dark nights leading up to the actual day, had been known to creep into the garden on silent tiptoe mission to purloin the gathering mountain then claiming it as their own. They too had an objective! Each year 'others' were determined that THIS YEAR, their own November 5th would be the biggest, the brightest!

Yes, there were other families in our street but at our end there was only one family with four boys...us! There were some with two, some even with three but not one who could match the output of our parents in the creation of macho boys to collect the much needed fire material. Sometime then these 'others' comprised a collection of various different male members from several families working together to pilfer our hard gotten kindling to claim as their own.

Some years one or two boys from different families would join forces to capture our collected but not yet brought home wood piles, secreted under hedges by us for collection at a future date! The result could be that once we knew the identity of the pilferer, all manner of horrid things would befall them. This could range from simply having all the stolen stuff regained by one or more of us, together with anything they had collected themselves.

Placing 'penny-bangers' against the letter box of their special 'front' doors, or even providing the ingredients for them to find that overnight, their letter box had supplied the entrance portal into their warm house for a family of frogs which had been dug up from the deep slimy mud of the local stream where they had settled to see out the winter. You see in this 'war' much was done to ensure that once again this year, ours was the biggest, the best.

Now to describe, as best as I am able to, whilst acknowledging that we children were always excluded from all that our father was, thought or did whilst we were growing up, with one major exception with me that is recorded elsewhere in this story, the role undertaken by our father in all of these annual events. Throughout our childhood it was always evident that money was especially conspicuous by its constant absence in our home. Pocket money was something that other children got given – not us. All my clothes were the re-shaped hand-me-downs from the older boys. My very first pair of trousers – bought from the local Woolworths just for me – was given to me when I was 12 years old. I think I was a teenager by the time I had my first pair of original socks! Our holidays during the summer comprised initially, until I was late child almost into my teens, of a day trip starting excitedly early in the morning, driving to Brighton beach then to return very late at night. These initially were courtesy of 'uncle' – my godfather – Lorry (Laurie) who lived next door! Then in our own car, the Velox!

Once we drove all the way to Herne Bay where we slept in a caravan for several nights before returning, all courtesy of our 'uncle' Laurie! But somehow, every year without fail, our Dad who was never out of work, would always have access to unlimited funds for the purchase of the biggest, the best available, the mightiest, the most colourful, the loudest fireworks ever for that years' bonfire night! Never was there any question that money was an issue when this infamous date was near.

Giant Catherine Wheels, Rockets that looked as if they were destined for the outer universe, sprays, Bangers big or small, Sparklers to hold, Roman Candles to stand in awe of. Another small fortune! All this was on top of what meagre purchases we boys had been able to make with monies earned via odd jobs done for weeks leading up to the explosive night! So in addition to the biggest, the best actual raging fire, our display of colourful sounds on those cold November nights became well known beyond just our local competitors in Patterson Road including several roads around our location, as being simply gargantuan. Sometimes this display attracted the attention of the local print media with occasionally a picture of this wonderful family happening appearing in the local rag. Much to the mortification of some, I have no doubt, but not all of our neighbours.

Then came the year of hollow steel tubes, wrapped penny bangers to be converted to flying exploding rockets! I was perhaps just thirteen when I think the number of fireworks in our possession was at its greatest. Greg was working, Chris had a job at weekends I think. Andrew also had a part-time job. As for me, well I was by then a Registered Chorister, having completed over five years of training with studying for oral as well as written exams, the result being that I had finally been inducted as a member of the Royal College of Church Music, just a month before my twelfth birthday.

This illustrious status afforded me the privilege of being paid to sing at happy functions outside normal services at the church such as weddings, Christenings, celebrations, although there were the sad occasions like funerals as well at which a young Choristers' single voice was used! I, by the time of this particular bonfire night, was being paid the magnificent amount of two shillings plus six pence (12,5p) for each wedding or event I sang at. The buying 'power' of such an amount was far greater than the current buying power of 12.5pence!

As there were twelve pennies in a shilling, each such payment of two shillings plus the six sixpence, provided the opportunity to purchase the fantastic total of thirty penny bangers! During the summer of that year I had been made joint lead chorister – in my other life – the one I was leading along with the current one at home, so my piggy bank was reasonably well stocked from singing at sometimes as many as four or five or more weddings on a single Saturday! Autumn weddings had continued at a pace so thus I was able to contribute to the collection of explosives for the annual family bash. So by now then, this former wet wimp, this boy of the wet whimper history on such previous similar occasions, this little angel of the choir, was as much a part of the Bonfire Wars as indeed he was when perfectly turned out in rich blue cassock, brilliant white ruff, scrubbed hands and showing a clean face, all with the ability of reaching a top 'C' in the boy soprano range with such clarity that grown people were sometimes moved to tears. But, that is a part of this child's story yet to be told.

Now back to Bonfire 1959, or was it 60!

You must remember the garden shed that wasn't in the garden? You know that place to hold sick, dying or recovering animals – the initial home of Percy the crow who thought it had a human mother – Chris! I'm referring to the shed that ran along the side/end of our two-story house that also provided a porch for the 'back door'?

Well what I haven't told you is that it was only one storey high. Neither have I told you that the back yard entrance to our home was actually like a passage without a roof. A plastered brick wall ran the same length as the side/end of the house. It was free-standing wall separating a piece of our garden from this 'passage' entrance. The only place where the wall was joined to the house was by an arch which rose across from the wall, over the small back entrance. This arch then linked the wall to the roof of the shed at the front of the house facing the street. So, if one wanted to, one could climb up the wall, walk along it, over the arch to find oneself standing on the roof of the long garden shed. Standing that is, looking out across the street to the homes of some of our natural enemies! If you then, as only a child could, lay on your tummy on the shed roof, your head could not be seen because the top of the wall was higher than the roof itself. So by using a handy catapult, one could propel a missile towards one's enemy then duck down out of sight behind this wall edge! What fun!

All the usual rubbish had transpired in the build up to this Bonfire night. We had expressed our annoyance so often when Chris had what seemed to be a great idea so I joined him on the roof. We had both had enough! Together we spent some hours tying penny bangers, purchased using money gained from singing on others joyful or special days, to the wooden tails of standard firework rockets. This was a serious business as we had to make sure that the banger was positioned along the shaft of the rockets where it would not unbalance the flight ability too much. However, to add a complication to the task, we had to ensure that at the same time, the bangers blue touchpaper would definitely be set alight by the rocket propulsion flames.

Having created a large supply of these altered rockets that not only flew but now had the added capacity to also explode – hopefully on reaching the predetermined destination of their flight – we then looked for the next piece of apparatus – something to act as a launch pad. In the shed we found several hollow steel tubes, the sort used to provide the handle of a pram for example, that were approximately eighteen inches long. These tubes were just wide enough for us to 'drop' into them an already ignited 'altered' rocket.

The secret was to somehow seal one end of a couple of the 'tubes', light the blue touchpaper of the rocket with a match, safety matches of course, drop it into the tube which was then supported by the top lip of the wall and aim it at a target across the street! Lying flat on our tummies on top of the garden shed roof, armed with our homemade bazookas, we aimed across the road. For ease of loading, I would set light to the rocket, drop it into the steel pipe held by Chris, who then using the top of the street facing wall as a fulcrum, raised or lowered the tube as needed. As the rocket inside the tube burst into flame, this would set light to the blue touchpaper of the penny banger attached to its tail! Wooooooooosh! The rocket flew from the steel tube across the street into the garden of an enemy exploding either before or after but never really on moment of impact. Whatever each result, we ducked down behind the wall edge giggling with delight!

It was not too long before all hell broke loose!

The fundamental problem with scientific things like flight for example, is that no two flying things are exactly the same. Nor do they behave in the same way in flight. A Boeing 747 400 for example will carry a specific load time after time to the same destination from the same place of departure, but its own level of fuel consumption during each flight as well as the point to point time taken to complete the same journey, will often vary. A second, identical, aircraft may require less time or more time or less fuel or more fuel to complete the very same journey with the same load. In both cases, should the configuration of the load change, a complete reassessment of the fuel needs together with the time required to complete the flight, will have to be undertaken. In addition, changing atmospheric conditions can either assist or have a negative effect on each individual flight. In any case, even with an identical projectile, you make a great mistake by expecting it to match the experience gained in the flight of the first or even subsequent ones! It must also be recognised that the wood used in the manufacture of the firework rocket for the 'stick' or 'tail', was not always exactly the same shape or specific density. Often it was not the same wood! Therefore, with each of the bangers that we attached to these sticks, our missiles never acted in the same way. On first inspection by the untrained eyes of one early teenage boy along with one know-it-all gloriously voiced almost but trying desperately to be a teenager (me), the bangers, the sticks of the rockets all looked identical. Therefore, it was up to us to challenge the forces of all that was natural within the structure of the banger adjusted rockets. Buoyed (forgive me) as we were by the apparent success of the initial 'test' we then, keeping our heads down listened to the inquisitive urgent shouts from one enemy house to another, hearing exclamations in partial panic across the road as we both were desperately trying to suppress a violent urge to burst into triumphant fits of laughter, we launched a barrage, of multi-flying explosive rockets! In addition, we found that using the bigger, fatter, noisier more expensive three-penny bangers as missiles fired directly from our Y shaped catapults, they would often reach a few seconds after the inbound amended rockets. Well actually just across our front lawn area, across the public pathway then mostly across the 'road' where cars would often be parked or pass by, these missiles sometimes landed on the front lawn area of the enemy homes.

As the afternoon moved inescapably towards the early twilight of that time of the year, as big then bigger brothers returned to discover the results of our wonderful manufacturing, we fortified ourselves for the fun. Volley after volley had been tried with spectacular results although…

…I seem to recall that one or more dropped just in front of our own back gate whilst others hit lampposts or parked cars with only three quarters of their expected journey completed. However, as planned, some flew across to the front porch of the homes opposite exploding as designed! With more practice, we started to compensate for the imbalances of our amended rockets. One such weapon almost smacked into the front door of the home directly in line with ours, exploding on impact and adding to the general cacophony!

The boys across the road were never cowards so within a short while they had determined that they were now under attack. They rallied together forming a collective answer to this unexpected barrage. Bangers flew back at us in waves. Amended Rockets flying one way exploding at various stages in the journey sometimes in gardens, others in porches, whilst others only halfway on their journey across the road. All this activity was before November 5th but it was as a result of that date, almost a legacy attached to the annual bonfire challenge. This exchange, this explosive shower lasted for a while. I concede that at several times during this barrage, I started to regret ever having shared the concept in the first place. The noise was astounding. The younger children in the street must have been as terrified as I was when I was their age. However, this 'battle' continued until with tired arms, munitions exhausted, the battle faded, ended. The firework smoke hung thickly around the now illuminated street lights. Although never very powerful, the street lights struggled to provide any clarity to the murky atmosphere. The participants never forgot.

Repercussions from that day continued for many months with skirmishes often springing from minor issues. But in later life we, as adults, look back on such events with a degree of bitter-sweet sadness. How could we have behaved in that way?

What started as fun in these Bonfire Wars often ended in that established passion with anything to do with Bonfire Night – we had to be the best. Was I guilty of bravado? Was I guilty of stupidly carrying on this family abhorrence year after year? Of course! These growing-up years of my life were full of such silly things, like poor Mr Sloan (not his real name) having worked at the local brewery for many years, who was often to be seen in the summer walking his bicycle home after a days' work. Walking being a very kind word for, staggering or weaving his trusty machine which always seemed so impossible for him to mount on his ride home! Clearly this was because he was so often unable to balance on it in the afternoon apparently due to the fact that the ground moved strangely each time he attempted to climb on board at the end of his shift. Each morning however, having recovered from the effects of 'working' during the previous day, he could be seen on his way to work peddling with confidence on solid terra-firma which, as if by magic, had returned overnight. Oh how we often mistreated this unfortunate man. Having just stood the bike against the wall of his house the previous evening, when Mr Sloan would often take some time to ensure that the wall was solid, not moving, we would sneak up later to loosen the chain off or ensure that a pedal was just balanced on its spike. As the fully sober Mr Sloan leapt on his trusty steed the next morning, his little legs would whip around with him going nowhere! The back wheel of that big black roadster must have been loosened so many times but at the end of each day when the obviously drunk Mr Sloan would be seen wobbling his way down the road to home, never really knowing why his bike always seemed to be so troublesome at the end of the day!

End of the fifties, rolling into the sixties was a time when the 'after-war' new generation were building a head of steam for change; angry young men, 'Rock-n-Roll', the explosion of demand for change.

The greatest dirty joke of the 1950s was the statement by Prime Minister, Harold Macmillan, in 1957 that "Britons have never had it so good" became the final trigger, pushing the baby-boomers over the edge.

The collective rebellion of the young in all things was set to dominate the coming decade, then beyond. Those first teenagers, babies for the future, tax incentives to restock the nation with cannon fodder after World War Two were now flexing their minds; self-recognition, rejection of class statuses, mounting a public outcry of the young for the application of their own state of being. The parents, the uncles, aunts, the doctors, the church leaders together with politicians of all colours were lost, not adding to or encouraging others to understand this society impetus. The needs of the Band of Brothers from Number 44 were part of this change by the time of this Flying Rocket story. For my part, much of the background to my future had already been established along a separate path so that at twelve or so years of age, I was already moving out of the cognizance of my family. My activities at twelve going on twenty but still awaiting that wondrous teenage period, were such that I was now firmly set along a road that would lead to the inevitable step in my life, my physical divorce from my family to accompany my already social separation.

However –

I digress yet again.

There is so still much to tell about the period six years six months to the beginning of my teens, so I ask that you now Dear Reader, come with me back to the era recording the end of my regular meetings with dear Mrs P. Followed by the arrival of the time when I was to follow all my brothers' footsteps subjecting myself to fathers' piano lessons in our front, special room.

During this same period I will introduce you to three people who were to shape my life forever.

A choirmaster, who was also an amazing organist of note! He was a registered master of the Royal College of Music, the Royal College of Church Music, a man of musical passion who had no regard, time or recognition of 'second-best'. Mr John C, a man as destined to become my voice guide, as I was destined to be his student. An artist in all things musical dedicated to the teachings of the church, a man to offer a portal, a fascinating gateway or insight into a life of music.

John C was an accomplished voice training master and a linguist with a passion for elocution. A diction expert capable of linking sounds, words, music, in a collective truth! "That word has a 'D' on the end of it boy! Pronounce it"! Yes, John C could 'hear' the colour of words, regularly saluting the abilities of each of his charges in public or private with consummate ease. Constantly he would DEMAND EXTRA SINGING training to GET IT RIGHT! Even though as my time at the choir progressed, we boys knew that our best was excellent, we had not nor ever could reach the end of our collective or own potential as seen in each of us by this wonderfully dedicated music master!

The second individual to grasp my consciousness, pulling me into a world of expressing dreams was an accomplished well respected actor, author, turned educator, Mr Alan G. Here was a man of the theatre. Classically trained, he elected to become involved at 'street-level' after playing his part in the recent war. His aim was to bring performing arts into the lives of the youth of the day. Holding a reputation of some standing in the professional theatre, education circles but also in the entertainment community, here was an educator of 'life' reflection, with a gift in sharing that artistic talent with the developing often angry youth of the day. Again, it was as if we had both been waiting to meet. Finally, our separate life journeys were to cross.

This merger of the singing young me with the duel universes of the wise in music, now together with a guru in the world of classical theatre, was to provide a platform for allowing this non-conformist family boy, the non-wanted, sucker of the hind tit, runt of the litter, who never stopped asking so many stupid questions, the combined opportunity to have some insight through their art, into other lifestyles that not many would or could ever experience.

The third individual is a special magic friend called Richard T. Richard (it was also his first name – actually his only Christian name, not like mine) who also shared with me my officially recorded birthday! He had no doubts at all about his day of arrival as the only child of his folks, so instantly recognised something we could explore together.

The first two people mentioned above were already adults when our paths joined so here were meetings directly as a result of me, nothing to do with any members of my family.

Richard however was my age, indeed exactly my age, as I was to discover. Although we did not know it at the time we first met, he was to become my best mate at school for many years to come. It was Richard who in my first year at junior school invited me to sing after an announcement at the end of one playtime from a visitor from the Aylesbury District Church of England Parish Council. From then on, we were so often together, sharing time in common interest with common friends. In our early teens however we drifted apart possibly due to hormonal changes that first boiled in me when I was offered, one cold wet Saturday afternoon under the footpath bridge across the canal in town, an opportunity to explore the feminine wonders of a young teenage girl! In my case, this specific education was given with amazing devotion to duty by one very well defined sixteen-year-old called Sandra C. Thereafter, the girl bug took hold with the resultant fading of wanting to be in the company of boys, other than the choir of course. Whenever spare time was available from then on, members of the other gender captivated wide-eyed testosterone filled me with their flowing shapes! Although still good friends, having spent some years in the choir together, it was recognised without real understanding, that our own needs were changing. Having left the choir for personal reasons at the age of fourteen, Richard T had also moved schools so by a process of gentle but natural osmosis, we moved forward as my other friends in the music world replaced his position of constant companion status. Without really appreciating it at the time, our individual journeys into adulthood had begun!

Before my Teenage Period.

As with all people, I assume my childhood was impacted by all sorts of external positive influences alongside those of more challenging effects. There are several such matters that I now believe helped to shape me which should not therefore be excluded from this record of my life journey.

A special pause in my story then Dear Reader, to allow for the opportunity to provide some further understanding of the then prevailing circumstances surrounding my little life.

Our sister, Penny (not Alexandra as you now know – sadly) cannot ever appreciate the impact her arrival had on us or how it made the lives of her brothers from that point on so very much inconsistent. Having applied fear by using the divide then rule practice over his male offspring which provided that status as the 'master' over us for so long, the entire demeanour of our father changed with the arrival of what was to become his last child, but, more importantly, his daughter! Although such a change had much less of a negative impact on me, imagine please if you will the impact on poor Greg! He who had somehow stood firm in the full face of this fear regime for twelve years or so by the time Penny arrived! Well, assuming that he would not really have been exposed to it too much in the first two to three years of his own life, but then the following nine or ten years however must have been pure hell. Such is the strength of human spirit, that Greg no doubt had amended, or tempered his own world to compensate for such an authoritarian modus-operandi practiced by our father.

How strange then it must have been for him to see over the next few years, those of his own teenage years where boys usually seek to exert some measure of identity, the way his fathers' behaviour towards the new offspring, his daughter, as well as to some extent the younger boys (mainly me I tend to think) started to show signs of mellowing! Whereas we had on some rare occasions, often just Sunday mornings, been given sweets as some 'inducement' some very 'special treat', the appearance of these oh so brightly wrapped delicacies now materialised on a more regular basis, more often than not on Friday evenings at dad's return home after his working day. Sadly however, also more often than not, these were for just one member of the family, Penny!

Note here that I have referred to him as dad – also a rare word used thus far in this record of my childhood journey. No doubt I am reflecting in this remembered attitude, a softening, a change, perhaps even recognising a change in myself at the time? His voice seemed to be less harsh, his temper still quick but with less of an overt anger, more a suppressed warm steel instead of a bitter iced blue steel! So, as far as I was concerned, the first noticeable benefit of having a sister was the tolerance level of my father (back to that title again!) towards his sons. This relationship improved measurably. As a result of this, for the first time perhaps we, the boys that is, seemed able to stretch a little further than previously although if the result of this newfound freedom was seen as over-stretching, instant return to the disaster of the normal but somehow strangely comforting apocalyptic previous order of things was the immediate reward. I can only record here of course my memories of this period so must point out these are not those of my siblings. Therefore, I must stress that the views expressed are mine alone.

Others may have differing memories. Where this is true, I mean to offer no contradiction or accusation or judgement of any sort where others views may offer conflict to my own.

Allow it to be noticed that over the next ten years or so, the change in our father was beyond obvious, well to me it was!

In the event that I have unwittingly drawn a picture in the mind of my reader that the family side of my existence during this phase of my life was continuously harsh, I must ask for it to be accepted that this same period was also filled with shared fun, warmth and laughter, all reflecting an occasional recognition of the developing personalities of each of us as we gained experience from drinking together the learning joys of life. The very existence of Penny, without her knowing it I am sure (well initially anyway), provided her male siblings with sight of a person residing in the body of our father that we had not seen before. At such times our home environment may have seen subtle changes, where fear was reduced, creating a phenomenon which provided a space for shared warmth between the family members. This impact of having a sister/daughter was to also contribute to the easing of relationships between all the male occupants with the 'master'. This also had the result of easing the tensions between the boys themselves. Was there jealousy of Penny? Oh indeed yes, as could be expected, but the benefits of a lowering of constant tension far exceeded the jealousy levels.

One good moment of fun involving Penny, although very embarrassing at the time, happened when adhering to an edict to take her to the morning service at the new, recently built church directly behind our house, Chris was given the responsibility as the eldest for this adventure, accompanied by me. We had been instructed to take her as apparently there were a number of local children attending the Sunday school there. Sunday morning! Yes, Sunday mornings became that very strange time when all the children of the family were given 'tasks' to perform away from the house! It was not until much later in life that I began to realise the connotations of such instructions as to "Go for a long run all the way around the playing field." Or things like "please take this 'object' to the shop across town, tell them thank you". Or, as in this remembered instance, "Take Penny to church today, its time she started to attend Sunday school," not that they had shown any signs at that time of ever encouraging any of the boys in attending a Sunday church service! Other than my own Sunday choir duties of course but that was my 'thing' not theirs.

All these demands from our parents were usually accompanied with statements like, "It should only take you an hour or so."

Anyway, back to Penny, her first church visit story.

This modern brick box building was dedicated to yet another variation of Christian worship, separated by yet another quirk of ideology or text interpretation or argument. I'm not sure but Penny was close to five years old making me about nine, heading towards ten so Chris was possibly looking forward to his twelfth birthday. In this 'church' Sunday school, membership demanded that all children participate in the first half of the main service with their parents. In our case of course, Chris was acting purely in a surrogate fashion as parent to Penny supported somehow by me! Not one of us though had ever set foot inside the place before. Halfway through the service then, children would be invited to attend Sunday school which required them to leave the main part of the church to gather in a side room used for the purpose. Here sat the two of us dressed in our Sunday best. Two junior men under strict orders to behave! Two boys charged to bestow an example of proper conduct, in teaching piety, to introduce their younger sister to the ways of Christianity. We were instructed to adopt a proper stance by entering into the spirit (forgive me) of the event. Here we sat with blonde haired, blue-eyed, sweet little Penny, resplendent in her best Sunday dress, squashed between us in case of trouble. People, adults mostly, had acknowledged our being in the church with half warm smiles, little knowing nods of their heads toward us as adults do when uncertain in such circumstances but must nevertheless acknowledge our presence, all showing us their sighs, their signs of welcome into their fold. We were after all a threesome of young sweet innocents who had never before been seen in their midst. Hushed, expectant, eerily quiet conversations, half whispers, surrounded us when the early congregation members arrived. However, on approaching the time for the service to begin, the congregational hubbub reached an almost expected crescendo with the church almost full of unvarying 'meet to greet' salutations between chattering people.

Why do you Dear Reader, think it is that those really embarrassingly public moments, those real instances when there is an urgent need for somewhere to hide but there never is, those moment of panic that will always happen when all noise in the crowd around you suddenly without any warning of its intent stops, ceases, ends? When all shuffling of feet – stops. Even the sound of breathing, coughing, or rattling of handbags instantly falls to a deafening silence! Why is that, at that every long lasting second in time, does 'it' happen?

As the service was about to start, a curate appeared carrying something of import towards the altar; walking with a proud purposeful stride across the chapel in full view of the gathered, expectant congregation, this semi-official, this not yet fully qualified person of the church now heading towards the altar being watched by all in the now perfectly silent congregation. All sound everywhere in the whole world disappeared, ceased! No birds singing outside, no Sunday traffic on the road outside, nothing! In that appalling empty silence, that vacuum, that void where sound simply did not, had not ever existed – a little blonde-haired blue-eyed almost five-year-old girl, having no recognition of or respect for the occasion, or knowledge even of precious silence, emits a bellow that would put a foghorn to shame!

"Why's that man wearing that long black dress? Is he a lady?"

Each word, although formed then produced at a normal speed, expanded! As each was released from the throat of this sweet young thing dressed as she was in Sunday best, the words themselves grew in individual stature! They became longer, apparently in competitive battle with each other for self-importance! How those words echoed around the church! Bouncing off the walls, multiplying in decibel intensity upon reaching the waiting ears of what seemed now to us, two of the boys from number 44, simply hundreds or even thousands of people!

Each one of these now millions of congregation members seeking justification, even answers as to why the wondrous, spirit lifting, Sunday silence had been obliterated, were all now turning to stare at – US! Oh please, please give me a hole to fall into! Billions of eyes that Sunday morning, turning first then seemly having to drag their slightly unwilling heads around in the direction from where this sound had originated, eye muscles on each face straining, seeking to get a view of the offending child who just happened to be sitting squashed between us!

Oh, it was not that I wanted a hole to disappear into because of the shouted question. Oh no, it was simply because of the instant explosive sound bursting through the following silence into wild imbecilic laughter with such compulsive uncontrollable gusto – filling the soundless world. Unable to hide or suppress in any way our mirth that somehow was so out of place in the silence of that morning! The boys, the two of us that were under strict instruction to behave, unashamedly chortled out loud! This continued for what felt like ages until we were able to compress the noise to a level of giggles that we both eventually managed to partially contain, then slowly subside to nothing. But it was far too late! The damage was done!

The infectious bout of intermittent child giggles in such an enclosed environment took hold of the congregation as with all such infectious laughs or even diseases – it spread! There can be nothing more contagious than a gathering of seriously minded people caught in a giggle-trap! Each sudden outbreak of uncontrollable sniffing, the swallowing back of the 'down-my-throat' giggles, the bum on seat shifting suppression giggle, the hand clasped over mouth giggle suppression were all attempted, but all failed, each failure causing yet another giggle-tickle to be ignited elsewhere within the congregation.

Each outburst only added to our own uncontrollable giggle smother attempts. So much so that the entire service was delayed for some time until we the visiting children were invited to excuse ourselves from that first half of the service to play in the Sunday school room until the other children joined us. Some of these children were also afflicted with the giggle bug so it was not too long on that summer Sunday morning that although the service was delayed, Sunday school began much, much earlier than normal. I am convinced that even once we were out of the church, there were adults still smarting, still holding back giggles, not just during the rest of the service but for a long time thereafter! To the very best of my knowledge, I think that that was the only time Penny ever went to Sunday school either on her own or with any of the boys. Not one of us would take that chance again! I personally cannot ever remember attending a service there again. On arrival home that day, Chris took great delight in informing our parents with an attempt at keeping a straight face initially of the seriously embarrassing catastrophe the church visit with Penny had been. The story remained a family favourite to be re-told many, many times.

As was the story of the flying tomatoes!

Soggy Flying Tomatoes!
(Alternative heading – The Splattering!)

This sparkling event took place on a late summer evening after a long, noisy, shared dinner when as usual we, the boys, were attending to the kitchen duties after our meal. Our mothers' sister, our Aunty Elsie, was staying with us on one of her very rare visits to England from her home in America. Dinner had been accompanied by lots of exciting talk about America; stories of big cars, cowboys, airplanes had captivated us throughout the long family dinner. If I recall correctly, this particular visit by our aunt was for her to have some dental work undertaken on the teeth of her only child, our cousin, Dianah. It was apparently cheaper for them to fly to the UK from Seattle to get the dental work done on the National Health than for it to be completed in the 'private' medical system in the US. Anyway, as with all her visits, Elsie had a totally unique ability to tell our father to "Oh, shut up, Jim" when he was being his typical Edwardian, pompous self. She clearly used such brazen disregard for his imagined status that her visits always created a rare time for us of the collective male offspring, to relax a little, to enjoy the 'breath of fresh air' that marked the character of our Aunty Elsie.

We were talkative us boys, happy in the comfort of a relaxed home atmosphere. Jostling each other, gibing, perhaps talking about the current visit, wondering how long Elsie would stay with us. On a previous summer visit, she had argued with our father to allow us to sleep in a silly shack/tent thing that we had built with her in the garden during the day – she won! What joy! So there we were washing, wiping, putting away the (good) dinner things whilst they, the adults, sat talking in the special front room. Salad had been on the menu that evening so tomatoes had been a natural ingredient of the salad. A hot evening, sagging, wilting tomatoes left on one's plate were aplenty. Some remains were now squashed between plates by the stacking in preparation for transfer from the dining room to the kitchen. A silly argument, a shout of injustice! Andrew, who was doing the washing, was suddenly chasing Chris through the back door with soap soggy hands clasping soap soggy uneaten, squashed not quite whole tomatoes! Outside they ran, along the passage, past the garden shed then out through the gate into the street as dusk reached its zenith.

An evening time in summer when the dark of night is only a pale light blue, typical of a late summer evening at the end of the warm day. Shouts from the pursued followed by laughter. Raging bull shouts of the pursuer! Greg running ahead of me – both of us in hot pursuit of both of them! We were each enchanted by the possibilities of so many different outcomes, of such frantic, unexpected activity! Sprinting around the corner of the now flung-open back gate, we were both eager to see what happens next! The leading siblings having shot through that front gate into the street moments before us, Chris turned right running in front of our house, past our front door, along the narrow pathway then past the front door of the Irish family next door. In a hot, perspiring rage holding a wad of damp red-soggy tomato collection, Andrew is in pursuit. Thinking that he can achieve his objective on the run, he raises his strong right arm letting fly like any good fast bowler. But this is not a cricket ball, oh no, this is a handful of non-eaten, red-pulpy tomato, a soggy mass held together with washing up soap mixed with other meal debris.

Visibility was reliant now on dim street lighting, the very last remnants of sunlight having given way allowing night to be in full attendance. At that very moment in the time of men, at that interval of space, an interval that time itself ensures will never happen again, Mr Irish – him with only daughters, much to the annoyance of our parents – Mr Irish, that big tall man next door, so big in fact that it would be impossible to mistake him for our brother Chris even in the darkest of shadows or depth of night. But not by dear brother Andrew, oh no! The family cricketer of historic note! Andrew bowled at full speed, sending his wad of soggy tomato at the first moving thing he saw on rushing through our back gate out to the street beyond. He let rip at full pace as if to the waiting batsman.

This airborne soggy, mucky salad projectile struck poor unsuspecting Mr Irish on the side of his face just at the very moment he chose to push his bicycle out of his front door. Splat!! It stopped all movement by him or bike in mid-stride. This gift of airborne red splodge originally earmarked (I'm sorry!) for our brother Chris, hit poor Mr Irish with a resounding SLAP! The entire left side of his face caught the full explosive force with the result that hair, ear, nostril, eye, cheek to chin with some inclusion of the upper throat, all became one with soggy, wet squashed tomato. Fusion of half a human face to a heavy mass of squashed, uneaten, soap-bubble mixed tomato occurred!

There existed at this time a very real but somewhat unusual truth about our Mr Irish who lived next door, a truth known by many in our street but never too often spoken about. Our Mr Irish had no roof to the inside of his mouth! Yes, he had a skull! But he had been born with an unformed roof to his mouth, a sort of cleft palate problem that was never to be corrected throughout his life. Thus it was that the poor man, no matter how hard he may try, could not in any way sound like any other person on the planet when attempting to talk. The sound he emitted as speech was a high-pitched scraping noise, difficult to understand as it was simply very strange at the best of times. We had often heard him attempting to 'shout' at his girls which allowed us the opportunity without any pity whatsoever, to copy this verbal corruption, this strange sound. Whenever he spoke, if that was how it could be described, it sounded like chalk scraping on a blackboard that, or the high-pitched moo of a cow with a nasty cold!

On that fateful evening with soggy tomato sliding down the left side of his face, his neck, seeping under the collar of his open neck shirt, he did not attempt to talk – at first. An initial silence of disbelief was however soon followed by a screeching banshee howl! This eruption of agonised, tortured non-voice attempting some obscenities emerged from that nature-distorted mouth! The sound was so loud that it travelled the street as we boys ducked to hide anywhere, trying to hold on to the urgent need not to burst into violent fits of laughter! Our parents, having heard the commotion, arrived on the scene via our front door accompanied by our Aunty Elsie. After enquiring into the nature of the tragedy that had suddenly struck their neighbour simply in preparation of the need to offer condolences if appropriate, Elsie realised what had happened. Her immediate reaction through fits of instant laughter was to wrap her arms around Mr Irish, giggling, then explain what had hit him. Thrown by whom, at whom, utilising that wonderful urban myth statement, "boys will be boys"!

Taking the sting out of a potentially hazardous situation for us, she invited Mr Irish with his wife who had appeared at the scene into our home to enjoy a cup of tea!

That was the first time I had ever seen my father cry! Not through the showing of some pent-up emotion, but because he laughed so much along with the rest of us that tears were rolling down his cheeks.

So yes, events shared with fun did indeed play a part in my childhood, occasionally including my father.

That each of us had established friends outside the family circle seemed natural. I in particular seemed to have joined several differing groups of people who had a cross pollination of performing arts interests, which were things that neither my parents nor siblings had any interest in whatsoever. It seemed perfectly natural to me that spending so much time 'outside' my family was simply a normal accepted part of growing up. Put another way, perhaps my growing away from them was a type of recognition; an acceptance by me of my established status of family 'blithering idiot' and therefore a lesser member of the sibling pack. A place perhaps where it was best that I should not impose myself any further than was necessary. These other people in my young life, this collection of chosen friends, provided influences on me that supplied an external guide for understanding alternative choices for me, the foundation building process perhaps for the direction my life would eventually take. They, these non-family people, were by their choice together with mine I suspect, excluded from my home life or having any relationship with my family due to lack of interest by all parties. Very soon this group of friends with whom I was associating, began to surpass any real influence my family may have had, allowing me from an early age to explore differing views, developing even alien levels of knowledge, seeking, then creating my long term self independently, not following the lead of those in my family that were ahead of me chronologically.

Having started with Mrs P at perhaps four years six months of age, I was to finish infant school some fifteen months later, moving to junior school in the September just before my sixth birthday. Chris was still at this (big) school, so again no doubt wanted as little as possible to do with baby brother Richard. Here I was following his life road to the same school as him, possibly from time to time seeking his help – an intruder in his world.

By now I had been given the opportunity by the wonderful Mrs P to learn the basics of how to read that 'stuff' from which music could be made on the piano. At age six I had, well, sort of had, mastered the art of allowing the fingers on one hand to do things quite differently to those on the other hand. Not yet at a distinctly differing tempo, but almost. This ability was used later on in my early teens when learning to play the drums. In senior school, I had become great friends with Nicky M. We both made a noise on guitar so would often 'jam' together. Nicky's brother Nigel M at the time was a well-known pop group drummer who was, when at home, happy to attempt to share some of the basics with me. But that's another part of this story to come later. So, by the time I started at junior school I was, albeit with cumbersome, slow results at times, nevertheless able to read this printed magic 'stuff' well enough to make a noise on a piano. During my first year at junior school, as the separation from Mrs P was underway, due mainly to the fact that my new school was much further away from her front room, it became time also to follow in the footsteps of my older siblings and start regular piano lessons under the auspices of a new, more frightening, more demanding piano teacher – my father. Plonk, plonk with more plonk, plonk to follow. Scales, octaves following scales. Then when finished – even more scales, practice followed by more practice. Finger exercises after more finger exercises, plonk with more plonk day after day, miserable hour after miserable hour. Instinctively I already knew that had I simply sat exposing my knowledge of this wonderful instrument by playing some piece I knew at the time to my father, life (the relative safety of it at the time) as I had come to know it would be in jeopardy. I knew that knowledge of my relationship with Mrs P would cause much consternation resulting in additional angst in that private space that was my world. So, plonk plonk – day in, day out. After school for an hour then having to show father on his arrival home from work how well I was progressing, or not. Nowhere near how well dear Chris was performing, but sort of 'on my way'. Although not a spy in the true sense, our mother would report on our practising habits to father. Not that she could play at all, just that we the 'students' did actually spend time at the piano in practice. So it went on. No tunes, no fun, no warmth, no holding fingers that were reluctant to do what was wanted of them, no laughing at finger behaviour at all! It was just a sort of hard labour without any reward. Dear Chris, the one who so often on a Sunday was rolled out like some little performing monkey dressed in his best whenever our parents had visitors; walk in say nothing, sit, play. Then be excused.

Initially this plonking was fun for me because to a degree, it confirmed that all was progressing as expected in my home family life. Regimented, controlled, all was subject to chronological event dictate! I had expected this change for what seemed like ages so I became safe in the knowledge that my young life was moving forward. It was also fun, because I could make it so. Whereas with Mrs P the awe of the magic itself was in control, sweeping both of us majestically forward to some form of pleasant comprehension.

It was however this very same awe, this understanding, this hidden, concealed ability that finally was to let me down so early on in my home pianoforte lessons period. An action, any peek at my private reality even then was to endow my parents with some knowledge of something possibly abhorrent to them in or about me. Such knowledge generally may not be received with kindness by my mother but more particularly by my father!

The split, the real divide, the gulf that I knew existed, separating me from the other members of my family, would force itself out into the public light of day often but rarely was ever noticed. Now however for the very first but sadly not to be the last time, I was to unwittingly show my hand! I had before this incident but managed to cover my error – but not this time! Exposure about to happen was as a result of relaxation of concentration or even as a foolhardy lack of consideration to potential future dangers. In truth, as a result of my own silly stupidity! But, Dear Reader, I already knew it was to happen.

Just not the when!

Way back in this epistle, Dear Reader, I referred to two items located in that 'special' room of our house – the front room. A piano yes, do you recall the other?

Yes, that's correct, that very large old fashioned valve driven radio. This object was, on the one part, full of countless possibilities; music of such a variety emanated from this large wooden box when switched on that I remember often thinking that there was far too much music in the world. However, this radio was never our, the children's, domain. It was simply a very uncommon activity to allow any one or more of the children access to this wonderful magic box as we grew up. This changed during our late childhood to early teens, when we were sometimes allowed to listen to some programmes. These programmes were considered 'light' listening. Things such as 'forces favourites' as food was being prepared over Sunday lunch time where BBC voices from places with strange exotic names around the world, played music requests for members of the armed forces. I knew how to turn this box on, to wait for the lights to glow from an early age! Listening to this radio provided a link for me to the world far beyond our home, far beyond our road or even our town! Not until much later then were we to be allowed opportunity to listen to this monster piece of furniture – for me though, a window to things far outside our world. Once again, following forces favourites after lunch was 'Around the Horn'. If we boys had finished our meal chores in time! In addition to this radio but located in that long passageway leading from the front 'special' door to the kitchen door, stood an old wind-up gramophone with a 'scratch' needle set in its own 'foil' stylus. I had spent many happy hours cranking the wind-up handle poking out from the side of the cabinet, just trying to maintain the correct speed, (the clockwork mechanism was broken), listening to whatever I could from a small collection of solid 78 inch discs of classical music. This too had added to my desire to make music somehow!

The very existence of this gramophone in the hallway passage together with the radio in the front room, played a large part in bringing about my first real lapse, or falter, leading to the public exposure of something I had intuitively withheld, a hereto hidden 'Piece' of me- a stumble from conscious control. You see when no one was around I would spend my piano 'homework' practice time listening to whatever music I could find on the radio or those scratched, chipped records. This 'wasting' of my allotted practice time was how the wheels eventually came off the then music relationship I had, pathetic as it was anyway, with my father. It was however also to bring together for the first time, a shared but never directly voiced understanding in our relationship; a quiet sharing, a knowledge or recognition of something unique, something quite different.

A capacity, an ability, that other than one shared episode yet to happen, neither of us pursued until I was a late teenager, early adult and only then with a great amount of careful circumspection or extreme caution. I will try to elaborate.

Dear Reader, the explanation or information contained in this next portion of my childhood story is, for me at least, to be perhaps the most difficult to divulge, to tell or offer. I have agonised over its inclusion but without your insight, without giving you an opportunity to view what I am about to present here, a central 'Piece' of all the 'pieces' of me that are recorded in this tome, would be missing. Therefore finding the best, the most acceptable way to take you to the core, this core piece, the heart, this very individual thing that has always been the unique essence of me, has to be included here. Please humour me a little when I suggest we can all accept that we are, each of us, born with a clean clear opportunity full of potential to learn, to give. Each new human life engineered if you will, is swarming with untested possibilities. Throughout my life I have however come to accept though, that whilst each new human life has at the time of arrival multitudes of yet unknown capabilities, these are generally soon lost as each person develops.

Uncounted gifts waiting to be explored, tested, even shared. Capabilities unknown are inherent in each individual but all requiring strenuous encouragement. Needing to be understood or cultivated. But with the exception of just a few individuals, the vast majority of these abilities resident in all of us are discarded as we grow. They are never to be used because opportunity or motivation or both do not present themselves. Perhaps the culture of repression of the unknown into which we are born, corrupts opportunity? Either in the lifestyle to which we are introduced to the world or when such skills are attempted, the attempt alone may cause consternation so powerful around us, a fear of the unrecognised in others, that we as children are encouraged to look like, behave like, to be like the current considered safe version of 'normal'.

So fear by peer supported by prejudice surrounding the infant toddler, often demands that survival requires us to ignore these potential gifts to the extent that eventually most of us become frightened to explore such gifts further. The inevitable result is our wanting to be accepted by our peers as normal, and this results in the majority of us losing, the potential abilities. Where these abilities are not used during the first few months or early years of existence even, our intuitive knowledge of them remains minimal; without reason or facility to apply them the capacity to do so vanishes and is therefore perhaps banished forever. I am aware that some abilities do resurface later in life usually however only in times of great, emotion, trauma or affliction but they are there! An autistic child may suddenly without any feasible explanation be able to perform very complex maths in milliseconds, or play the piano without any music lessons. A journey 'towards the light' in near death experiences or the sudden recovery from a long-term coma are all such examples. That feeling "I knew that was going to happen" that we all experience at some time during our own life journey. Although I'm not sure if it will help at all but I ask that you allow your mind some freedom, some space to wander, to explore possibilities that may frighten or challenge your own status quo. Gently nudge around the edges of the 'seventh child of the seventh child' syndrome. Not convinced that this may provide any acceptance of the potential possibilities expressed but may at least offer some strange logic to what now has to be written here as part of my own journey.

Also, please be aware that until now, I have never attempted to put to paper before anything of what you are about to read even though I have always known, even as a young child, that I would undertake such a task as that I am doing here today.

The incongruity of that last statement calls for a pause, a contemplation, a reflection, as you will see.

With just a couple of specific special exceptions, I have not talked to anyone on these differences, have I tried? Oh yes! Has that gleam of fear or apprehension instantly appeared in the eye of the listener? Oh yes! Have I seen, even listened to ridicule as the attempted wash away with closed reply? Oh yes! Having tried but failed so often to even start the discourse but failing constantly, leaving suspicion, even guilt in the wake of such attempts.

Oh how I have over the years so many times wanted others to help or share, listen or to simply know. If I fail again therefore at this written attempt to give meaning, or if my words confuse or frighten, I seek your mercy. I cry for your patience to indulge me. However, to give insight to as much of me as possible, the following must be included. In fact, excluding the following would create a void in recording what or how I am or indeed who I am.

Knowing Things!

As a child, my own inner essence, that single thing that is unique to each of us, was exposed to others the results of which were, as I had known they would be, ignored, drawing labels such as 'Blithering Idiot', as a self-defence stance. Even though I knew ahead what was to happen, there was nothing I could have done to prevent such exposure!

Here then is another example from my 'controversy' birth companion, that constant 'controversial' life companion.

I had known from a very young age possibly even as a babe in arms, that there were some things about my very existence that to others, were at best just strange or askew. Uncommon! Therefore, to avoid potential awkwardness it was less stressful, safer even to keep any manifestation hidden. I hid behind whatever 'normal' was as a child, continuing to do so many times since. Perhaps this need to conceal was not even an intuitive thing but some inborn knowledge, some throwback generic comprehension in my physical being that placed a secure deep-seated knowledge even at early 'newborn' life stage, that it would be unwise to expose too many differences to others. That these 'gifts' as some may say, these 'things' existed from the moment of my arrival on this planet, I had then nor do I today harbour any doubt at all. For example, it was not too long before reaching a stage when as a child I became aware that somehow I was able to see things that others seemed totally unable to comprehend at all. Without any conscious effort, I started to realise that I could see the structure of, well things! Or, put another way, if for some reason I needed to see what or who was in the next room, I was able to simply 'look'. I didn't have to walk or crawl, I could just look, not necessarily in any referenced direction but into a space in my head. This was so perfectly normal to me that it very soon occurred to me that others around me couldn't! How scary was that to this little life to realise that such was clearly not 'normal'. If I wanted to know what was happening in the next street as a child growing up, I did not have to leave what I was doing in the house or garden to walk down the road or around the corner, I could simply look! I do not mean that my eyes popped out of my head like some silly cartoon character!

I mean I was initially able, if I wanted to, somehow 'see' past or through physical matter, natural or manmade into the 'space' where the answer was to the question I was asking myself. Realising how strange this may be to others, I abandoned doing this in blind panic.

Only at times of real comfort or joy, or fear, or imminent danger have I attempted to use this since. Putting this into perspective, I could 'see' things that at first I thought everyone else could see but soon learned that others obviously could not. 'See' is really not the correct word it is/was more a 'knowledge of' or the ability to 'perceive' happenings in a given space. Initially it seemed perfectly natural to this tiny person who had yet to develop simple, let alone, complex language skills to be 'seeing' through obstacles, this was as unchallenging or as common as breathing or having big brothers or hands attached to one arms. It was not though until I was old enough with minimal language skills enabling me to construct basic sentences that my never-ending 'stupid' questions began to CONSTANTLY invade the life of my family or anyone around me. It was then I started to realise that something was very wrong! Along with speech ability, I became that 'idiot boy' who blabbered, constantly asking silly questions – my need to ask 'stupid' questions, to seek answers began almost as soon as I was able to construct a grunt or point! Here then I record a simple memory living in my head forever that may encapsulate as an example, where those silly questions arose from, so often articulated from this very small crawling, waddling, toddler child. Firstly, you have to know that pipes, yes pipes, near or over my head have, for as long as I can possibly recall, been my particular irrational human fear. Some people fear spiders for no apparent reason, others cannot abide feathered creatures; still others panic at the mere thought of snakes or open spaces. Me? Its' pipes lying overhead! Thin or fat, large or small, metal or plastic makes no difference at all. Do you hear the music in the last sentence?

The top of my neck tingles as the tiny hairs there rise. I cringe, my knees wobble sometimes I feel almost physically sick. So, humanly irrational, even psychotic as it sounds, pipes are to this day my personal silly 'fear' thing. Standing or crawling or sitting in the kitchen downstairs as a young human having first heard a bird calling as it flew over the house, I could 'see' it! Then returning into the house via the roof space, I would point at the big grey square thing full of water up there with all those pipes hanging from it making a noise, asking what it was! These questions at that stage were just toddler sounds waiting to be formed into words. Once these sounds became words of comprehension to others, spoken words like "Oh what!" followed by "Just ignore him!" or "What are you pointing at, what do you want now!" So it was that I became, as a toddler, the constant provider of 'Stupid' silly questions which were often accompanied by gesticulations, much to the obvious annoyance of everyone in my family. Thus it was that the "idiot" child title was created, the one child in the family group forever annoyingly asking silly as well as apparently un-coordinated questions, as a result of things unseen by others but very clearly viewed by me.

No wonder I was often left alone a lot whilst growing up! "What's that for" or "Who is that running over there?" Questions asked when inside our home. Even when going on those exciting day trips to the seaside or when entering a town or village on the journey to our chosen destination, I often 'knew' what we would encounter around the next bend in the road even though I had never been to the town or village before! Then the inevitable! One day, I revealed this strange ability. I started to tell the other members of the family that uncle 'Lorry' from next door was outside in his garden or, cleaning his car! This statement was made whilst inside our house playing some game on the dining room floor! Laurie Hollings (I learned later that he was my 'God Father') was there plain for me to see in front of his garage next door. 'What are you talking about Richard you idiot!' So, here was little me, the runt of the litter talking rubbish – again!

'We have never been through this town before so how do you know there's a funny building around that corner?' Of course there was! I watched a car once coming from a side road ahead of us. I saw it skid whilst turning, mount the pavement to hit a wall just around the corner from where we were travelling towards it early one summer morning when we were on our way to a day at the seaside! The car sort of bounced back onto the road, skidded sideways then came to a stop half on, half off the pavement. I was so frightened that I shouted, blabbering what was ahead of us only receiving a shouted demand to stop making so much stupid noise! But a couple of minutes later, we were forced to suddenly slow down, to watch people in a damaged car half off the road, struggling out of their vehicle which was showing signs of being recently bent. Father stopped, wound down the window to speak to them. Once it was established that no serious injury had occurred we continued on our way. I was naturally treated with fear, suspicion, remaining subject to dejection for much of the rest of the day. The conversation that I was hoping for but expecting it never to take place, didn't! Maybe they were all quietly wondering just how much of a lunatic I really was.

I would quietly immerse myself in self-pity in bed, sometimes simply angry that this 'thing' was wrong, was not right! Why is it me? But not too often, accepting that safety was hiding away, bury deeply such things inside to try to never to speak out again.

So from my early beginnings, I learnt to hide deep inside, to push an impossible understanding away, to play the role of silly little brother or behave in a way that reflected the 'Blithering Idiot' status which was so often awarded to me by my father. I also learnt how to buy time, to hide panic, developing a cough to help squash my own nervousness. I deliberately forced this 'thing' away from my mind by slowing down my thoughts. So much so that only on extremely rare occasions as an adult, have such abilities resurfaced – usually in times of real stress.

Colours! That was another thing! Colours! At will I could change for me only the outward colour of something, soon recognising that as with 'seeing', I could manage to control this. Such changes could be speeded up or slowed right down to almost nothing. Gradually throughout my life, by continuously burying such 'things' with a fierce determination to be as normal as possible, I created a variety of ways to distract me from these differences as they invaded my head. Slowly, even gently, the capacity for these strange 'things' faded. Growing older however, another inexplicable capability started to be displayed although this was less frightening to me because I discovered there were others able to do this particular 'thing' with ease.

As a child not only could I somehow gauge 'what was to happen next' in a conversation for example but I started to really annoy whoever I was listening to, either as a part of their dialogue or not, then ahead of them I knew what they were about to say next! This became embarrassing to all concerned because often I would say the words, at best with them, but worse, by saying the words just slightly ahead of them! Here was Richard, seven or eight years old talking to Mrs Irish next door perhaps but finishing all her sentences for her before she did! How annoying was that!

Try the same with some of my teachers! Worse still, my father! So too, this capacity had to be amended, hidden, buried out of sight for fear of hurting people around me. This horrible ability to understand what was to happen next has, over my lifetime, been very dangerous also. I once, for example, saw a man fall off a lorry minutes before the event. Stupidly, without thinking clearly at all, I thought that I could stop this event from happening so I ran down several flights of stairs to a loading bay at the back of the building I was in to warn this poor guy of his impending fall shouting 'watch-out' as I got to the side of the loading bay. He looked up at me, lost his footing then crashed to the ground! It was me! I was the reason for his fall! I was an adult at the time quickly, very desperately attempting to hide my shame. I should have known that he fell because of me! Had I stayed where I was, I could have stopped him falling – perhaps not. I have spent more effort, more time on suppressing this single 'ability' throughout my life than all the others. This ability forced me as a child to cover up, close down, run away, not argue, be passive never, never telling anyone! I can provide many stories of how 'knowing' what was to happen would often lead me to try to change the inevitable! I recall my earliest lesson very clearly showing me just how inept or maladroit any attempt to change a known future event could be. It was as a child that I got to know that change or prevention of an outcome was totally impossible. I was at infants' school in fact, just before leaving at the end of the summer term when five years old. Once the summer holidays were over, I would be moving on to junior school.

Located in the playground of the Infants school, throughout my time there, I assume also long before my arrival, was a child's play 'house'. Just a single square box really with a gentle sloping roof, an arch entry at one end with open 'windows' on each side. Although small to an adult, this 'house' was big enough for the young pupils to run in to, out of or to climb on and off, stand on its roof, sit inside and generally have fun in during playtime. No manufactured soft ground in those days – just hard concrete! No soft plastic/rubber construction – just hard, splintering brightly painted wood! The only time I ever ventured inside this construction was the second last day of my time at the school. I had known what would happen from the moment I had seen this 'house' some almost fifteen months previously on my first day at the school! But knowing something was to happen then attempting to be 'in control' of that 'something' at the age of five, just simply confirmed my suspected status of first class idiot to myself at that time. But I took no notice even then! I was about to leave the school for the summer holidays moving on to the junior school in September. Having known all along what was to happen, I was attracted to undertake a silly experiment to prove something only I could possibly appreciate if I succeeded. Could I be in control? Could I 'un-make' an inevitable event? With just two days left at the school and quite aware by then of how to hide, to keep myself at peace with my peers, bravely, well I thought it was anyway, I went into this playground toy play house for the first, the only time! Challenging a fact, a known event of the future, I had enough awareness even then to desperately want to prove that I could be wrong, to somehow change the already known outcome. Hey, what did I know! I was not yet six years old! I had 'seen' the result of this visit many times thus avoided going inside since being at the school. But still I went anyway. Foolhardy Richard was in charge. I had determined that if I were to stay inside around the time the hand bell was to ring signifying the end of the current 'playtime', I would delay my joining my class line. I listened, looked around (through) to confirm unquestionably that all the children had climbed down, crawled over, run out of or jumped away from the play house. It would be safe to exit. I waited listened again, waited some more. I looked, out as well as through,

I was in charge! Soon no child or adult was anywhere near. Still I waited even knowing that the teachers may get upset with me for taking so long to show at the end of playtime. Eventually, full of an excited confidence that I alone could appreciate, standing up, I bent over lowering my head then ran bent over as fast as I could out of the archway door to anticipated freedom!

The huge boy, who I had 'seen' many times before, jumped down from the roof just as I reached the outside, still half bent over, still running. The downward motion of this plump little fellow had such a powerful momentum as he hit me from behind with a terrible force! I was smashed at speed hard to the concrete playground floor! My own forward movement adding its part in this silly melodrama, increasing my impact speed as I hit the ground. My face, suddenly squashed by simultaneous forward, together with downward heaviness, scraped along the rough concrete. My nose although not broken apparently, emitted that glorious red fluid as the boy who landed fully on me rolled away, stood up then ran to his class queue giggling. Cut, scraped, nose swelling, blood running, I walked crying from frustration more than pain to my class queue trying to hide the physical damage as much as possible. No tears of pain just frustration at my inability to prevent or just somehow change a known future event. So much for my ability to alter what I knew was to be! Now I knew that I was, never would be nor indeed had ever been 'in charge' of this ability at all. Since that day I have not offered any contests to correct or alter known future events, with the exception of the falling man in the warehouse! What's more, I still to this day shy away from this ability on an almost day by day basis but have a much better control on the 'knowing' side by having developed a way of shutting out tomorrow. So where did the plump little boy come from? I have no idea! Having 'seen' him often in my foresight then 'in-the-flesh', I never saw him again anywhere. Perhaps a fractured time/space problem around a potential dimensional cross pollination continuum issue…maybe? This ability though has, when I have allowed myself a 'peep' at the outcome of a specific instance, sometimes also provided immense comfort. A sort of 'let it happen without fear attitude' as I know things will resolve themselves naturally to my or others satisfaction. Very good for job or promotion interviews or wondering if your loved ones are or will be safe.

So, here at the age of about six or so, experienced at hiding these so called 'gifts', how then did something so simple as piano lessons at home act as a catalyst for the public display of one or more of these capabilities?

During those wonderful times with Mrs P, I had identified a singular ability that we shared with lots of joy along with some good fun. It was so silly really. Having been provided with the opportunity to find my way around a piano 'listening' properly to where all the notes were, I stored them in my head. That was the easy part. It took some time for me to remember which 'key' to press that would match each 'note' I heard in my head. In other words, I discovered that I was able to reproduce a single sound (note) or many notes of a piece of music often even in the correct order, most sounds that I had just listened to for the first time, reasonably well. Should I have a second opportunity to listen again to the music being played, I could sit at the piano playing it without any of the paper squiggly 'stuff'! I did battle though if I was not truly interested in or moved by a particular piece of music. Mrs P had encouraged this activity with such joy during my time with her.

This ability, as I grew up, was to manifest itself across many things not just with music but with anything that I really wanted to do or learn. It was so easy for me to listen to a piece of music then perhaps even select a single line of harmony in a whole group of voices singing or, to remember a sequence of words – for a song maybe or poetry or language, reproducing the same sounds or words or maths just by playing my memory playback facility truly by 'ear'. Actually ears, including the not so whole one on the left! I knew what people were about to say, not by any mind reading ability but by just listening to the 'music' structure of their words! I could 'see' all the pieces of the interior of the radio or other things, 'watching' what each piece did! Music was counting numbers, word rhythm was counting sounds. All these were attached to colours that I could change at will. These sounds, music in my head if you wish, became the simple counting rhythm of maths or words. Arithmetic became, well, just music.

So came the day when my mother was to walk into that 'front' special room whilst I was busy playing what was then a popular piece that I had heard just a short while before. It was a Lonnie Donegan Skiffle Group song that she recognised as not being any part of my usual plonk, plonk practice 'homework'. She wanted to know how it was that I knew it. I recall her face etched with a little concern, asking me how was it possible for me to play it on the piano without any music. I told her that I had heard it on the radio. I remember her asking me to start the piece again, which I did, pretty much playing the whole thing to her. That evening after dinner, just like a performing monkey, I was placed at the piano. My mother, who gave the impression that this was something really exciting, wonderful even, relayed the 'Lonnie Donegan' story to my father.

How I had not been undertaking the finger exercises given to me but had used the radio to listen to a piece of music then played it on the piano without any sheet music. Whilst our mother was sort of innocently excited in conveying this, the already icy cold ambient temperature of the room seemed to plummet! On went the radio, search for some music broadcast, find a suitable ditty that was being played. Eventually, having found something, told to listen to some of it, the radio was switched off. I was told to 'play that piece'! So, with great reluctance, not to say a little fear, I turned to face the piano in our 'special' room. After a slight hesitation, I started to play something like the music I had just heard. Both hands, no sheet music! I thought that as mum seemed somehow buoyed by what I was doing, perhaps everything would be alright. But you guessed it – I knew already what was to happen! A question from my father, "How long has this been going on?" In a quiet voice but with a fierce, deep angry determination (a very frightened man perhaps) "You'll not have any more lessons from me. There is nothing I can teach you"! A statement made by him that contained the inevitable foundation for the next real point of departure from my family. I had known already that my life would take on another change that day but was simply powerless to delay, stop or change it. Yes, I had known all along what was to happen. Here abruptly ended my home piano lessons!

Here the divide, the no-go fractured space existing between us, cemented into place without any hope of developing a close understanding or empathy for many years to come. A frightened man perhaps turning away from a frightened boy, shaken but not too scared, not anymore, just resigned. As indicated earlier, there was a shadow of recognition that neither he nor I would explore until much later in my life. Mother also started to change in her approach to me, sort of holding back, sort of knowing, sort of unquiet but exhilarant, sort of expectant.

These strange gifts or abilities are still a part of me. However, like learning a new language, use it or lose it applies. Since a young age, I have hidden or managed these things as best I could into in-abilities.

Sometime after the piano incident (but not entirely purely as a result of it), I was taken by my father on a bus early one Saturday to a large house in the countryside. This was apparently located near High Wycombe, about an hour or so ride by bus in those days, where we met with a number of other children who seemed of similar age. The range of ages was around 6 to 11 years. We were given games to play with. Games with numbers, music, shapes, moving of multi-shaped wooden or sometime glass objects, we were asked to read, study drawings. Generally be exposed to silly conversations with a lot of questions. It was an almost all day event which included lunch. Like many of the other children there that day, I suspect I remained hidden away deep inside. I knew, as I'm sure some of them did, that we were somehow being 'looked at' or 'tested' or 'watched'. I remain convinced that I was not the only child that day to ensure by the delivery of deliberately stupid answers to often stupid questions, together with generally pretending to not understand the silly games, that we remained closed, locked away, safe. By late afternoon we made our goodbyes, returning home by bus. To the best of my knowledge, the events of that day were never mentioned in our house other than Richard's 'school' day out with dad neither was the day ever referred to at any time thereafter. I had undertaken something called an IQ test several weeks before this activity so convinced myself that it had led to this exercise.

The result of this? I promised myself then and there that if asked, I would never again submit to being a performing monkey, a freak, to be touched or prodded or ridiculed.

Nor will I again allow myself to be pushed to any state of emotional anger because I fully knew the results that such activity may herald! I am a real pacifist who will, without fail, turn the other cheek! Rest assured Dear Reader in the knowledge that my life has been, and continues to be wonderful, full of real love, full of acceptance. I have for so many years been very comfortable as to who I am, thus experiencing a continuous exquisite quiet peace within. I am truly blessed by those who love me, so very, very lucky.

Far more importantly though, I found a peace with life at a very young age, with a state of mind that sadly few can ever truly attest to; I remained comfortable in my own truth. I have often stated that 'no matter how hard I may try, I cannot damage what my life is today or is to be tomorrow.

JUNIOR SCHOOL! – Age 5 years eleven months. September 1954.

On my arrival at this really big (junior) school in September, two things happened almost simultaneously. I cannot remember with specific clarity which was first but logic of today would lead me to accept that the meeting of a boy with the same first name as me was probably first. Richard T. We somehow managed to share a desk in the classroom into which we had both been slotted on the first day. There must have been a level of natural magic as we later discovered that we were both, well one of us officially anyway, accredited with sharing the exact same birth date! On investigation however, Richard T was able to confirm that his time of birth was "during the afternoon" according to what he had been told so no argument about the date had greeted his arrival. Neither was there any complicating controversy in his arrival nor was he a twin or seventh child of a seventh child of Romany heritage. Nevertheless, we shared 'Richard' as our first name! Such meetings can only be pre-ordained! Two Richard's with the same birthday starting at the same school at the same time are allocated to the same class – sat at the same desk, each as nervous as the other! Richard T had no interest in playing music at all but oh boy did I discover that he could he sing! This newfound companion accepted me as if I had been a part of his life always. No questions, no challenges, just immediate unconditional friendship. After a few weeks of settling into the new school, an announcement was made one day at line-up in the playground, that the Aylesbury Parish Church of St Mary's, was seeking boys to audition for the church choir. Richard T looked at me, "I'm a member of this choir are you interested?" Well I sort of made music, had sort of sang Christmas carols at infant school assembly as well as some songs on that radio thing, so why not. A few days later, off I went one afternoon after school to meet the choirmaster of St Mary's Church of England in Aylesbury which was just a stones' throw away from the town centre.

Oh the plans of angels for individual men are so sure footed!

Meet one truly magical individual, Mr John C, Licentiate of the 'Royal College of Music', a registered organist of the 'Royal College of Church Music – Organ Master of note, now set to become the second great mentor to provide major influence on my childhood development, in fact all the way to my leaving home at almost seventeen years old!

That afternoon I walked into a very, very old vaguely lit, cold, dank-smelling hall next to that consistent companion of all such churches in England, the graveyard! This particular portion of the 'place of the dead' happened to be the closest to the town centre, a suitable place for meeting purposes, some clandestine, others not, but always known as the 'town side' section of the graveyard. This hall was literally an elongated box with just one double door entry, high windows along each side, very small raised area – the stage – the whole building being some four hundred feet from the main entrance to the church. In England, September to late October had the ability to present both fine summer weather (an Indian summer?) but also at any time, the first warnings of a fierce winter to come. Often it was possible to experience these extremes on the same day! I remember entering this building and instantly recognising the cold of too many years even though it was just about four in the afternoon on a fine October day.

A lingering, almost vague memory of summer warmth outside! The construction material of this church hall was primarily of stone where each piece had been hand chipped to the required size, inserted into its allotted place then simply ignored for many, many generations. At first sight, the unsuspecting would perhaps think the hall to be an original adjunct of St Mary's Church. The church however had been standing for much, much longer with records reflecting that this site had been a place of Christian worship for well over a thousand years by the time I was to be drawn into its authority. There is, on public display within the church, the name of every Right Reverend, Minister or Cannon etc., to ever serve this area from the early Eleven Hundreds. On inspection of the church hall it would not however have been difficult to recognise that it was of a much younger vintage, perhaps just three to four hundred years old at the time of my arrival in its interior for the first time.

Looking back on that day, I sometimes wonder if this building had been specifically waiting throughout the centuries for predetermined people to enter its space. My tiny feet crossing the threshold, stepping into its care, represented just the next expected arrival. As I just wrote those words today, now, generations later, a shiver of cold has passed over me often referred to I understand as 'someone has just walked over my grave', how very appropriate!

However this structure, this building that had been welcoming potential choristers for generations, was about to share significant human time with me. Less significant for the building though its' silent acceptance, almost expectant recognition of my arrival within its sphere of stimulus perhaps conducive of agreement that I existed, even if only for a half of a nanosecond in the great scheme of the universe.

Such time would be noted, recorded for eternity, to be held within the solid embrace of its very walls. St Mary's Church had enjoyed a choir of repute, some periods better than others of course, for hundreds of years, producing a number of well-remembered exceptional choristers. The church itself was the information centre for all events within its community, not just the town of Aylesbury but the surrounding districts as well. Recording much of the local history over those centuries with written archives of Births, Marriages, Deaths, social trauma, changes in local civil laws, together with all manner of things attributed to the apparently insatiable need of man to record in this universe his mark during the micro-moment of his being. Records date back to the eleven hundreds, the twelfth century, with some evidence existing that Christians worshiped here as early as the tenth century. On my arrival into its midst, St Marys Church was the proud owner within its physical structure of a relatively modern, perhaps close to 150 years old, magnificent German built full-size organ where the base 'pipes' were equal in size to that of well-established tree trunks!

But more about the church itself later. First though back to my initial entry to the hall. Other than a few chairs, the hall contained a piano. Naked electric lights strung between open rafters providing at best on complete darkness, a general yellow-grey gloom. The floor was old-wooden with the main floor space comprising of approximately twenty-five yards wall-to-wall at the narrowest section then about fifty yards in length. The high windows on each side were leaded, tall thin and arched with pretend colours of dark-ages type hue. This colour or lack of colour had joined forces with many, many years-worth of accumulated grime! This opaque mess was by far beyond the help of a good clean.

All this accumulated dirt had combined to create an atmosphere of particular foreboding not yet fully experienced in my short existence. Visions of sullen, very tall, hooded even, church elders holding secret clandestine meetings with monks of a long gone era would not have been out of place in this hall. The incumbent C-of-E official lived in his large abode just around the corner from this hall so perhaps in former years it had been a staging post, a waiting space for those seeking an audience.

The church with its ever busy graveyard together with the hall had all collectively become known as 'Church Square' acting as exactly that. A large plot of English green with, as its centre point, a massive stone grey place of worship built atop a natural land rise. St Mary's could be seen across many miles of Buckinghamshire countryside, a focal point drawing in country folk to join their compatriots of the town offering protection to all. As mentioned, the church, as in so many locations across the United Kingdom, acted as the recorder of a multitude of events some important, others of little stature, a magnificent, dominating feature then, the centre for so many lives.

Thus it remained. Until the mid 1960s when it was popular to create 'sky-scraper' lookalike office buildings of which the Aylesbury Civic building is an amazing example. That this new edifice, comprising architectural delights of steel, glass in huge amounts all rounded off with broad areas of grey concrete, destroyed the all-round country view which had been so much part of the regions life for centuries. This modern edifice so stupidly with pride was justified by being called progress!

There is plenty of additional ground around the entire structure of the church for the planting of local citizenry when needed. A cobbled path stretches along all four sides of the graveyard from which several cobbled accesses link the church to the town – a sort of spider's web of passages providing thoroughfare in any direction. So here I stood in this semi-dark hall in the shadow of new friend Richard T, relying on his own recently acquired knowledge, he having himself been involved via another boy for about two months. He was my comforter, the one to subdue my trepidation on entering the mouth of this waiting cool stone structure. Once inside I noticed immediately that there were already several other boys there, some I had seen around before but also others I had not. Milling about expectantly, waiting in that strange 'full of movement without movement – fidget' stance that only boys in the age range of six to seventeen are able to display. A sort of side-shuffle stance, an impatient, milling around group waiting in anticipation of something but not really knowing if or why they should be concerned or more importantly, quiet. I acknowledged those boys I knew, shunned the ones that were strangers whilst remaining very close to new friend Richard.

No one talked! Well, boys were talking but in such a subdued manner that it was as if the entire protocol of being present in that ancient, sacred place reduced these boys, irrespective of their individual rowdy abilities to 'rule-the-world' outside of this building, to be reflective, showing respect for things nebulous, unknown!

In all, there were approaching twenty boys ranging in age from approximately six to sixteen years. It was not too long after our arrival when, with little fanfare, a collective but orderly shuffling movement by the gathered boys began with each moving towards a previously allocated seating position, leaving the two Richards standing abandoned, exposed. In my case anyway not knowing what to do next! We had both been talking together in the same hushed, conversational mode so neither of us was aware of the arrival of Mr C, who had walked into the hall, and gone straight to sit at the piano.

The sound of quiet talking faded to a hushed almost reverent, respectful silence, turning into full silence. A pause of expectant waiting with all assembled eyes now focused on the back of the head of the only adult in the room. We, the two Richards that is, were now completely obvious to the world due to our non-sitting posture!

A voice I later recognised as my friend Richard said, "Mr C, I have brought another boy from school!"

Almost twenty pairs of eyes turned in unison in my direction following my progress as I was led, head almost bowed, to stand next to this man seated at the piano. A final deep quiet settled over the gathering again as Mr C asked if I could sing. I felt more than could see an almost imperceptible, almost concealed rustle of limbs on chairs, stretching to hear my answer. "I think so", was the humble reply. Then, "can you sing this note?" he hit a key on the piano, (I did) Good! This one? (I did again) Good! Do you know 'Away in a manger' the Christmas carol? All the time the collective boys behind me watched, listened, quietly each appraising this new pretender – me. Although it was October with Christmas still forever away, an entire lifetime away in fact, he played an intro to the mentioned carol so I sang. I recollect, trying to look around at the boys seated behind, but I was held in fixed concentration due to also being not a little bit embarrassed. At the end of the first verse without warning he changed key, increasing the pitch! "Sing the same verse again" was the command as I stumbled to stay with him.

Each time I got to the end of the first verse, he changed key again, each time raising the pitch! Again, time after time until the pitch was so high that it became impossible for me to continue! I stopped somewhat out of breath, red faced not knowing what was expected next! In solitary desperation I sought, found, looked directly at my new friend Richard in that sea of expectant faces. He stood just to my right but slightly behind me, staring back at me with a huge grin across his face, his eyes shining encouragement.

Most boys' choirs of repute, throughout the world I think, work on the basis that the established choir members, not the master of the day, must first approve or 'elect' the entry of a 'new-boy' to the choir. So it was with this one. Mr C turned to the boys to ask them if they would accept me into their number. Instantly, new friend Richard's hand reached for the ceiling in the recognised gesture of approval. Support of several other boys soon followed; thus started a wonderful journey in voice training, breathing exercises and religious behaviour. Religious training lessons which also included lessons in Latin word appreciation. Not to mention music appreciation with sight-reading. All this was to be a part of my everyday existence for the next nine years or so!

Richard had explained to me on the way home that I was only accepted on a probationary level. Much would depend on me as to when, if ever, I would be able to be accepted to sing in the full choir. At that time Richard was himself a probationer learning the ropes. At that time we were two of just five new boys but became the only two to stay for more than a few weeks.

Thus the continuous request to all the local schools for any interested boys to audition. I remember arriving home that evening, somehow full of warm pride almost gushing forth to anyone who was there with my exciting news.

'Oh that's nice, your tea won't be ready for a while yet' together with things like 'singing' training each day except Monday, that's nice'. 'It's a long way to walk to St Marys'... as always the perfunctory response to the runt of the litter. This did however give me a freedom that I will always be very grateful for. A message to 'get on with your own life' which provided a licence much broader than that which had been given to big brother Greg.

So now I was singing, playing piano, sometimes allowed to make a noise on that huge organ at St Marys. Then I received a plastic guitar the Christmas just after my eighth birthday.

What a mistake Father Christmas made that year! Guitar playing Rock-n-Roll, that abomination of the then modern era, that heathen noise emanating from America was about to play its part in the youthful drive to change, leading the 1960s explosion for social political change. Due to the portability of a guitar, my determination to transfer what little capability I had from the piano onto this music making device became a very long passion. Indeed, it was not until losing movement in my hands due to an inherited problem as I approached my sixth decade that I was forced to abandon this determination, having not succeeded at all. Nevertheless, from that Christmas, the start of this instrument journey, I was to spend many hours of lonely practice in the kitchen of our home most evenings. Year following year for the next few years as well! Oh what a wonderful path had been chosen for me to follow.

Dear Reader, when or if you ever have the occasion to enjoy a service in a C-of-E 'High-Church' where there is a full male choir, or you amble into a church of this ilk or Cathedral to be accosted with wondrous sounds of melody in harmony, be aware of the hours of exhaustive training, almost every day every week, that has been undertaken to bring to you the quality of sound you will hear. Expect to hear clear crystal voices resonating in such an environment. Understand also that many boys work very hard for long periods with no guarantee that they will ever be included in any of this weeks', or even those of next weeks' services. Also understand that the adult portion of the choir has usually met to practice at a different place or time to the daily training of the younger section with the two parts only to come together just before a service! The selection of Hymns, chants, anthems all being made then logged in the everyday events programme long before 'today', reflecting the current portion of worship within the church calendar. This provides for some continuity within the church, its congregation, but can only be learned by new boys to the choir over some years. As a 'new boy' my confusion reigned! Most really good initial voice training for young (on probation) choir boys aspiring to be full-blown choir members has, at first appearance, nothing to do with singing. In fact, it was only after two months or so of attending afternoon 'practice' that I was to sing solo again in that church hall. By then I had become entranced by the sound emitted from some of the older boys. In those early days, I was constantly astonished each time I left practice walking into town or on my way home that 'over there', carrying his school stuff, was registered chorister Malcolm W who had the most amazing voice. There he was, a boy just simply walking along the street – no one knew him! No one stared at him or pointed to say "look, that's Malcolm W"!

Over my years in such illustrious company, many new boys joined us, and established choir members moved on to other greater choirs in the UK, to well respected Cathedral Schools across the country, others still to smaller environs. Malcolm W included. As could be expected, many a boy of promise who was elected to the probationary status of our choir faded away to relinquish their place in the choir. They left for many reasons.

Throughout my many long years in the choir, I was to be continuously, truly blessed by the sounds emanating from so wide a variety of long, short, clean, dirty, thin, fat, bright, dim individual boys from across the entire spectrum of our society. Some with blue eyes, others with brown, some with glasses others without, but all having voices that provided a range so enormous with such depth, that with little effort they could have inspired a town, even a nation. To be selected to sing in the 'first' choir at a service required one to dress in a long rich-blue Cassock (dress as sister Penny had called it) if you ever got that far, to place around your throat a starched white Ruff, with similar display of white at each cuff. This 'dressing-up' resulted in some boys questioning their participation in such activities. Also driving them away was the incessant training; each day at four-thirty or five pm – Tuesday to Friday, then seven am Saturday. On Sunday, seven am practice for the day followed by a minimum of three services, sometimes more subject to the season. This level of required commitment drove away many potentially good choir members, sometimes long-serving established members too. These later individuals no doubt found more 'manly' interests in which to participate that perhaps demanded less time commitment. It was always the magic of the sounds that held me, transfixed me. This was to be reflected in my long-term commitment to the choir.

The calming of emotions or fears inherent in the music, the feeling of solidity, of foundation but always with heart thumping amazement that I was a part of it all, that was what captured me, and held me in this world until my departure from the choir in the summer before my seventeenth birthday.

Breathing! Stretching arms, stretching shoulders, standing erect, standing still, arms stretched out as if reaching for each side of the world, more Breathing! Swallowing, hold your breath, standing straight. Breathing, running on the spot, STOP breathing, Keep Running! Breathing! Sing those scales, hold that note, hold it still, still, keep the volume, hold the air, still – STOP breathing – hold it still! Now slowly, inhale! Take a long deep breath open your mouth wide DO NOT LET OUT THE AIR! Hold it – hold it! Slowly now release, oh so very slowly! Scales – one breath up now, hold that note— hold it! Softly, sweetly, now LOUD hard! Do not let out that breath! Hold your breath boy! Now down to middle 'C' –hold it! Hold it! Hold it! OK now relax. September, October, November, all through the winter into next spring, throughout the summer then back to winter – September, October, November! Breathing to sing!

One breathing control exercise that proved to be the making of some or the breaking of many others during my association with this choir was known as 'The Mist'. I will try to explain in words the physical process of 'The Mist' knowing however that I lack sufficient skill to define in words, the sheer depth of emotional impact on all participants. Only during the cold winter months could 'The Mist' be used to real effect. Not only was it strenuous beyond imagining but by its very nature, had to be out in the cold in full public view!

Usually this activity by the selected choir would only take place in the early mornings of Saturday or Sunday or before any of the special Christmas services. These public exhibitions by the choir on Christmas Day often attracted the crowds on their way to the next service who would stop, and listen to the choir sound before moving into the church. There are, I know, photographs of us standing outside in the snow preparing for midnight mass on the 24th of December using 'The Mist'. Being involved in this was a really great way to warm the voice as well as body prior to any service at this time of the year. Other photographs were taken of us standing outside surrounded by ground covered in frost or looking like ghosts emerging from the foggy air-frost conditions in the early mornings.

Here is how it works.

Having all taken a single breath, we would all sing the same note for a 'time-target' that constantly moved!

First it would be fifteen seconds. Twenty seconds. Thirty seconds followed by 'who can last a whole minute'! One minute! One minute more! During these time segments, all of us held the same single high note. Between the extended time-targets on occasion was a command to return to thirty seconds at the next note! Or ten seconds at the next! Each boy taking just a single breath before each note! Three minutes! Very few could hold a note or even a single breath for that long! Again, then again! The last of us to stop at the end of each note in this madness became some fake hero for just a short while!

Why 'The mist?'

In the production of each note, breath was not allowed to be seen escaping from any mouth! So imperceptive had to be the release that it was only possible if just a gentle waft of exhaled air was properly controlled from each open mouth. Not just singing a constant note but also controlling the air output at the same time.

However, the sound level had to remain fully constant at the instructed level from FULL BLAST to tiny whisper! From lip-tingling humming of an A or M or O or U! Expelled air must simply drift, hiding from view, slipping bashfully away from each wide open mouth. Watching this was, I am told, like seeing a very thin slowly moving piece of fine softest silk moving over then down the lower lip of each boy. This 'Mist' gently following the contours of the chin of each boy before sleeking unhurriedly away like a departing lover before dawn with oh, such sweet reluctance! All the time the crystal-clear chosen note, depending on the current volume instruction, echoed, resonating around Church

Square. It was reflected evenly from nearby gravestones to bounce back across the square hitting cottage walls on all sides, seeming to gather more strength from each blocked direction. A single sound, one clear note multiplied by surroundings seeming, attempting to be, the conveyor of life into winter sleeping tress, caressing the pathways to the church doors. John C would move along the line of boys who were all identically dressed in the choir uniform standing just outside the hall on the path to the front entrance to the church, with a glint of passion in his eyes. Maybe perhaps even a tear? Resonance was not allowed to change with the meeting of each target! Ice cold air gulped down, wide open throat filling tired lungs with rapid urgency (one breath) now hold, now repeat!

The real enchantment for any listeners though was when after what seemed to us to be an eternity singing the one note we switched to a static harmony. The boys were grouped to switch, on a hand signal from John C, to a five or six-part harmony made up of a constant note from each section to the single note sound. Again each boy/group stretching to reach a set time-target for a single breath! Although these times may have seemed to each of us that were participating in them some form of sadistic torture, devised then constantly perpetuated by that non-human genius musician Choir Master, I clearly remember the exhilaration, the fear of failure, the absolute need for each of us to prove that, 'I could do this'! And the really warm internal glow of achievement on reaching the target, the often hidden, shameless, secret pride when others failed along the way!

Exacting? Oh yes, but the results were there for all to hear.

My first three months as a probationer in the choir then were as if I did not exist. I carried books, turned music pages at the piano, spent hours learning breathing techniques, trying to hold single notes for seemingly an eternity at a time. Stretching to build a straight back to ensure that I would maintain the best posture needs. None of the latter ever really stopped as the years rolled on. The only difference or change experienced by me, or any other, was that of 'status' change within the group as we completed voice exams, exams of a written nature for sight-reading plus the practical voice note recognition/ replication 'tests'. These were at a recognised national standard level, all part of progressing toward that coveted status of Registered Chorister! Also, each younger boy was constantly seeking recognition of his peers alongside that from members of the main choir, with of course that of the choir master.

Even having reached the main choir, further training was essential to become a 'lead', requiring ongoing dedication, constant voice training, learning followed by tests. In addition, ability to 'play an instrument' was simply a requirement for being accepted then to be inducted as a member of the Royal College of Church Music as a Registered Chorister. Just before the age of twelve, this honour was finally bestowed on me in a dedicated special section of the one Sunday morning service at St Mary's.

Now obviously my family, parents, siblings were aware that Richard sang in the church but I cannot recall other than once, any interest in this activity whatsoever. I know that my participation in the choir was to mean that I would spend a lot of time out of the house. So I record here that the very first time my mother was to hear my solo voice in that august place, was as a result of an invitation to attend my induction as a chorister. This absolute lack of any interest in me or my activities was simply standard practice, so to think or even suggest that such lack of interest in any way scarred me at all, I must deny as a possibility. My parents never attended a parents' evening at any time throughout my entire schooling period. I had become accustomed to being on my own, being my own person on so many such occasions. Thus it was that by the age of 11, nearly 12 years old, I had already accepted the existence of an inevitable growing void between me, my parents, even my siblings. This latter statement is a very convoluted way to let you, my wonderful reader, know that they 'didn't give-a-care!' Throughout all the years I was to sing solo at many churches across many counties in England. At services at school, in music recitals, I stood shoulder to shoulder with the other Richard singing, playing, studying (Ha!) and generally growing up. He, the choir, with all that we did collectively, started replacing my family as the principal influence on me as life-time marched on. Each week from that initial audition onward, week after week, year after year, as a member of the choir on very many 'happy' occasions, I would sing (get paid for even!) at weddings. Each Saturday during the slightly warmer periods found within the months of May to October in England, my capacity to earn real money with my voice allowed me a small level of financial freedom, not just to spend on Bonfire Wars or Bonfire Nights, but to buy sweets and books but more importantly train tickets! The latter taking me to local stations just for the fun of it, then initially just sometimes all the way to London. There I walked the famous or infamous streets of the big, bad city, all alone. My vice had given me even more freedom to explore my world.

There are many instances, some unique, others repetitive remaining in my memory today that will always allow me an opportunity to call on some of the spectacular things that happened during those choir singing years. Bells frozen solid, followed by a silly jingle, is just such a typical fun memory!

January, it was really cold. Snow lay unusually deep. Where it had been cleared to the side of road or path, a freezing ice layer had developed to form a hard crust. Leaking pipes were now not leaking at all, not due to repair but because the water inside was frozen solid! Our outside 'boys-only' toilet however, whilst still working, simply had much larger ice stalactites pointed down at the temporary male visitor with even more grotesque intent. Yet, as if in defiance of the elements, a young couple chose this month for their wedding! Never privy to the reason for or even times requested for the service to take place, we were simply summoned (selected actually) on this majestic winter Saturday morning. The church was almost full, my "Oh for the Wings of a Dove" still resounding high in the rafters as I returned with proper grace, bearing the solemnity of the occasion, to my place amongst my chosen peers. Movement, a church steward, leans whispering to John C. The congregation waits expectantly for the arrival of the newly married couple from the vestry after signing the register. Next was to be the all-important triumphant march down through the full length of the church past their family, their friends, to exit the building through the enormous double wooded West Doors of this magnificent edifice. A march to be accompanied by the booming sound of 12 bells high in the belfry! John C rushed from his place at the organ to the attending curate who is also awaiting the entourage that will be preceded by his boss – the Cannon. More urgent whispering! The curate running down the full length of the church to the bell ropes off to the left of the West Door. Not a single campanologist in sight apparently! Actually they were there but were busy attempting to actually get one or two of the bells to ring. Some had climbed up the circular stairs to inspect the bells because no matter how hard they tried, they could not move them. Apparently one of ringers was a local fireman who had inspected the bells earlier that morning only to have found that one or two of the metal wheel things through which the ropes rode when pulled, were frozen to the axel. He had taken it upon himself to try to warm the central spindle of the bells without too much luck! Prior to the commencement of the service, he together with his colleagues, had managed to un-freeze most of the non-performing machine parts. The usual peeling of welcome prior to the service seemed to confirm that all was well. Put another way, nobody noticed anything wrong at the time! The bells had not been used at all throughout the service of course so our bell-ringing colleagues just sat to await the triumphant march at the end of the show! Judging when this march was about to happen, they pulled on one of the ropes only to find that the bells' movement had again frozen. Thus the sudden panic! After all, the couple starring in this particular show, had paid for the ringing of the bells, the churches across the world are good businesses. Anyway the rope-dancers were there to perform then receive payment for such performance. As time to the final moment was fast approaching there seemed to be nothing else at hand. The bell ringers were aloft trying to manipulate the reluctant peelers!

Above the heads of the waiting congregation just towards the end of this choir boys' solo piece, a CRUMP! SNAP! THUD! SPLINTER! JARING BONG noise was heard! Apparently it was discovered that part of the wooden support structure holding one set of the 12 bells, ranging in size from little 'ping' to giant 'boom', having been standing for many, many generations, took its vengeance on this rude violation of its space, deciding to collapse at one end! The result, a wedding, but no triumphant march accompanied by the crisp sound of joyous bells across the countryside announcing to all the arrival in the state of marriage – the happy couple! Just one poor man, an unfortunate bell ringer, who had his foot caught as the structure collapsed around him.

The happy couple however were greeted by bells as they emerged from the church porch out into the world together as a married couple for the first time. Due to the injury to the bell ringer, his fireman bell ringing colleague had left the church, run across the place of the dead that surrounded the church to a public phone box located at one corner to dial 999! The new couple having paid handsomely to hear the special peel of bells were greeted on leaving the church by the single somewhat shrill sound of the ambulance bell as it raced towards them to collect the injured party.

Here then was a world of activities, interests, outside my family. Difficult or hard study, frustration, friendship but most of all, understanding, not challenging even replying in gentleness to my constant questioning!

So, now alongside that separate life at home, Mrs, P, Music (Piano, Guitar), the very magical Percy, Bonfire

Nights, Snowball Wizards all this Choir Singing activity, all this ran concurrently! Oh yes, my official education was also underway. It was not too long before I learned how to keep a low profile at school, soon keeping myself about the average pupil until the next big mistake I made early in my Senior School career one day.

Having to some extent been a part of so many couples' happy days, I often wondered how many of those whom the Cannon in our church had 'joined together forever' – sometimes as many as five couples on a single day, on behalf of his God – had at some time later been 'separated' forever by man without any reference to any God! The thought of all those young women, some beautiful whilst others simply looking their personal best on their one (supposedly) special day, those often blushing, sometimes fragile looking young (mostly) women who had smiled so very serenely at whoever was the soloist on the occasion of their marriage, who went on to live the dream or would be haunted by what might have been. How many were destined to be used, sadly abused then discarded, cheated on then loathed? As soloist on such occasions I would concentrate on nothing other than my voice, always embarrassed if requested to stand alone to sing. However, standing alone in front of the two young people to sing on their day was a way of having significant impact on them. I sincerely hope their joint dream at the time won through all the trials that life would throw at them. Whilst this man-child had little or even no regard at that time for adult male/female relationships, no real knowledge of life behind the closed doors of the matrimonial home, I was aware, had a knowing foreboding deep inside, an opaque view if you will of some of the things that could cause such shared joy to be dashed, or 'cast asunder'. I had no understanding of the external, erotic or not, threats to each of the individual members in a marriage or what they may face together or separately as the years rolled around. But how could anyone with any human compassion, smash, bash, cheat or hurt in any way those young women?

I do remember also thinking clearly during my final choir years, my early to mid-teenage years as a red bloodied male adolescent, that if I didn't hurry there would be no 'oh-so-beautiful' women left for me when I wanted to wed! This, after my own innocence had been lost, my body changed, brains dipping, slipping south to explore the new rich hormones that were driving me closer, inch by inch, to be near or in the company of young women. Like all good males at the time, my voice also attempted to drop as did certain other body parts together with my brain. In the early years of singing at weddings though I was still a boy when all girls of my age were plain, spotty with no display of curves at all! I do recall conversations I sometimes was privy to where Chris would agree with Andrew about being suitably impressed by one Carol C who lived just around the corner in Prebendal Avenue. Carol was much older than me but still I had been drawn to her quite full, fascinating with lots of smooth interesting body curves – especially for a fifteen or sixteen year old girl. I remember seeing her several years later, silently approving of what a shape she had become! It seemed at the time though that most girls of the age twelve to mid-teens had faces that must have been resting or nesting places for some strange insects that repeatedly left faces covered in pink (though not scratched or picked) spots!

The sound of a single well trained boy-soprano voice trilling around the high vaulted rafters of St Mary's in Aylesbury where I was lucky enough to sing during those years, still manages to evoke in me a spontaneous reaction of goose bumps along my arms, down my back, across my neck, in recognition of the emotions such a sound can often awaken in its listeners. There were times it was difficult for any one of us boys not to be moved at the sight of tears on the faces of total strangers in our congregation at Sunday services, weddings, or christenings.

Singing at funerals however, even though quite sporadic, required a solemnity for the occasion by all boys attending. Maintaining a stone, poker face countenance at all times.

The illusion of a young boy clean, chaste, with apparent angelic voice to match his apparent untouched maleness, was often just too much for some. Whilst it was our strict intent to provide the level of respect demanded by our choirmaster, outside the church it was difficult to always maintain that 'dear thing' image. As a choir member, there were very strict levels of behaviour taught then expected when inside or near the church, dressed in choir cassocks, hair combed or not, as well as expected 'good' behaviour when in civilian clothes away from the church. Proper, social performance must be displayed at all times. As indicated before, there was extensive training in the choir covering all aspects of religion, specific religious doctrine, deportment, generally including an instruction in the 'finer' areas of etiquette in all expectations of the then civil society as depicted or currently interpreted by the C-of-E. My knowledge of things religious along with, in particular, how man was 'expected' to treat his fellow man and that man was made in the image of God, initially created such a wonderful picture in my early days as a choir member. But you already know Dear Reader do you not, that I, the stupid, stupid boy that I was, always wanted to know, to appreciate more of anything I found of real interest at any time! Any subject of interest, I could never, nor would ever stop digging until my desire to understand, measure then challenge if needed, was satisfied! This insatiable need drove all around me to distraction but of course in particular, those within the Church who had a variety of both public as well as their own private agendas!

It was not to be too long before my eyes together with other personal 'gifts' supplied me with a very different view of humanity in general, specifically, a broader comprehension of the 'behind-the-scenes' environment in the church. (Proof again that 'familiarity indeed may breed contempt'). I was soon to learn that the statement attributed to a very tired, exhausted Christ 'suffer the little children for they alone shall inherit the Earth' may have been true, but in the world of the present day – only by political expediency linked to selection coupled with social status or educational standard, would individual progress along the ladder of authority be possible! With progress through the ranks of the choir together with an own accepted status as a 'good boy', came a trusted status offering some access to areas or people that perhaps others were not privy to. Slowly, awareness of the day-to-day, often bitter, often very twisted inside track of the people who 'were' the church, from the lowest of the low lay-person to those in exalted high places in the ecumenical command-chain, crept into my consciousness. A deep illness was rife, hidden yes but as real as the stone walls of the church. An internal conflict for personal gain which had itself been a part of the fabric of the institution since the stones for the walls of this magnificent building had been hewn from the earth. A constant conflict driven of pride, of greed, of seeking recognition, of secret domination whilst all without exception outwardly preaching human love, human understanding, human comfort, shared fellowship! This non-public, persona, raising yet more questions in me that demanded I seek answers and finally with sad realisation, smashing all sweet innocence of childhood in my mind! There were, over the years, continuous revelations of the corrupted attitudes of the old, together with some not so old churchmen. Stories kept as the property of the church that raised questions about the sincerity (a word commencing with SIN) of men at the very heart of this social institution.

All the politics, Christian church members who constantly polished the sharpened, sometimes theoretical knives to stab, to achieve, perhaps to enrich at the cost of others when clambering over, up toward the next perceived 'best' rung of an imagined ladder, to greater personal import or heavenly placing! These fights had for generations also existed among local families of apparent 'good' breeding having social or financial standing! Generation after generation of local 'important' families ensuring that the historical behaviour or social positioning of their ancestors was not wasted, by getting closer to their God via the physical location in the church of their 'family' pew. 'Our' family gives more among the congregation and thus expects to be regarded by all with respect or import! Such sentiment overtly or covertly expressed never, ever ceased to amaze me! I became aware sometimes of (sick) private laughter in the offices or vestries directed at the real people who really did believe in salvation, perhaps seeking solace at a time of personal crisis. They may have been fobbed-off quickly because it was drinking time so not very 'convenient', the incumbent man of cloth 'indisposed', unable to help or offer guidance. For 'indisposed' read drunk!

All of this was to entrench in me a violent reaction, a permanent deep disgust at the lies in a place where truth is the espoused fundamental! This knowledge forced me to build and to live within my own moral code based on me, not any book, not even a holy one. Based on the way I wanted to be, the way I wanted to treat the world of people, hopefully with respect, dignity, without fear or violence or intimidation.

Not some counterfeit ideology employing fear to the populace, advocated even practiced by the few for their own personal benefit with control over the many!

I, the real me had to know, had to understand within me, that if I were to make a promise to another human, there must only be one reason for me not to see such a promise through to its conclusion. Thus developed a very private but comprehensive range of the way I would act or react to whatever life was to present to me. I agreed with me, a contract for life, that I would never knowingly let down another human. I would never knowingly fashion a situation that would humiliate anyone! Or abandon, or discard those dependent on or relying on me. Nor will I seek revenge or pass judgement on any other or refuse to offer a helping hand when needed if I had the resources to do so. This is how

I shall be judged, if I am ever to face any external personal judgement. I am of no significant importance where other people are concerned but if in need of my truth, it would be given without question until no longer needed. Thus at thirteen years or so of age, I started to search for my own truth, my own foundation where 'truth' was not to be bent by or for expedient reaction or statement; my own sense of moral code in my behaviour with or towards others. A beginning of a very long journey with many failures, but also providing a quiet peace as the development of my person life truth took hold. Discipline, church indoctrination, music, singing training together with a strict family environment had by then, battered me into someone semi-human who, although has had such a wonderful, albeit sheltered life, would not knowingly harm anyone but engage in only those rules of civil society that I deemed as fair or good. Challenging all others when needed and take responsibility. I guess that, if asked, this was the prime legacy of all these described growing-up years together with that constant urgent internal need to 'read-between-the-lines', to question the answers received constantly about all things.

This is the very essence of me.

Throughout all the above, my life continued to pass as normal as any other with school, some football, not too much, with tennis, a little cricket, always closing my mouth when attempting to catch a high ball. Sharing many fun times together with Richard in or out of the choir; cinema visits, trips on trains, although the latter was often just me wandering around London on my own. Normal illnesses afflicted us, some easier than others to overcome. I once drank a whole bottle of sweet tasting pink liquid penicillin simply because it had a great taste! Shock! Horror...nothing happened! Dr G (the one always allowed to enter our house through that special front door) rushed to visit, finding me sitting on the stairs where he asked a lot of questions, poked, prodded then told my mother to just watch me. If anything happens to contact him immediately!

Then one day at nine years old entering the kitchen on this school day morning seeking some breakfast, my mother looked around at me as I came in then after a few seconds asked if my face was very sore? No, not at all said I, why?

I didn't make school that day. Instead the next six weeks were spent in the children's isolation ward section at Stoke Mandeville Hospital being further prodded or poked by all manner of interested humans. All who were to be allowed to enter my room however were hidden behind white face masks with feet in special shoes, whilst wrapped head to toe in surgical gowns topped-off with sterile head coverings. Injections every six hours, or as it happened with me, at exactly midnight, six am, midday, six pm, then midnight again. Day after day for six weeks! Exposing my buttocks or thighs to all-comers who were carrying needles in kidney bowls! My life took on a new shape! By night to enter sleep only to be shocked awake with a needle in bum or thigh at midnight then at six am. Great start to each day.

As midday approached wishing time would stop but failing as the nurse arrived in my room on schedule carrying that ugly shaped dish armed with needle!

Read, hide under the sheets awaiting the next jab. Throughout this time in hospital, the world continued to live beyond my isolation room windows, ignorant of my pitiful state!

Without any pain whatsoever, I had managed as a child to develop an adult infection referred to as 'Streptococci Gingivitis'. This affliction is usually only seen in adults of senior age who suffer from swollen bleeding gums, falling teeth, all accompanied apparently with plenty of pain.

Here was little me, no blood, no falling teeth but gums so swollen that eventually my lips could hardly meet! The antibiotics resolved the swelling but was not at all assisted by the huge amount of poking, prodding, swab-taking or the x-raying. Those allowed in attendance to this child trying to discover what had inflicted itself on my mouth, finally made a discovery that I had not got just one set of teeth, not just two sets but was the proud, albeit reluctant owner of THREE sets of adult teeth! As each milk tooth fell, three replacements were ready to march into the breach to replace the one now gone! Other than taking some out to make room for others over the years, our dentist had, until then of course, failed to notice this state of affairs and thus address the potential problems of this array of eating implements hiding in my gums!

This strange bug, this interloper in my mouth, multiplied so fast that it had destroyed almost all the nerve-endings in my gums. This disaster, this terrible unseen bug also attacked the nerve-endings in each tooth so it was that I experienced several multi-tooth extractions over a period of time. The result? The infection was finally cleared. A note was handed to my parents at the end of this enforced solo stay in hospital concluding that in the view of the attending specialists, the chances of me having any of my own teeth by the end of my teens were remote indeed. The damage done by this strange bug was of such grave concern. I remember being reasonably upset at the prospect at the time but soon lost any caring on the matter at all. Six weeks off school followed by the long summer holiday period what more could a boy want? On returning home from hospital, there were just less than three weeks of the academic year left so I was officially excused. A reward perhaps for the time lost or maybe a small fear that so little was known about the infliction that it was thought best to keep me away until the start of the new academic year in September.

At the time of my hospitalisation, the open ground beyond our back garden at home was being developed to become a new Presbyterian Church. Construction was well underway on my return home, with builders, cement mixers, front-end loaders, steel scaffolding, wooden planks aplenty, all reflecting the building process. Continuous shouting of men across the rising building, lots of movement with much hammering throughout each day. With not too much to occupy me, I watched through the garden fence this edifice grow.

Some of the builders, realising that I had become a regular visitor or watcher to their progress, started to wave or to say hello to me. Then one day I noticed there was a regular member of their bricklaying team who had not said anything to me at all, just giving a nod of his head from time to time with a faint smile. His role seemed to be to collect bricks from the stacked pile just beyond our fence. He had a long metal pole with a very wide 'V' on the end into which he would load many bricks, then lift this long pole up with the V over his shoulder to carry this weight to the nearest scaffolding ladder. Here he would climb the ladder, placing the bricks on the platform for the bricklayers to use. After watching him do this for some days, I changed my daily 'wave' of hello, to a verbal one but only received a sort of 'grunt' in return. This happened several times until one day, with some time on his hands possibly, he came over to me at the fence making 'signs' that I soon managed to interpret that he couldn't speak or hear.

Here was to be my first known contact with a real person not just unable to speak but also not able to hear. As my own confidence grew with this newfound friend, I started to ask questions of this individual, having soon learned that he was able to 'lip-read' if I spoke slowly. He was really good at 'lip-reading' so was happy to share with me, using a massive amount of patience, some basic sign-language. After a few sessions using lots of gestures, and making many mistakes, we found a way to communicate that allowed us to become friends. He wanted to know my name so using a stick in one hand whilst pointing at himself he wrote the following in the sand 'ERIC'. I then wrote 'Richard' pointing at myself. From that moment on, Eric always attempted to say my name aloud when we first met. I do know that with the pronunciation so often being just a sound blur, I did learn to learn to encourage him by saying how good the sound was. Eric invited me to help carry bricks, showed me how to hold three bricks in my hands then throw them to him to catch…no gloves used by either of us! Also he showed me how to throw this same number of bricks from the ground up to where he was standing on the first level scaffolding platform. After a while I was able to throw three bricks simultaneously that he could catch! Between us we didn't break too many! Away from school, heading towards the summer holidays, I received an education that few children ever have the chance to! Climbing, standing on scaffolding, throwing bricks but more importantly, learning that people such as Eric, although unable to hear or speak properly, were just the same as the rest of us. In fact, many would suggest that they have proven long before us that such disabilities are there to be beaten. Oh how I wished that there could be some way for Eric to hear music, or singing, a very important lesson, more so than any other, as to how very fortunate my life was. Once the brick-work was completed on the church, Eric moved on to the next construction where bricks were being used. I did not see him again.

Mr Alan G!

At about eleven years old I was invited to participate in a culture festival run by the Buckinghamshire county education department. It was during this youth weekend event that I first met the then County Drama Adviser – Mr Alan G! It was not until about a year later that we were to meet again at a 'Mime Drama' event directed by one Mr Alan G. I was later to learn that Alan was a well-respected professional actor, who had abandoned his profession to work with 'talented' children all over the 'Home Counties' which of course are very close to London. His work had been very well publicised with a number of television appearances and performances including for many local (Rep) theatre productions. In addition, Alan had written two books on the journey of talent in young people of the day. By chance it seemed he had simply walked into my life. My hometown is just forty miles from London, so many people from the entertainment industry lived in or between the towns or villages in the countryside around the Chiltern Hills, including the Vale of Aylesbury.

These locations provided easy access via train to the city with a number of the then major UK film studios also located nearby; Denham studios in Buckinghamshire is just one example. Roald Dahl, Sir John Gielgud, David Tomlinson were just a few of a collection of famous nearby residents, along with many other celebrities from the performing arts.

From when I was about eleven years old until his death some seven years later, Alan became my real introduction to the world of theatre, acting, miming, shape movement. He seemed to see in me – his words – 'a stage presence rarely seen', a 'status of character' in my acting ability. He led me to the world of theatre, to being a student at the Bristol Old Vic Theatre School. It was to be with Alan, that I was able to travel across the country, when not committed to school or choir or music making, working with a very talented group of young performers some 18 strong, presenting sections of classic or modern plays to schools located in villages or towns. It was as a member of this group that I stood in front of cameras in a production of a mime drama based on the final days of Christ. It was as a member of this group that I first travelled to Germany to present traditional English youth drama works with music in a cultural youth education exchange programme.

All of this taking place at a time when I was making music, singing, schooling, eating, sleeping, in fact just living like everyone else! Well, perhaps not washing too often! Throughout this time I was constantly drained by the more important development issue of my physically growing up. In reality, with 'twenty-twenty' hindsight, my divorce from my family with the subsequent independent development of me began at that wonderful time when Mrs. P had entered my little life.

The separation wedge was driven further between us by my participation in the choir, the determination of John C to enlist my voice as an asset to him with Richard T supporting me all the way. Finally, taken fully away into a world that had no place in my family – acting, by someone as special as Alan G all helped towards sealing my future – well at least until at twenty years of age, my need to live up to the emotional promise to myself, the moral standard I had set for myself, the follow my heart truth never to let down another human, allowed for me to close my eyes to this world, to follow my heart in changing my life forever. I married my wife Eileen.

Looking back on my life between the ages thirteen to twenty I can say without conflict that I saw, achieved, met, had the pleasure to be with, to learn from so many very talented people. During my teenage period, I visited many amazing places, perhaps experiencing more in those few years than most ever have the opportunity to do in a lifetime.

Early Teens to suitcase in hand!

Spots!

I really waited for them to arrive!

Well why not?

Almost everyone else had them! Their very existence on one's face was therefore something of a symbol, a sign, a badge of office indicating a sort of early 'man' status. I was missing out! Something was very wrong with me. My sweat glands were working, that was a fact, but my pores, those tiny apertures destined to be the dispenser of unwanted icky stuff living inside this growing male human-kind, did not once get clogged with gumph.

This can't be happening!

I was being passed over, ignored, not even given the option of choice for this particular 'growing-up' joy-of-joys! How I recall the rich emotion of envy as I watched with polite contempt those of my peers so afflicted, who surreptitiously attempted to hide their personal horror. They did however have every intention of showing their corrupted potted faces to all. After all it was a matter of pride! Which itself, at the individual level, created a conflict. On one's own a level of shame for this ugly infliction. However, with one's peers, a show of pride! This wanting to hide but show – a simultaneous desire – was evident in many of my friends. All the boys around me were seeking to gain public peer affection for owning the most ugly, the most repulsive eruption of the day. You know, those gorgeous, lumpy pus-filled ones, as well as those that are the small next to the large, lying prominently side by side on the same face. Some white with strange red or yellow coloured dots whilst others were red with white or milky-blue dots. Then the 'grotesque of the day' in the often really good shock award, winning the 'best' "open" ones that seeped multi-coloured gooey glutinous stuff!

Me? Nothing!

Just no spots, plain, pale-faced me taking a back seat on these joyous hide or show confrontations. Morning after frustrating morning, the same sweet clear creation with eyes would stare back at me from our bathroom mirror. Mockingly this unwanted reflection smashed the expectation of joy that nightly dreams had created providing a wishful awakening expectation.

There I was following such dream inspired expectation, an almost excited hope, that just one of the ugliest, the largest, bloodiest facial explosions of pus ran wild on my countenance but – NO SPOTS! NOT TODAY! Keep dreaming young punk! Day after day, off I would trudge to school, my head hung low in desperate shame from the lack of facial mountainous perfusions. I would often attempt to hide the publicly exposed areas of me, hunching shoulders, chin tucked in shirt collar or scarf wrapped around my face as the other boys had. I was now excluded from the peer group with whom I was sharing my puberty period. There I was, excluded from the spotty experiences that were being seen, discussed by others as a perfectly normal way to start each day.

Normally, that first meeting each day behind the bicycle shed for the showing of the newly arrived during last night skin blemish, together with the previously picked scabs, was a practice undertaken with a huge amount of verbosity mixed with swollen pride! Discussion, laughter, 'mine look worse than yours' mixed of course with the whiff of smoke from a stolen cigarette. As was the showing off for inspection of yet another oily eruption on the side of a left nostril, I could do nothing other than mentally crawl away with my clean, fresh face for I was not to be a part of the ugly 'in group'. Whilst I experienced all the other strange even wonderful bodily changes, my entry into my journey through these early teenage years was marred by the continued absence of abscesses or of pus-eruptions of any sort on any part of my body, not just my face. Those other less conspicuous – meaning not on public display therefore lacking in trophy hunting conversations with others so afflicted with the dreaded but secretly wanted spots – changes moved in quiet recognition that progress was being made on my personal journey from child to adolescent man. Hair appeared in places where virgin white skin had been the norm. Armpits, groin areas grew progressively darker.

At the same time, a fine fluff sprouted around the lower portions of my face, nowhere near to being visible but present nonetheless. Up to this point in my life, having a history of being a primarily soft, generally dangling personal gender identifier, my middle appendage now started to develop an often-time inconvenient movement programme all of its own – a sort of better than stirring but not yet fully operational attempt to stand for its design rights! Having soon to experience the sudden arrival attention of the, initially rather cold hand of dear Sandra C, clearly learning its real place of importance in my existence would not take it too long at all. Which statement I must now confess also proved true of its ability to perform fully as designed!

Also, combined with the appendage development, the lower spheres that would generate billions of life creation opportunities for the rest of my life had, lowered. This, together with the correct, much improved blood flow to, and then from that particular region of my body ensured that all was as it should be.

But not a single bloody pimple arose to challenge my clearness of face, not a spot seen anywhere! "White Boy Virgin" was a title, amongst others I acquired during this period. Such a title separated me from the pack and that in a strange way compensated for my inability to be a full active participant in the face spot eruption parade! This same title was adopted by many of my fellow choir members adding to the growing awareness that I was somehow unclean, not pure because of the no-show spots. Strange boy!

I doubt the absence of such natural wonders visually reflecting the effects of the human chemical change of development, was due to some unexplained consumption by me of a secret or as of yet unidentified spot eroding, pus excluding stuff.

I had eaten, had drunken (forgive me) from the same trench as my male siblings. Therefore, little had been imbibed by me that was not effused in the blood streams of the whole 'Band of Brothers from number 44'. I had even shared their space during the period when each had paced the streets proudly exposing THEIR spots to any interested parties. Even to this day I have continued to be denied the dubious pleasures of or indeed access to, if any, the benefits of that status-defining, life changing outward experience – acne! I suspect that being devoid of this affliction has, over the years, enabled me to often jest that having 'missed out' on this portion of the metamorphosis, I was never a real teenager. In fact, perhaps this particular outward definition of child-to-man development may also indicate that, as yet, I have still to reach full maturity – although I doubt that to be true from a physical perspective.

However, some who have known me for a few years now would today be very likely to concur that I remain or retain something of the child in my everyday demeanour. They may also express concern that should I develop the dreaded spots at this late stage, any attempt by me to undertake the final conversion to a teenager must be avoided at all costs!

To compound the impression of non-visible development, thus confirming to the world that somehow very little was actually changing, my voice, now a fully recognised instrument in its own right anyway, was also deprived of the often funny, often sweet but always embarrassing slip/slide of pitch changes that all males go through as a part of this physical adjustment period of growing up. Over many hours and during many months, not just me but other choirboys as well; Mr. C 'trained' each voice down with determined dedication to retain as much of the 'soprano' ability as possible. Training down was really nothing more than very hard voice control work outside of, therefore in addition to, normal practice!

It was generally a scale exercise, soft in the middle but pushing hard to hold single notes of the top or the bottom of each boy's range. We were introduced to the falsetto sound then spent time learning to use this, moving from octave to octave. Apparently such activity on a regular basis – twice daily – acted as a sort of controlled 'stretching', 'thickening', 'slacking off' of the vocal chords. The object was twofold. One, as previously said, to prolong the boy soprano ability further into the teenage period than would normally be the case, whilst at the same time attempting to create for the singer, a comfortable ability to change tenor into falsetto then visa-versa, making such a change sound as natural as possible. The only thing I recall about this rude interruption of a natural human bodily change was that often it didn't work!

The unwanted result of all the hard scale work manifesting itself during the presentation of a solo piece by the unfortunate boy who would suddenly break into a slip-slide of a note, which would waft around the rafters of the church hall or, as on one or two occasions – in the church itself! The appalling, devastating result was that such an uncalled for abrasion of purity caused huge grief for the poor unfortunate boy. Imagine, if you will, the loud breaking of wind in a passage of silence by one amongst a group of say twenty boys ranging in age from six to seventeen, with the resultant inability for some amongst the gathering, if not all of them, to remain outwardly calm and not collapsing into fits of hysterics! Such similar outbursts were uncontrollable when an event such as a slip/slide note penetrated the explicit defined order of trained voice melodic! Just one of the many trials and tribulations of being a choirboy!

But it was this very wonderful ability to sing, together with playing, reading music enough to make something of a noise on a piano, organ or guitar by then, that was to shape my world in so many different ways.

It was 1961 in England! Well actually it was 1961 all over the world but in England it was the beginning of the infamous, the dark, the bright, the happy, the light – Oh hell – it was the "SIXTIES"! Yes, I was an early teenager in that wonderful period of substantial change, driven mainly by those 'baby-boomers' who were now in their late teens or early twenties, educated, demanding a different world, following on from the devastation created by "Look Back In Anger", a play that shook the very foundation of the then established British civil society. 'Kitchen Sink' reality on public display! The four year period from May 1956 when the play first opened in London included the advent of Rock-n'-Roll a modern music that was an irritant to the authority of the day but by its very nature, was 'pop' with the powerful emerging 'new adult' community. Pirate Radio stations in full disregard to government controlled broadcasting took to the airwaves. Young workers' demands for a real better deal erupted across England. The volcano of pent up dreams accompanied by suppressed emotions burst forth spraying CHANGE then more CHANGE forcing a nation to listen, to take notice! This was the decade that spawned outrageous new designs in teenage clothing, free love, the boom in illegal drug use, in effect, drugs-for-all – a prelude to the 'Good Morning Vietnam' attitude of the next decade! It included Elvis, swaying his hips, clean Cliff Richard, then came four guys from Liverpool with strange haircuts – the magic of 'She Loves You' or 'I want to hold your hand". Miniskirts, sounds of the Mersey, all with London's new fashion centre, Carnaby Street! England – Rosy-Red-Cheeks, all supported across the arts world including the musical 'HAIR' with everything swinging free! An explosion of colour together with popular protests at all things considered communally oppressive! Flower Children with 'Free Love', the introduction of – THE PILL!

Here was I, at thirteen years young, playing guitar, piano, acting, singing with a voice recognised by a mighty royal musical institution, a registered chorister of the RCCM.

It cannot then be too difficult to understand that my life was set to be so very different from my siblings.

The youth theatre group that I was attached to via Alan G comprised some amazingly talented individuals. One such was Nicky M. Actor, dancer, magician, clever playwright. He was fifteen when we met! Although I lost contact with Nicky when I left for Bristol, I know that he moved into the pop music production world with his famous big brother, the UK's highest paid rock session drummer, Nigel M. During our days together with Alan G however, Nicky became my mate. We shared space together for several years. Nigel, at the age of 12 some years earlier, had crushed both his hands in an accident. He had been advised at the time to take up playing the drums in order to restore their use, the rest, as they say, is history! At 19, his hands carried the highest insurance cover of anyone in the popular music industry in the UK at that time. The three of us enjoyed some special times just jamming together – making music simply for fun. Nigel worked on a regular basis with many individual 'Pop Stars' of the hour as well as some who were internationally famous groups. They would employ Nigel as their drummer for their UK tours. Via Alan G, we were also able to experience times with members of The Actors Studio in London, participating in some of the 'fun' sketch sessions at the studio. I recall also having the opportunity to attend rehearsals for productions by the English Stage Company at a time when the resident director was George Devine.

English Stage Company at The Royal Court Theatre in Sloane Square, London had become a basis for theatrical challenge, or as Mr Devine would often say, a theatre for writers, not necessarily for actors.

With a special group of young teens including Nicky, we were requested to perform in Germany in a youth cultural exchange. Nicky helped to create "The Mask" theatre in the county town of Herefordshire. Having the opportunity to meet so many wonderful people of the day, with others yet to become household names in the future, continued to shape my life. Other than school, this was my life at thirteen to twenty leading me to be constantly pinching myself on a regular basis as I walked onto film sets, into television studios or theatre rehearsal rooms.

The speed of life activity for me during my teens caused the years, thirteen to nineteen, to become a blur, passing by very quickly indeed. To even suggest to you that I can today remember in any real specific detail more than 50% of the first four years of my teenage period, would be nothing more than a huge exaggeration. Attempting to 'put-to-paper' in a fashion that may provide enough insight or comprehension of my life during this period is a very daunting task. Staring down at the keyboard of my computer, I notice how my now broken hands tremble at the magnitude, the real impossibility of the project I have set myself for you Dear Reader. I will therefore try to make sure that I am at my very best when opportunity presents itself for me to work on this epistle. This must be the case in order for me to be able to record those very special things or events that due to their nature, have burnished themselves into my memory to shine forever.

Even so, I may not be able to do justice to any one individual item with sufficient descriptive power to leave you in no doubt of the colour, smell, taste or texture of the events. Your patience with your acceptance of my inabilities as a writer is truly appreciated. I will try to place some chronology to these events but this too may also contain holes in the sequence due to a memory today not fully able to reach its top or even bottom floor!

Here I go!

MY EARLY TEENAGE YEARS.

French, German – oh hell, Oops' – Caught in the storeroom at school – no more German! The wonderful Sandra C. The amazing Elizabeth M. Oh yes! MATHS!

On the really brave assumption Dear Reader that you're still with me having thus far somehow remained interested in this old man's recollections of his ages past. You will I am sure, remember that as a child, I was the one who frightened some individuals in authority resulting in my having to perform as a monkey! Subjected to, or instructed to, by some so-called specialists/experts alongside some other children in that large house in the Buckinghamshire countryside. Each was tested which in my case simply confirmed my own determination to hideaway with the subsequent life-long devotion to providing an external image that matched my oft' espoused status at home of 'imbecile' or 'idiot' or 'stupid'. From that Saturday onward, it had become an essential that my outward actions or comments in or of public view, demanded concentration skills so that I would not be seen to represent any other demeanour that was not reflective of my stated capacity. Initially though, some thought that as a child I may possess different abilities beyond such stated comments.

Isn't it funny that even those highly educated, apparently clever individuals of the day who were often (stupidly) regarded as intelligent people, then as still today, find it difficult to create the 'link' between known, proven or recognised ability with the required intellect or capacity to ever employ such abilities. Some perhaps have seen then been scared, shocked into denial with deliberate reason and supressed these 'gifts'. I am aware of people with very high IQ's for example who drive public transport buses for a living. They may indeed lack the capacity or, more importantly, the will to employ their talents. My own brother Chris lacks the inclination to employ the obvious abilities he possesses. Such individuals may simply be scared to! However, these very same individuals have a massive capacity to look or to behave in such a way as to remain unobtrusive in or to the society of their time. Some of the very best criminal minds in the world have IQ's so far off the scale they are unreadable! In other words, it seems that these government appointed so-called 'experts' were of the view that abilities of this nature must be regarded as somehow singular, or separate; that an individual owner of such talents would never or could never cross-use, 'mix-n-match' at will, including the ability to hide some or all of such ability, at random! Stupid aren't they hey! So missing in the process, the great flaw of intellectual thinking on these matters in the mid 1950s – like the missing link – was the simple lack of knowledge by the experts regarding the capacity or will of the owner of such strange capabilities, if indeed they existed at all, to want to employ them…ever!

So, day by day keeping low, I conducted myself in all things according to official rubber-stamped edict depictions of me issued by authority which was correctly stored in the correct place for future reference if needed. Always in everything I did that may have been or could be scrutinised by parents or others, where any form of alarm may potentially be the result, I remained in line with accepted and expected norms.

Me being one simply lazy individual always acting in the expected, accepted manner of then current society, agreeing with official school reports that 'he can do better'. Just with different interests or conflicting outlook to my parents or my siblings, that's all. I do recall however where expediency lost out to emotion or my own distraction, cover-up was a well-used, successful tool. So, there I was, concentrating on always being as, behaving as anticipated by all those around me.

Oh what a joy for me. It became such an easy method of behaviour, hiding away. Living, from an external viewpoint anyway, always within identified expected, well accepted patterns that by the time I entered the academic senior schooling period of my existence, even I had come to accept myself to be academically slow to average. After all, no other eminent personages than my mother or father on a regular basis would often refer to me as stupid or their "Gibbering Idiot!" This latter was one of several special favourites of my father, used in direct reference to me on many occasions when his perception was that I had not done or had done, or had said or had not said, something that by its very nature afforded reason to attract his attention. These titles though were partly as a result of my own doing anyway because, as indicated, my concerted effort was to always present my 'lazy' slightly detached approach in all that I did. Not, however to singing, singing training or music making or discussions on life, religion, sunrise, death or laughter with my like-minded friends. Here was my constant salvation, my escape, my pressure valve release! But anywhere else, slow, quiet! Silly fun at the beginning but sadly something derived from necessity. Therefore, as those not in my other (music, singing, acting etc) life who had any recognised authority had been indicating for some time, it was best to write me off like some unrecoverable bad debt, one with no specific potential to achieve anything of real value in my future earthbound existence. Singing was fine but a far cry from the aptitude needed as an indentured apprenticeship… such employment being our fathers' single dream for all his sons. Get a skill, be a plumber, an electrician or a carpenter. The skills of the tradesman or artisan provide earning capability for life! Activities such as writing a one-act play at age thirteen, read by my soon to be sister-in-law, another blue-eyed blonde called Penny, sadly reflected no potential for me to be a useful artisan of any needed skill. Singing therefore or even acting could not be considered attributes needed to attract the attention of such people to build a safe future life. In any event, the music or theatrical world was seen to be full of "strange" or "funny" or "weird" people. People I could not possibly want to associated with. A decision made on my behalf as I was informed by my father on many occasions, without any reference to or input from me on the matter.

So a clash was inevitable, a mistake in my perpetual personal shield had to happen.

Then – oh dear...

I got lazy about being lazy! Inevitable knowledge again, but could I control the known inevitable?

I am not at all sure that had the following event somehow not come to pass, what difference if indeed any it would have made to the outcome of my life. Suffice it for me to suggest with the usual clarity of 'looking-back', that it would have happened somehow, somewhere, sometime. The inevitable is simply that – inevitable! Planned, one could argue to transpire regardless of my/our own best efforts.

At the beginning of my second year at senior school I was rumbled! I the almost academic buffoon, the 'about Mr. Average', the 'plodder' of all plodders before me – one day really leaked my true reality like the village fool or the absent-minded professor. At the time I was so utterly shocked at my own lapse that later I clearly remembering silently screaming at myself! But as I have said, it was inevitable.

MATHS! Oh what a silly subject.

Our class, our group of spotty boys – well some at least – plus some girls, I recall that 'generally' girls were academically always further ahead of boys thus the proportion of girls in my class at the time was much less than other, higher streams in the school; however as for characters, shapes, hair or eye colour mix to anyone who was interested, we were a broad collection of the just below the 'Mr Average' ilk. We, this collection of new youth, were the recipients one day of a new maths teacher. Well 'new' is a relative word in this case. New to our class, even to our school yes, new to teaching maths, not at all! This man appeared to us as perhaps one of the oldest individuals ever to still be walking or talking! So old in appearance in fact that to us in discussion, we agreed it strange that the government would allow someone to be teaching at such an obviously well 'past-it' age! What little hair the poor man had was just as white as the chalk he was using to write on the board! He was so old that it was possible he had not stood erect, as humans are apparently supposed to, for a very, very long time indeed. In fact, the poor man was almost 'folded' in two. Nevertheless, he was our new teacher of that $1+2 =$ something stuff that I had always found to be so dreary for so many years. In order to get to know his new charges, this re-warmed human-like figure, this antique teacher, as we thought, set a class test at the level which he had apparently been advised to expect us to be at. Only later did he discover that his expectation of our collective maths level was far above this particular gathering of pupils – with one (about to be exposed) stupid exception! The shocking discovery that these particular pupils were not at the level he seemed to think we should have been at was however made too late to save me. The result of the inability to be lazy was that I (yes me) was to progress with sudden rapidity up the academic ladder at a speed that was breathtaking to some, very scary to many. I was to be poked then prodded again.

In spite of his apparent status as the oldest man still alive, this bent-over teacher displayed a demeanour that was something enchanting, almost magical that had not previously been experienced by any of us. He had a capacity for humour! A teacher with an obvious joy for all things including sharing FUN with us! Emanating from this poor bent man was a sparkle, a life, a physical zest, a real personal agility beyond his obvious physical impediment. But more remarkably, there was a love for his chosen profession accompanied with a blatant passion for his subject. He projected a ZEST for all things, possessing the ability to mentally grab hold of our attention, demanding without anger or command the right to be heard. He very quickly proved to be a person to whom we must listen.

The class test he set was 'Trig' or 'calc' or one of those very obnoxious subjects designed specifically to frustrate, even irritate, the mathematically challenged or those classified to be bright but lazy or even those who simply didn't care. I became so enthralled, fascinated even, by his awkward stance, his wonderfully open behaviour toward us as a group that I simply finished the 'idiot-quality' test without any concentration at all, handing back the paper without even checking or granting a casual sideways glance at my answers. Do you start to see the problem now? I, as you know, always want to understand something new! Silly questions about to stem from that stupid, stupid (Gibbering Idiot) boy again! Here was a man so fascinating, so full of life yet representing such a contrast to his appearance. I simply had to understand more.

Thus I was, rumbled! In Public!

A sound, his voice "Please stand up Mr S..." Broke my reverie! From the mouth of this exhilarating new teacher, a sound blessed in oh so gentle tones that the words almost floated directionless across the classroom but with extreme clarity of diction that all could hear the demand some fifteen or so minutes after we had handed in the silly test. As I said, he possessed this extraordinary knack of touching each of us with the effect of an electric shock. Snapping us all metaphorically upright (an ability he had clearly never lost as a person or a teacher). So polite but with soft intent was the request that at first I thought he was trying to address my father who had, by some never before experienced extreme magic, materialised amongst this class of almost average pupils. I clearly remember being lost in confused comprehension. Attempting to answer the question as to why having achieved such an outstanding piece of enchantment, had my father chosen then to sit down amongst us thus causing our teacher to request him to stand up! It took a long strong measure of cool to realise that the request was directed at me! Once again in perfect diction that soft polite request "why are you in this class?" was aimed straight at my now standing form. A silence, a pause, a moment of extreme horror sprang from deep in my gut. Guilt flowed through my heart not blood. A hot blushing guilt climbing across my 'oh so un-spotted' face. Heart racing, with no answer to the question, experiencing a subtle shifting of multitudes of eyes, feet, faces moving to locate me I was made to stand at the board to 'show' the class how to answer each of the questions in the test correctly as I had done. Walking towards the front of the classroom, having gathered some of my lost composure but boiling inside at my self-inflicted agony, I realised what I had done, instantly knowing that I could not now 'pretend' not to know how to answer each question, because dear, clever, crafty, conniving very old but NOT SO DEAD, MR B held in his wrinkled steady hand my answer sheet! 100% correct!

It was this stupid lapse by me that resulted in a flurry of activity. Within a few days I was shipped up the academic ladder by four places to what was then said to be the second 'best' or 'smartest' bunch of pupils in our year. There I was to remain for the balance of my formal education. But again, once exposed to the accepted, expected levels of comprehension of this group of my peers, I was very soon able to return to the position of class plodder-of-plodders albeit at a, supposedly, faster, higher learning capacity. Never again however was I to allow myself to be distracted to such an extent by the unexpected behaviour of anyone in general or any teacher in particular.

Such luxury of distraction I resolved to keep only to myself well within my chosen domains of activity far removed from my family or any type of officialdom. Where I was at peace where others simply knew me, accepting me as I was without probing or question or having some strange unspoken need, desire even to alter or challenge or so much worse – CHANGE me!

Looking back now, the above episode seems very small, perhaps insignificant in the grand scheme of all things; yet it was to be my unwitting entrance to a level of academic comfort or contribution that enabled me to later receive a full government grant to attend tertiary education at the Old Vic. Having apparent talent, according to some anyway, was not seen as enough on its own. (What will you do if you cannot get work?) Having also some recognised 'standard' from an academic perspective was regarded as absolutely essential. (I could always sign those awaiting indenture papers to be an apprentice!) Having represented young

English artistic talent in music as well as drama around the county on many occasions, across the country then also in Europe, perhaps also helped. But there is no doubt that dear 'not-so-dead' doubled-over Mr B played his role in ensuring that my path to the future was secure, irrespective of my best attempts to thwart the Grand Plan that the Gods had agreed upon prior to my arrival on this planet!

Talking things academic I had, at about the same time in school, started to learn French. I had come to enjoy the concept of being able to converse in another language, 'speak-with-forked-tongue' as it were, so after just a few months I was putting conversational French together, starting to provide a new "life-skill". However, due to the loss of my concentration on the 'oh-so-stupid-level' on that strange day of maths resulting in Mr B, pushing the sudden subsequent rise in hierarchy within the academic stratum, I joined a group that were all learning German not French. Even though my protests were obviously full of venom – the established 'time-table' into which my stupidity had placed me, made it impossible for me to continue with my French lessons. I remember being very clearly offered special classes after school but as you may probably understand by now, my non-school activities just allowed time for a little sleep prior to the next school day! So, how to study German? As it turned out – not the way we were experiencing it! From the depths of my soul I have searched the murky remnants of my memory but must nevertheless concede utter irrevocable defeat in the objective of trying to find the name of our German language teacher. The utter loss of this name must be for a good reason as may become apparent soon. It may therefore be fortuitous that my memory refuses to submit or give up prior ownership of his name because I'm sure he would want to sue me about this story, even though it is true.

Whilst I cannot remember his name, I am able to recall many things about this, now nameless, man. Firstly though something that was quite a rarity at the time – he was actually German! (So I shall from now on refer to him as Mr. German!) He had lived in England prior to the start of World War Two after marrying an English woman some years before hostilities began. I can only assume that during the conflict he was one of those 'Aliens' reporting to his nearest police station on a regular basis. Nevertheless, here he was, German, teaching English teenagers his mother tongue in the late '50s early '60s in England. I can only guess at his age but he must have been somewhere in the thirty to fifty age range, a very large man, with broad shoulders, cropped grey hair displaying expansive and distinctly bright, large blue eyes!

Thus it was that I now started to learn German having abandoned any attempts to force the authorities to allow me to continue with my French. I was behind, very uninterested, clearly pissed-off!

As an 'alien', Mr German was suspected by the boys in my new class of all sorts of acts of nastiness against dear England during the recent war period as was depicted in all those boys comics published during our childhood. These comics would always show the entire German army as comprised of totally stupid villains with a collective IQ of just over 3! Our Mr German must have been working for Hitler, passing information via a network of agents back to Berlin. He was, according to some theory I recall, possibly acting as a saboteur at every opportunity. We talked up a storm about this poor man without any foundation in truth whatsoever. Stories purely created in the murky fertile imaginations of the teenage idiots that we were.

However, within twelve months, our Mr German was, to some degree at least, to provide the possibility of credence to support our dubious thoughts on his character by his very sudden and unexpected departure from the school. It was the next school year. My German was awful due to my lack of interest in it at the time. However, I had been accepted by my peers in the class as the plodder of the group, having achieved this status in accordance with my want. Other things were happening in my life of much greater import anyway so I just continued to accept that unless the current subject was singing, music, theatre, poetry or time shared in the company of some very talented 'others', the current subject was of little consequence, more a function or formality of life, like using the loo, than providing for any future meaningful endeavour.

But by his actions Mr. German was to supply us with a wonderful opportunity for the wildest most breathtaking range of teenage 'boys-own' speculation! "They finally caught the spy". 'He was captured in a huge gunfight but to avoid capture he took the instant 'Death Pill' to ensure his contacts would remain safe.' The speculation was fun, there was an unannounced nervousness in the school corridors for some time; a private, very hushed whispering dominated the sounds of the playground, whilst many senior pupils together with some of the teachers were desperately attempting to lead a normal day as if nothing had changed. But it had! As with all such things, a version of the truth regarding the disappearance of Mr. German finally surfaced, to become after a time at least, regarded as the de-facto reason for this unplanned departure. Looking back with the usual clarity supplied to one by worldly experience gained from observations of general human behaviour, it is difficult now to understand why the accepted truth took so long to reach the common public arena.

The story, as we began to understand it, caused enough giggling alongside quiet smirking for all of us to enjoy for a few weeks of whit, a time when many a crude, often not very funny joke reigned supreme. It seems that our Mr. German had been discovered in one of the class storerooms shortly after school had finished, providing a very different 'education' to a young sixth form female pupil. He of course was subject to instant dismissal with, we understood, being banned from teaching; the young lady pupil (who was never named publicly) simply moved to another school.

Thus here was I with two half languages, left to wallow along with my classmates with only one half language awaiting the appointment of another teacher. They came, stayed, attempted to teach us something, proved to be inadequate, moved on. So we as a group were never able to complete the course to examination level.

Penultimate Pieces.

My dear, wonderful reader, there are now just three areas I must cover here as we reach towards the end of this epistle which I hope has given you not just an insight on, of, and about my childhood but also a view of the times that affected me. Some shaping me to help secure who this seventh child twin (well nearly) of a real seventh child twin has become or is today. I hope that you have seen some laughter, some love, some horror, even some fun, some tears of both joy or sadness with perhaps a reason why today it is you for whom I have toiled here? You, who have been my encouragement, my motivation to share with you as much of me as possible.

"Pieces" is the only way I can think of to provide answers to the request for information about my life. What created the fundamental character basis for the development of the person I have become? Only those who have travelled with me through my life journey will know if I have, in this first written down memory of the period from before birth to the day at sixteen years eleven months I stood on the Aylesbury station platform with luggage in hand to set off to Bristol where I had been accepted to study at the Bristol Old Vic Theatre School...the divorce from family completed.

It is possible for this perhaps to be the only portion of my life to be encapsulated in writing to give you a picture which I hope will address your need to understand who I am or was. If I have failed, please find it within yourself to forgive. I apologise today in the hope that you will rest assured that such failure is due only to a fumbled memory, or my inability as a writer or story teller. It will not however have been for lack of the need for, or the want of, trying.

The first missing 'bit' is very easy, my first guitar! I was seven years old when Father Christmas provided me with a four string plastic guitar. I was hooked. After all, it was mobile so I was able to carry this instrument around. The sound it made was simply terrible but immediately I started to understand how it worked. Piano, guitar, singing etc, I am sure that Father Christmas must have known something of my future but then attempted to stop that future from becoming a reality later. My first real guitar was given to me by a friend in the choir when I was nine years old; this was the moment of my conversion to playing this instrument. This was how it started! In fact, if I could still physically play today, that conversion would still be regarded as being a 'work-in-progress' even though I have been fortunate enough to entertain many friends over the many years with my ability to play this wonderful instrument. By my early teens, when time would allow, several of those very talented young people I have referred to, had formed then disbanded a number of 'groups' with my guitar playing by then, both of the solid-state electrical as well as classical acoustic types.

The second missing 'bit' is that I promised to give you the reasons for the loss of the family fortune when my father had wanted to train as a Medical Doctor in the early 1930s. The demise of his father, my grandfather, was to be a precursor to our family monetary loss. Grandfathers' death has to do with that basic but most powerful of all human emotion – love.

Actually two types of love, one – that of religion, the love of a God, the love of His Word, blind total acceptance to His teachings as interpreted by the Roman Catholic Church. The second love refers to – love for a woman by a man. Often where these mix, disaster is the inevitable ending!

My grandfather was born in the early 1880s into the family wealth that was by then well established. His upbringing was strict adherence to the doctrines of the Roman Catholic Church with all its teachings as had his fathers' before him, following the path of many previous family generations. This fact of religious belief was the domination in all things. Our grandfather's life foundation then was of an existence that was to be set by his complete conviction to all that the Roman Catholic Church had to offer. Thus it was not an unexpected event for him when he presented his first-born child, a daughter, to the church via a known convent located in Brighton on the south coast of England as a 'gift' representing his conviction. My father's sister was, in the words of my father however, "sold to the church" to enhance the standing of my grandfather in the eyes of his church; perhaps moving him up the ladder to be closer to his Lord. As more children arrived to my grandfather – my father being just one of eventually five that we were ever made aware of – they too were all subject to the essence of the rules of the Roman Catholic Church with all that such unquestioned following entails. My grandfather was well educated at Stowe School, although we have no proof of this other than from verbal information provided by our father but it would follow in his world, that any male offspring would attend 'his' school automatically. As our fathers' education was at Stowe School therefore we must assume this too was where our grandfather was also educated before him.

Grandfather took up his position on the main board of the family business at the appropriate time, married a good Roman Catholic lady from a good family where together they raised their children in their world to the convictions of their religion. As the years rolled past, he lived in accordance with his religion, it sustained him, providing peer expectations until in his late '40s (my father now in his early '20s) the unthinkable happened with an absolute catastrophic outcome!

He fell, with total honesty, really, with debilitating brutality, completely, body, mind and soul in love with a young woman who happened into his life one day!

This cannot be true! What had he done! His religion forbade such a thing! His church will send him to hell! Even to think of the word 'divorce' would mean damnation for eternity!

He stumbled!

We understand that whilst there was no affair with the young lady whom he apparently shouted at in public one day to "get away from me", this outcry of shame, this was a shattering human misery being noticed by all! (Imagine that!). There was no attempt to crack the fortress walls of his religious doctrine – his central life foundation He apparently confessed to his wife, telling her of this absolute infliction, this abject horror that led him to question why such a thing should infest his mind! What had he done to his God that the result was such anger of the Almighty to direct such a challenge at him! How can he be true to his real 'being' as required by his beloved church when such an emotion had inflicted itself upon him, in him, to his core, dropping him like a heavy sack to the ground on knees no longer able to support him! Must he now deny his conviction to the doctrine of the church? Was his life until then a lie? All the cores of his being a waste, an evil corruption even? Could he accept or even recognise this new awakened emotion as 'real', yet remain close to his God or even as a member of Christian humanity? Can he, after everything he had done for the church in His name, truly be 'just another human full of dark sin'?

Over the next few years, I have no actual elapsed time information, my grandfather locked himself away tormented, struggling with his conflict of Love of God – via the Roman Catholic interpretation – against that of a man who was (human at last, some may say) truly lost in a love of another woman who is not his Catholic wife! His remorse was relentless apparently. It gouged a heinous hole in his soul. It is said that he ignored his life, his family, starting to sustain himself more each day by consuming bottle after bottle of liquor. I cannot say if the liquor gave solace or simply killed the terrible pain, or the torture of the emotional bewilderment. He did not attend any business meetings, was eventually removed from the company then distanced from the family. Over some three years, he sold assets including houses for next to nothing, abandoned his family, seeking to quench his thirst for understanding, buying books on all subjects to find a solution that would perhaps place him on the road to peace for his troubled mind. Reportedly attempts were made to squelch this emotion with advice from quacks – then at the end of it all, after a lifetime of blind conformity to a religious doctrine, he committed the ultimate sin against his church, his God, his society – abandoned without an answer, knowing that what he was doing would confine him to hell for ever. (According to the RC Church anyway). Despite being warned, his consumption of alcohol became his new master, dawn-to-dawn it played its role of welcoming chaperone on the journey to oblivion.

It is said that our Grandfather committed suicide by alcohol, alone, lost, outside of his safe known comfortable cocoon. Thus the money, the assets that would have supported my father were lost at a time when my father was in his mid-twenties, when war in Europe was by then inevitable.

Girls (Women!)

I will not draw this child's journey to young man to an end on such a sad note!

The third promised missing 'bit' was my first incursion into the world of adults, in particular that developing period of physical attraction to members of the opposite gender, in my case…GIRLS! Having three older brothers was itself an education on its own, with whispered stories during shared washing-up chores. Embarrassed, red-faced recounts of personal adventures all helped to offer confusion, intrigue, along with open mouthed wonder for this follower of the pack. But we all embark on this aspect of life in simple innocence, passing though total disbelief to a period of acceptance that it must be true. In my case, I clearly remember walking home one day with my brother Chris. Having been to the 'pictures' in town to watch yet another war film where the Americans were again the saviours of Europe with multitudes of brainless German soldiers slaughtered by just three chiselled-chinned CLEAN GI's with all their activities bolstered by rousing heroic Hollywood music. We were talking about the film when, without any warning whatsoever, Chris informed me that I had a thing called a penis! At something like nine or ten years old, I seem to recall thinking 'that's good' now wasn't that a good movie? Unperturbed by my lack of excitement at this really good 'news', although more for his own appreciation I think, Chris stumbled on.

"It's how we make babies," he said. Now I had heard something about this somewhere, where there was an apparent relationship between my appendage linked to the birth of children so I forgot about the film, listening. Oh was it frightening! Apparently our dad put this penis thing of his into our mum so that we, Chris, I, the others, could be here. Apparently, according to Chris anyway, our mum as with all girls, had something that he tried to remember the name of but failed, although he was sure that the first letter was a 'v' he couldn't remember the rest of it. "This" he said "is where men, 'which is what we will be one day' push this penis thing into this 'v' thing with the result that babies would then be born". This was all too upsetting for me so I ran off ahead to escape such horrid thoughts that were now accompanying scary pictures that arose in my head! However, somewhat later, these strange imagined pictures were to start to lead towards tiny 'stirrings' below that would not leave me. I remained very confused, wanting desperately to find out more but reluctant to do so just in case – it was true! So after having had secret battles with myself I sought out the only one that would know the truth of such matters as he did on all things – Greg. I can see his face even today as it wrinkled then crushed into explosive laughter that seem to continue forever as I expired on the spot, shrinking with burdened embarrassment, head bowed, hot faced! "Of course it's true" he said, "It's what makes the world go around"! He then gently proceeded to unburden my troubled mind with talk of attraction, the 'love' thing that would happen naturally between two people of different sex. That was really scary, so much so that I then convinced myself that it would never happen to me! I would keep my penis thingy to myself!

It was easier for a while but oh it seemed such a horrid thing to have to do! Then just so very few years later however, the innocence was gone, the hormones were tripping the 'light-fandango' reflecting how different my feelings were then.

A year of life beyond even that period, I was to be a fully-fledged adult male, but that's another story for another time perhaps.

So to my escapade one very cold, very damp November Saturday afternoon – I was a clean, pale-faced tall, solid young man (ha!), just sixteen a month ago!

The rapid hormonal change from child to young man or woman is perhaps the most splendid but often most brutal of the entire range of human natural metamorphoses. Birth by its nature is brutal even traumatic for both parties involved, but memory ensures that particular experience remains blocked for most of us. Death comes in so many shades but always has the colour of nothing after. Puberty however is just as inevitable but contains a mystery, an excitement, an element of 'special' reward with its brutal change challenges. The puberty period of what in reality can be a short few months where boy becomes man physically, often will take many, many more months for the individual to catch up mentally or even emotionally. It will, for example, be suggested by a very large portion of the adult human female population that most men never actually make it through that mental or emotional development to catch-up. Remaining part child for always! Or are regarded as never having completed the course, to reach the end of the process so as such remain in a perpetual state of emotional deficiency! Be that as it may, my own journey through the physical translation was swift, with only the demand for spots lost during the progression. As to any observation of my translation in the mental or emotional areas, I leave that to others to form their own conclusion. As I did not suffer at all from acne as most teenagers do, I argue that I yet have to experience this portion of the physical translation.

Also, our choirmaster managed to 'train-down' my voice during this time so I cannot ever recall experiencing the often very funny slip-slide pitch changes of the spoken voice of young men in this transition phase. So here I am at senior school, hormones now rampant, awash, brain lost in a teeming ocean of emotions unknown with, just over there across the passage in another classroom almost two years although a lifetime of experiences ahead of me, sat one female pupil…dear Sandra C.

Fully developed in all aspects, eyes wide, mouth seemingly, yieldingly soft, she had agreed to meet me tomorrow, Saturday, in town. My boyhood nervously sponsored by the 'knowledge' espoused by my peers behind the bicycle shed, with stories of carnal escapades along the local canal provided by the enchanting Sandra C! Challenged to be the next to discover these wonders then promising to report back fully on Monday, I had gathered the nerve to ask Sandra to meet me in town at a well-known teenager hangout where coffee, tea, cool drinks etc., were to be enjoyed. Aware of some potential veiled mystic-happenings 'experienced' by some of my peers who had taken this road before me followed with excited (exaggerated) report-back times in the bicycle shed I was, in reality, without knowledge of what to expect! I had been told of her reputation in secret, giggled verbally (yes boys still do that during this transition period), conversations that included 'knowing' but hidden knowledge of or apparently by some of the other boys – oh how brave I was in that group!

Oh how I trembled through the night! Oh how agonisingly slowly Saturday morning seemed to pass, with choir practice even extended for some special service the next day. Time seemed to crawl to an almost STOP! Even so, as the morning moved on inexorably, almost every second I sought with trepidation any way that I could duck out of this assignation!

But how could I then face my giggling information hungry co-conspirators as arranged behind the bicycle shed on Monday morning. Eventually it was time to venture into the unknown, armed with an agreed time to meet, an agreed location, a pocket full of money earned by singing – I set out in grim determination to meet a 'girl', to face my future!

What a let-down!

Yes, she was waiting at the allotted corner of the High Street, yes, she smiled when I arrived as we walked to that popular youngsters' café. There we sat by the window looking every-which-way except to or at each other, drank milkshakes, made small talk about people at school, music, films, even some teachers. Then she informed me that she had to be home within an hour from now, this was after one of the most trying hours of my life already! So we walked to her road where I left her at the corner then walked home…Well, let me say that we did take a detour on the way resulting in a journey that even walking very slowly, should take no more than half an hour, much less at a good walking pace, but we took about an hour. She had done this before! The detour was down to the canal where without any warning she suddenly reached out to hold my hand as we walked along the towpath.

Now by itself, this I could handle; we smiled, looked away then walked slowly on holding hands, trying to look as if we had done so for many years, ha! It was now about four in the afternoon of a grey, dull, damp, very cold winters' day – flesh was not meeting flesh in this hand holding, gloves were meeting gloves, we were both wrapped against the cold.

Nevertheless, the 'electricity' of positively charged expectation made me feel very naked! Then as we walked under the walkway bridge which ran across the canal, I was hauled against the bridge wall; suddenly without any warning I found myself pinned by the full, well developed remember, weight of dear Sandra. Cold mouth met cold mouth (I think) my nose seemed to be pushed away to allow for the convergence of lips! I had no recollection ever of being this close to anyone! Too late! I was involved now! It was not really too bad! It was sort of cosy, sort of warm, nice with a stirring slowly deep below then–what the?

Down below, under the overcoat, the woollen jumper, the thick shirt, below the belt, amongst the cloth of the upper trouser, an invasion was taking place. A de-gloved (obviously experienced) hand was casting aside all obstacles, slowly burrowing towards my middle appendage! For its own part, it was growing in stature without any regard to my needs! It was independently reaching to greet this intruder with such abandon! Dear Sandra, who by this time was obviously seeking some reaction, some service from me, had reached with her 'free' hand to one of my own, guiding it, pulling it towards her lower region...! All the time my mind is racing, what is this? I hope no one else is going to be walking under here any time now! What should I be doing here! The feeling of being so close lasted forever but was over in nothing other than a long instant. She withdrew from me with a smile, adjusted her clothing leaving me with an enormous ache, an uncomfortable bulge. I readjusted my own attire as she took hold of my re-gloved hand again whilst we walked the rest of the way to the end of her road in a silly, red-faced almost sweetly giggling way. The walk home later for me was one of having done what was expected by my peers, I could now plan how I would enhance this recent activity to enthral, to excite! This I did on Monday morning behind the bicycle shed – as expected.

I never attempted to speak to Sandra C again. My groin was aching for most of the rest of that weekend but now I had a much better understanding of the attraction of male to female relationships. A world of knowledge...armed with an example of one! So why should I bother again? But just over a year later, in a warm comfortable studio dressing room, one Elizabeth M, an actress aged 20ish in the youth group I had been with for some time, introduced me to a real exchange of the potential pleasure of sharing each other as adults! Well me almost an adult! Having been provided with the opportunity to work with many of the Alan G group on some challenging youth theatre projects, it was not too long before I was first exposed to having to get used to finding time to become involved in rehearsing a particular piece/play or mime or movement presentation for production in the theatre world. So it was that often with just one other person rehearsing a section of a piece, or waiting to rehearse ones' own piece – generally just having to wait. Such is the nature of these things in the entertainment industry. One such waiting occasion led to the full deflowering of my innocence with the returning to the world at large a fully-fledged, young operating male human. Dear Elizabeth M! She took unto her that day of waiting, the 'child', sharing some 'education' time. Later, with an exhausted ache, perhaps even several shades lighter – she returned to the world – THE MAN! All I can say is that I THANK MY LUCKY STARS – well Elizabeth M really for making me her 'challenge' on that day of dawning in my still young life! It must be said that there was no malice/anger/hate/force/corruption or other negative intention in this shared activity. Neither was there any alcohol nor drugs inducement, it was just a natural human 'need' by one for release with a natural human 'need' by the other (me) seeking knowledge, experience, understanding but not as a 'blithering idiot' anymore. Elizabeth M continued with her life, I was soon on my way to my new life.

As I continued however to develop physically over the next few years, there was from time to time opportunity to practice a little of that which Elizabeth had taught me. After all, this was the full 1960s, free love to flower-power etc. involved at that time as I was in making music, theatre, choir in the first half of this magic decade and most of the second half in the world of a theatre student.

With that in mind, I sometimes today think it was very sad that our Mr German got caught at his activity even though both participants consented. Whilst I cannot condone his behaviour, I must concede that perhaps they too were both also seeking to fulfil one of the most powerful of human needs for…each other.

Sixteen (well almost seventeen) going on thirty-five – this child walks to his future!

So, here I was, from a controversial arrival to stormy early years. One ear not quite the same as the other anymore. Being a seventh of a real seventh both with accompanying twins. Having a passion for music, to some abilities best not placed on public view. From keeping a low almost lazy profile, I had somehow managed to already have enjoyed so much, so much that was outside my family influence. From dancing with Percy on long summer evenings, to independence of thought leading to my own actions or interest; from study to acquire only knowledge on those things that interested or challenged me. From learning life skills of choice to constantly seeking always to understand the simplest to the most obscure, from the complicated to the straightforward, questioning with more questioning, holding on to new life experiences almost daily. I was now to officially step out from under the world of child to that of independent man. From knowing that constant risk of difference, to seeking answers to millions of yet unasked questions, it was now time to abandon for always my family roots. I would from this point on never again live in the family home. Visits yes, but they became an exception.

Knowing much of what was yet still to be, I walked one morning just over a month before my seventeenth birthday, to a waiting train at Aylesbury railway station. Small suitcase in hand, single ticket to Bristol via London! Excited? Yes, yet simultaneously terrified at the same instant. Feet nervous, eyes darting around every-which-way, I climbed aboard that train, turning to say 'goodbye' to my mother who offered a gentle kiss on my cheek whilst clutching a damp hanky in her hand. I managed to sit down in anticipation to start the next 'independent' chapter of this life journey.

So Dear Reader, the passing of this child to young man has been written here in 'Pieces', the passing of this young man through early adulthood, into parenthood, successful business career, through to very old age has yet to be written. But from my first day of study in Bristol in the September of that year after leaving home when almost seventeen, the next four years contained for me so much more than an average full lifetime of experiences by most people.

Standing side by side with people yet to become award winning film stars, others who would become household entertainment names in just a few years, to being on soundstages in some of the UK's best known film studios, and meeting so many talented, very special people in the world of entertainment.

Then at the age of twenty years, my heart had been given to a young woman, Eileen. Together we were to embark on a shared amazingly wonderful life journey, building our own family, sharing joy, laughter, love with a passion for sharing, talking, learning…but that is another story!

So for now my Dear Reader, thank you.

PS: Final controversy!

Remember my not too shy companion arriving on the planet alongside me on that October night? Yes, controversy – some food for thought!

Both my parents had blue eyes. All my siblings had/have blue eyes. My eyes have always been of a clear strong BROWN in colour? Hmmmmmmmm! The 'odds' of two blue-eyed humans producing a brown-eyed offspring are, I am advised, massively against such an outcome!

As adults, all three of my brothers became Type 1 Diabetics, reliant on daily insulin injections; Greg in his early twenties, the two others both in their thirties. I am not a Diabetic. Our father died aged 64 following an operation for pancreatic cancer, the Pancreas being of course the villain of this dreadful disease. Hmm!

R.A.